D1256165

THE NOVICE

WHY I BECAME A BUDDHIST MONK,
WHY I QUIT & WHAT I LEARNED

Stephen Schettini

GREENLEAF BOOK GROUP PRESS

Published by Greenleaf Book Group Press
P.O. Box 91869
Austin, TX 78709

Distributed by Greenleaf Book Group LLC

For ordering information or special discounts for bulk purchases, contact Greenleaf
Book Group Press at P.O. Box 91869, Austin, TX 78709, (512) 891-6100

Design and composition by Stephen Schettini
Cover concept by Tanya Hall; design by Stephen Schettini

Publisher's Cataloging-In-Publication Data
(Prepared by The Donohue Group, Inc.)

Schettini, Stephen.
    The novice : why I became a Buddhist monk, why I quit & what I learned / Stephen
Schettini.

    p. : ill. ; cm.

    Includes index.
    ISBN: 978-1-60832-005-9

    1. Schettini, Stephen. 2. Buddhist monks–Great Britain–Biography. 3. Spiritual
biography. 4. Monastic and religious life (Buddhism) I. Title.

BQ984.H48 A3 2009
294.309/2 B   2009925202

Printed in Canada on recycled paper
First Edition

To Mum

Gwenda Keary Schettini
1920 – 2007

THANKS
To Dad, for the grit; to Mum, for the stories; to Lama, for the role model; to Geshe, for the details; to Gotama, for the end of views

SPECIAL THANKS
To Caroline, without whose tireless support this story would be but a pale shadow of itself

NOTE
Some names have been changed at the author's discretion or by request of their respective owners

Attention is living; inattention is dying.
The attentive never stop; the inattentive are dead already.

—THE BUDDHA, DHAMMAPADA 21
translated by Thanissaro Bhikkhu

TABLE OF CONTENTS

Preface

As a young man I struggled and failed to escape my Western patrimony. For better and for worse, I discovered that the pretensions of scientific objectivity permeate the ways I think and write. On the other hand, my incurable meditations as an attempted Christian and Buddhist unleashed a storm of subjective realities. Buddhism and life have shown me that both these truths, objective and subjective, are relative, conventional and contingent; and although I believe in right and wrong I also know that nothing's black and white.

The trickiness of writing honestly didn't even dawn on me until I put pen to paper, and I was embarrassed to find my own hand attempting to paint me as a hero. Fortunately, that approach petered out for lack of evidence. In time, a more balanced tale emerged; but the stark shades of gray that I'd hoped for turned out a misleadingly one-dimensional tale. Therefore, in order to render their full color I leaned on narrative and its foremost device, dialogue.

This is where some of you might take issue, and so I place this page in your path and ask, how else would you have me paint these times and players? My memories of the fifties, sixties and seventies aren't the happiest of my life, but they are startlingly vivid. Quotation marks may lend my characters' words the appearance of journalistic truth, but if they're not always a word-for-word record, I can vouch for the veracity of the voice. To deny their idiom would be to suppress their substance.

Their marks are on my life, and if memory's imperfect then so be it—I have no other resource. I was there, the times were alive and so are the recollections. I've consulted with others who were there too, though in the end this is my interpretation.

In a broader perspective, storytelling is the currency of the Jewish Bible, the Christian Gospels, the Muslim Hadith, the Hindu epics and the Buddhist Sutras. I trust that there is no more fundamental vehicle of human truth than the stories shared by our ancestors around their evening fires. Memoir may be more ambitious and more subtle than reportage, but the greater fabrication would be to pretend that memories aren't more strangely poignant than life, or that only facts have value.

I bow to the core teachings of the Buddha Gotama Shakyamuni, which put dualistic thought in its place and help us see through the tales we tell about who we are. In trying so self-consciously to recount my tale, I was forced into a middle way of sorts, and in the telling I learned truths more whole than I ever imagined possible with mere words.

Finally, this story is more true to the mature emotions of the narrator than the protagonist. After all, I the storyteller have the benefit of hindsight, while the "I" in this book is still wet around the ears—a mere novice.

WHY & WHEREFORE

I wrote this book because I was mystified by my own life. Why would a middle-class, privately schooled Anglo-Italian Catholic boy from rural Gloucestershire abandon his education, career and family to travel to the Tibetan refugee camps in India and become ordained as a Buddhist monk? Why would he then abandon it all and spend twenty years trying unsuccessfully to write about his failure? After dozens of fruitless attempts I finally found the courage to put down the facts one at a time and arrange them into a coherent narrative.

It was a frightening task, and more strangely enlightening than all my years as a monk. I was horrified to see how many secrets I kept, but as I dragged them into the spotlight I took courage and eventually dispelled much bitterness. I learned to accept, and finally to like myself. I also realized that profound existential bafflement wasn't mine alone.

It isn't simple to tell the simple truth. In an early draft I wrote, 'If only I'd known how difficult a task I'd set myself . . .'; but the fact is, I knew very well. I had to trace all the conscious and subconscious motives of the young man I was thirty years ago, as sophisticatedly confused as my own culture, itself struggling through the awkward growth spurt of the sixties. It all came down to two very persistent questions—why I became a monk in the first place, and why I subsequently left the glorious heights of solitude to resume the daily, stressful grind. The truth was elusive, for every answer seemed woefully inadequate; the words rang hollow in my ears.

For years I wrestled with these two questions in conversation, prose, poetry and fiction. Two decades of my life are littered with false starts and dead-ended manuscripts. Only in middle age did I eventually find the voice and endurance to carry my story through from beginning to end. I rose each morning at the crack of dawn to rake through the embers of my past. Exhilarated at first to put pen to paper and see the story finally taking shape, I soon began to wonder what I'd do when it came to an end.

This is a true story but not a work of simple nonfiction. During the two decades covered by this book (from the early nineteen sixties to the eighties) I lived by denial, too proud to feel pain and blindly pretending I knew what I was doing. The narrator, however, is a relatively disentangled product of thirty subsequent years of reflection and analysis. These paragraphs took shape each morning over a period of eight years, during which I was sometimes startled by the clarity of my recollections. I'm certainly aware that memories evolve and are embellished over time, and that they're more than a simple reflection of life as it was. I accept these traces of the past as a gift, a legacy of the person I once was, and take fatherly pride in the lifelike shape they've taken on. I've been as painstakingly honest as I can, have no agenda other than to hold your attention and trust you, dear reader, to come to your own conclusions, if conclusions be necessary.

I don't know, as some people say, that our society is entering a golden age of spirituality, but I'm heartened by those who can face their weaknesses, or do good, without having to resort to some proprietary belief system. We all want to be happy. We know at heart that we're better off facing our truths, no matter how unpalatable. I grew up spiritually terrorized by totalitarian religion, searched high and low for refuge and, for a while, thought I'd found it—but I was just clinging to an elaborate signpost. The real journey began only when I let go. The day I gave back my robes I fell precipitously from the imaginary heights of spiritual ascent, and it took me twenty years to clamber back onto dry land. Now at last I have worth in my own eyes and scars enough to expect no guarantees. For a brief, shining moment, I aspired to an Awakening of transcendental light and bliss. The illusion faded, I cried bitterly, but in time the simple truth settled down again, plain as day. It was, and always had been, staring me in the face.

Even if we are in a period of unprecedented self-examination, I don't believe in any inevitable march of progress. The notion that we're continually bettering ourselves, through either technology or faith, may be the great myth of our time, the bickering of science and religion just another vanity. The industrial revolution laid the ground for unprecedented leisure, an opportunity for reflection and awakening, but the communications revolution steadily consumes free time faster than we can create it. Our predicament is stark—we're stressing ourselves beyond measure, and our planet still more. Of all roads to sanity, the quiet good sense of the Buddha's *end to views* may be just what we need to regain our balance.

Life in our day, as in the Buddha's, has flung many a soul into a personal search for peace, truth and good sense. This book is for them.

ORTHOGRAPHY

This isn't a scholarly work, but it does discuss scholars and scholarship. I've avoided Tibetan, Sanskrit and Pali words in the body of the book whenever possible, and explained them when not. Terms such as *karma* and *buddha* long ago passed into the vernacular and are found in all English dictionaries. Unfamiliar ones are spelled phonetically in context and scholastically in footnotes. Words like *lama, buddha* and *geshe* follow common English usage by being capitalized when proper (e.g., The *Dalai Lama*) and not when generic (e.g., *a well-known lama*).

PART ONE

HOME

The wind bloweth where it listeth, and thou
hearest the sound thereof, but canst not tell whence
it cometh, and whither it goeth: so is every one
that is born of the Spirit.

—JOHN III, 8

THE AUTHOR: *age 9*

1

HOME & DRY

I SQUEEZED MY EYES TIGHTLY SHUT and bowed my head. Nothing. I gazed up at the crucifix and watched Jesus hanging on the cross, shedding tears of blood, expiring in agony. The same figure was suspended above the altar at church, behind the teacher's desk at school and over my own bed. More to the point, a psychological crucifix was embedded in my head, my heart and my crotch. The Christ was always silent, his suffering an eternal reproach.

The good nuns of Saint Michael's Convent School taught me the ins and outs of the one, true faith, starting with damnation. Sister Theresa, face framed by a starched wimple, hands poking from heavy robes, expounded tirelessly about the two types of human beings, Catholics and non-Catholics. Catholics *might* get into Heaven. Also, the Lord's love for humanity was undying, and a few exemplary heathens might find Limbo and escape the eternal fires, but there was no guarantee; besides, they'd never gaze upon the face of God. At six years of age I and my classmates were at ease with words like *incorrigible, excommunication* and *perdition*.

We thanked God daily for our great good fortune. "God is merciful," Sister said. "He loves each and every one of you," she added, but constantly reminded us that the floors of Hell were littered with fallen Catholics.

I didn't know what to think. God may have loved me, but He scared me more. How could you reason with someone who populated the world with Jews, Muslims and Hindus and then punished them for it?

I tried asking. In her doubt-demolishing voice, Sister reiterated that God's thoughts were unfathomable, another nice long word for my burgeoning vocabulary, and that it was a sin to question His intentions; but things were obviously so, otherwise He wouldn't have made His son Jesus Christ a Catholic, now would he?

How we kick ourselves in retrospect for not coming up with a perfect retort. It was plainly written and oft repeated in the Gospels themselves that Jesus was a Jew, but no alarm clanged in my head at her absurd lie. With the smoke and mirrors of pious intonation the priests and nuns had trained our instincts to knit everything into the involuted fabric of Catholicism, staunchly lulling us from all doubt. My eyes were opened much later, when I saw just how much more powerful are stories than facts in weaving our beliefs.

Sister drew a large circle and filled it with white chalk. "Now children," she asked, "Who can tell me what this is?"

We chanted in unison, "A pure soul, Sister."

She put a finger in her mouth, held up its glistening tip for all to see, then dabbed it in the circle to leave a black hole. "And this?"

"A venial sin, Sister," we replied.

"And what is a venial sin?"

Hands went up. Paul Durkin was picked, took a deep breath and blurted out, "Please Sister, it's a little sin that doesn't destroy the soul so you don't have to go to Hell and if you die with it you can burn it away in purgatory and afterwards you're still allowed into Heaven."

Sister beamed.

She carefully wiped everything out of the middle until it was an empty black circle and turned. "Now," she said, "What's this?"

"A mortal sin, Sister," in unison.

"And who will tell me what a mortal sin is?"

My hand went up with the others. In my excitement, I raised my arse several illegal inches from my chair.

"Mister Schettini, sit down," she addressed me and turned to the other side of the class. "Marcus Williams, explain the meaning of mortal sin."

He rose. "Please Sister, it's a sin that kills your soul so you go to Hell and burn for ever and ever."

"Very good." She looked around the room. "Now, who can give examples of venial sin and mortal sin?"

I raised my hand with suitable decorum and was rewarded when the chalk-encrusted finger singled me out. "A venial sin is when you tell a small lie or you don't do exactly what you're told, and a mortal sin is if you commit murder or you don't believe in Jesus."

"Very good, Mister Schettini," she said.

I should have left it at that.

"So Sister," I pursued. "What happens if you kill someone in a war, or if you're born in another country where they never heard of Jesus?"

She glared at me for a second. Then she pursed her lips, gathered her saliva and said, "If you're in a war and God is on your side, you're allowed to kill. And the poor heathens don't have to go to Hell but," she shook her head, "you can't cleanse the soul of original sin without the grace of the Holy Ghost. I'm surprised you've already forgotten that, Mister Schettini. Now sit down."

"But . . . ," I began.

"Sit down!"

Doctrine was meant to be recited, not understood.

I was routinely accused of being contrary. I believed I was only being curious. I really meant to be a good boy. I'd been granted an opportunity, thank God, to save my soul. What could be more important? But at night, I was plagued by filthy imaginings. A bunch of printed flowers on my bedroom wallpaper was actually a secret doorway behind which naked women did unimaginable things to me at night. I was terrified by my own longings and prayed to be freed from them.

Most afternoons I returned home from school to find Dad asleep in the armchair, for his restaurant kept him busy every morning and late into the night. Mum shushed me judiciously when I came in, but sooner or later I'd forget myself. Sometimes he'd grumble in his armchair, but at other times he'd storm in, vein twitching in his neck, cane in hand and slashing from side to side across my arms and legs. I jumped, squealed and tried futilely to escape.

"Bloody hell! Keep quiet! Why can't I get a little peace around here?"

In later years Mum wished she'd done things differently. She once wrung her hands confessionally and asked, "Did you know I added sugar to your bottle? To keep you quiet as a baby? So Dad wouldn't get upset?" She was almost in tears.

"Really?" I laughed.

"Do you think that did any harm?" she asked, fearfully.

"Probably accounts for my sweet tooth," I answered.

Now that she mentioned it, I do remember being starved for attention. My bedroom window stood two stories directly over the restaurant entrance and my earliest memories of writing are of forming words on scraps of paper and casting them to the winds. An incoming customer saw them fluttering down, read that I wanted my mummy and handed

MUM: *wished she'd done things differently*

them over to the charming hostess, Mum herself. Pink with embarrassment, she fled upstairs.

I was standing on the bed with one arm still out the window when the
door opened. My strategy had worked! All dressed up and smelling deli-
ciously of perfume, Mum held my hand and warned, "Daddy wouldn't
like it. No more messages." She sat on the edge of the bed and stroked my
head as I dozed off, then looked at her watch, bit her lip and stood up.
"I'm sorry, I have to go back. Daddy needs me . . . ."

Lord knows what other fragments of guilt she stored in her volumi-
nous conscience. By the time I went completely off the rails her trickle
of contrition had become a raging torrent. "I didn't spend enough time
with you," she fretted.

"Sure you did," I lied as usual. It was always easier to feel sorry for her
than for myself.

Being alone came naturally to me from the beginning. Not that I was
preternaturally withdrawn; that came later. It seemed natural that I and
others should be incomprehensible to one another, and I was content to
weave my perceptions into realities of my own choosing.

I liked to explore, and before I was allowed out alone I took to indoor
nooks and crannies. An early favorite was a cupboard under the stairs
where a battered leather suitcase overflowed with photos from that surreal
pause between the World Wars. I stared into sepia photos of Dad, hair
on his head, in foreign countries with exotic people, clasping lion cubs.
Mum was there too in newer pictures, strangely contorted in dazzling
costumes. Some of the prints were hand-colored. These images were my
window to the future as well as the past, for surely these lives presaged
mine. At the same time, I inhabited their memories. When Mum called
me to tea I'd bring a handful of pictures and she'd begin with the stories.

She loved the blitz, or so it seemed. "There were no class barriers in
those days," she said wistfully. "Everyone stuck together and helped each
other out, the La-de-dahs and the Cor blimeys all mucked in together." To
this day she sighs nostalgically for the time when little England thumbed
its nose at the mighty Luftwaffe and lived to tell the tale, and when she
first met Pasquale the lion tamer.

"I was with my boyfriend, Pat," she said with an animation rarely triggered by the realities of the present day. "That was when I was an acrobatic dancer—a Millimetre Girl. The circus was on the road, a long convoy of lorries and cages and cars, you know. Suddenly I heard the roar of a huge engine, and honking, and this great big car flew past us with its top down. The driver had a leather flying cap on his head and a cigarette holder clenched in his teeth, and there was a huge Saint Bernard dog in the passenger seat with his coat rippling in the wind. 'Who on *Earth* is that?' I asked."

"'That,' said Pat, 'is Shit-teeny.'"

"'Shit-teeny?' I asked. "What sort of name is that?'"

"'Oh, he's Italian,' Pat said."

"'Well, what a show off!' I said."

"Oh dear," Mum laughed. "Your father was so arrogant."

She was twenty when Dad was dragged off to internment and asked her to look after his most successful act of all: Koringa, the glamorous female fakir, hypnotizer of alligators and pythons. Mum said her name quietly and politely, the English way, syllables dripping with disdain. "She wasn't oriental at all—just French."

KORINGA: *wasn't oriental*
at all; just French

I hung on every word. I had to pinch myself to recall that I never woke up to the smell of circus sawdust and lion dung, never trod the streets of Rio in silken shirts or crouched in a waterlogged Anderson shelter as the bombs fell.

In actual fact, while Mum was busy giving birth to all ten-and-a-half pounds of me, Dad was down on his knees at Saint Peter's Church in Gloucester praying that her third issue would be priestly material. Dad had been a bad Catholic for many years and was craving pardon. I was his unborn offering.

Just how bad he'd been isn't too clear, for he was intensely secretive about his early life. In response to my questions Mum just laughs quietly and says, "Well, he was quite the ladies' man, your father," as if that's explanation enough.

Pasquale Schettini grew up in the toe of Italy and came of age in the twenties, shortly after his father's untimely death from syphilis, which did nothing for his family's standing in the little town of Castrovillary. A picture of Pasqualino at age seventeen shows a good-looking young man, only too aware of the fact. He hated authority and avoided both the Mafia and the Catholics. But one day in Rome he ran into the Fascisti. Stopped on the streets by two Blackshirt thugs who demanded to know whether he was with or against them, he blurted out that he neither knew the difference nor gave a damn. They forced a bottle of castor oil down his throat and left him to ponder his politics while squatting over his vacating bowels. By the standards of the time it was a trivial incident, but it was the last straw for Dad, who rarely had anything complimentary to say about his country of birth thereafter.

He sailed to South America and was met by his crazed-looking older cousin Blacaman, who made a living hypnotizing lions for circus crowds. Dad's job was to go into the cages beforehand and whip the cats into a crowd-pleasing frenzy. He had the scars to prove it. He and Blacaman were apparently a couple of desperate kids who lived by their wits. Whatever I know of those days I learned from Mum, whom I've plied constantly for details, and who's always happy to tell both her own stories and Dad's, for he rarely told them himself.

Koringa started out as Blacaman's pretty French assistant. She added a touch of melodrama by appearing suddenly in nurse's uniform and dashing into the cage. I reckon she assisted him outside the ring as well. When she and Dad became "friendly," as Mum puts it seventy-four years later, Blacaman and Koringa had a huge row and the latter returned to France. With equally evasive perambulation Mum tells how a year or two later Dad happened by heavenly coincidence to be strolling through Paris when he came upon a seedy theater featuring an alligator-and-python-hypnotizing-female-fakir act. There was his ex-partner's ex-girlfriend, her face framed by a huge Afro wig. He took it upon himself to become her manager, build up the act and take it to the top of the bill at England's Bertram Mills's circus.

Mum had joined the circus by this time. The war, destroyer and creator of opportunity, separated Dad from Koringa and turned Mum into his business assistant. When I ask whether he and Koringa had been lovers, Mum looks vague and says she isn't sure. I haven't a shred of evidence that the two women were mortal enemies, but I've always presumed it. Mum doesn't say anything bitter about anyone except the Germans and, as the years grow cold, Dad.

So when in 1939 Mussolini aligned poor Italy with Mister Hitler, Dad was gratefully in England. The day the Axis pact was signed, the Metropolitan Police rounded up the Italian men and sent them off to an Isle of Man internment camp to pick potatoes, leaving behind the weeping women. In the damp of the Irish Sea Dad developed chronic back pain that stuck with him for life. Nevertheless, it was there he planned his subsequent life in the restaurant business, and eventually satisfied the authorities that he posed no threat. He was released to do "work of national importance."

Because the military brass worked night and day and never made it home for dinner, there was great demand for restaurants in central London. Mum joined him in Kensington, lost her British citizenship by marrying him, an enemy alien, and worked with him through the Blitz. Her father, a veteran of the Boer War and Great War, can't have been too happy about his new Italian son-in-law. Meanwhile, the restaurant was bombed, patched up and bombed again. My elder sister, Yolanda, was

DAD: had scars

nursed in a drafty caravan near Ascot while Dad tried to get things going again in town.

One day, when Mum had exhausted herself trying to keep the newborn warm and dry, Dad showed up. He convinced her to sleep in spite of the squalling infant and a mountain of unwashed nappies. "First you sleep," he said. "I'll look after the baby and you can do the washing later."

By the time she awoke he'd washed them all, hung them up to dry and spruced up the place. Such sensitivity was hidden in this man, but it sometimes rose to the surface. He turned out to be a generous provider who fought tooth and nail for his family.

When the war ended, Dad traveled to Montevideo to set up home, and wired Mum to join him, but as she was getting ready to embark he realized that the British authorities would never let him remove his pounds sterling beyond its near-bankrupt borders, and he was soon obliged to return. The stateless Mum and the enemy alien Dad became British citizens together. For this he was proud, grateful, and determined to be a good subject. Meanwhile, Mum's dreams of a future of international travel and a colorful life onstage faded as she grew rotund with my brother, and the nappies piled high again. He was christened Francesco Philip, but in post-war Britain found it politic to favor his second name.

England now faced years of austerity, and Dad found his circumstances straitened. No longer the fur-coated impresario he'd been in 1939, he broke up with his business partner, moved to Gloucester and bought a snack bar at the small city's busiest bus stop. As he sliced his excellent sandwiches and worked sixteen-hour days, he vilified the Catholic Church without compunction. He was only one among many of his countrymen with such resentment. Certainly, the church would have overshadowed his Calabrian childhood both at school and at home. As for publicizing his feelings, perhaps being an Italian in post-war England, where nationalist feelings still ran high, he was just chattering self-consciously and trying to disown his past.

Mum, on the other hand, had longed since childhood to become Catholic, and was now taking the plunge. Canon Roach of Saint Peter's church, with Mum's newly converted ear at his disposal, demanded that she silence Dad's foul mouth—a daunting task. Although Dad wasn't about to take advice from any woman, least of all his own wife, some dim childhood respect for the priesthood led him to Saint Peter's vestry where the good Irish Canon, as belligerent and assertive as Dad himself, accepted his apology and heard his confession. The prodigal son returned to the fold just as I was about to be tossed into the cold wide world. And so it was my fortune to be raised in the arms of Holy Mother Church.

Twenty-four years later I was delighted when Dad told me he'd prayed for me to be a priest. "Gosh!" I exclaimed, "your prayers have been answered."

He wasn't amused. Picture the scene: I'd just returned home with a shaven head and announced my recent ordination as a Buddhist monk. Out of deference to his image as the city of Gloucester's premier restaurateur I'd removed my maroon robes before arriving in town and hadn't shaved my head for two weeks, so it at least had a dark patina. This conversation took place in the chattering cocktail lounge of the Don Pasquale restaurant, the sweat of his brow and his source of pride.

"You think so?" he looked me straight in the eye. I don't know if he wanted to cry or laugh, argue or hit me. We often argued, though he hadn't hit me in years. As for his feelings, an underlying sadness seemed to infuse his every action, even his laughter. I was still too young and confused by my new Buddhist clarity to understand how such emotions could coexist in one heart. I silently prayed for him, hoping that in time he'd count my blessings. As for me, I was on the road to certainty and Awakening, quite intoxicated by a joy that would prove treacherous.

But I'm getting ahead of myself. My present-day parents, Pascal and Gwenda, were two harried grown-ups who ran a café and restaurant in Gloucester and lived in the upstairs flat.

I asked Dad, "Tell me about the circus."

"That was a long time ago. You don't want to know." He turned away.

I jumped up and followed him. "But I *do* want to know."

"No!"

I took an involuntary step backwards.

"I don't know why Dad won't talk about the past," said Mum. "He says there's no point."

"But it's so interesting."

"Yes. He could write a book."

"He should."

"Never mind dear. Perhaps you'll write one, one day."

I laughed. "Anyway Mum, what do *you* remember?"

And she'd launch into another of her romantic tales. A lot of water would have to flow under the bridge before the darker ones emerged. By that time I knew enough about Dad to not be surprised, but it was a relief to see Mum finally break the silence and reveal all her accumulated resentment. That was much later.

She was right about his arrogance, but it was his charm and unhampered generosity that won her over.

Nevertheless, the very day of their registry office wedding she was initiated into the Calabrian sense of natural order. Pascal expected not just her obedience and unswerving loyalty but also control over her spending, to which end he put out his hand and demanded her purse. She was taken aback, but handed it over. In those days marriage was marriage[1] and she'd made her bed.

They worked together from day one. She held her head up and considered herself an equal, but he treated her as an employee, albeit the most valuable *and* lowest paid. The way he saw it, she was privileged to share in his bounty. All she had to do was to bear children, care for us, keep the flat clean and tidy and, at the end of a long day, dress up, turn on cue into the restaurateur's elegant hostess and charm the customers.

We were four children. Yolanda preceded me by eight years, Philip came midway between us and Maria was another eight years younger. As the firstborn male Phil was supposed to be the head of the family in Dad's absence, but his orders fell mostly on deaf ears. Yolanda, his significant senior, had no time for patriarchal nonsense, and I was endowed with an instinctive disdain for authority. Dad scared me, but, as older brothers do, Philip annoyed me.

What with Dad's refusal to explore his memories and Mum's stiff upper lip, there was little sharing of feelings in our family. My emotions nevertheless spilled out. Bouts of frustration were accounted for by the inherent *bad temper* for which I was routinely upbraided.

"Control yourself, Stephen."

I called upon the highest authority I knew. "What about Jesus?" I demanded. "He was always making trouble for the Pharisees."

Comparing myself with the One Christ didn't help matters. My crime climbed the scale from belligerence to blasphemy.

The notion of self-improvement infuriated Dad. His mantra was "You can't change human nature!" I was never clear on exactly what he meant by that, but he threw it at me whenever I suggested that we could rise above the mire. I knew what I liked about Jesus, but just didn't *get* Dad's interest in him. Why go to church if you don't believe in personal change? What did he pray for? And how could he of all people demand that I control myself? It was all very baffling.

In the early years Mum used to park my pram outside the café window, where she could keep an eye on me. But as soon as I could walk, I took to wandering up Worcester Street and disappearing around the corner into London Road, where I'd explore the lanes of Gloucester for hours.

THE CATHEDRAL:
Gloucester's crowning glory

The ancient city was an inland port and came to prominence as a Roman garrison, so traces of ancient conquerors were everywhere, particularly to my imaginative eye. Any ha'penny lying in a gutter might bear the head of Hadrian, or any fragment of glazed brick might have adorned the villa of some Latin-speaking family. There were *bona fide* Roman walls and other ruins too, though never quite as exciting. I imagined soldiers in red tunics watching over leisurely colonists while the downtrodden Britons cursed them in their forgotten tongue. The thought of so many centuries and people, all dead and gone, sent shivers down my spine.

I didn't know just how famous Saint Oswald's church was, built by Æthelred in the ninth century, but I did know that its ruins had the best nooks in which to hide and let my imagination run free. As I crouched in old corners, I fancied I could hear the faithful whispering their prayers. Then, if the police hadn't already found and returned me to Mum's beating breast, I'd stroll up Westgate Street past walls of bulging criss-crossed timbers, fully functional remnants of Shakespeare's day. Richard II's parliament had been held nearby; the Dukes of Gloucester were always tight with the sovereigns of England. There was no end to the once rich and famous, and I took it for granted that the little city in which I grew up must be the capital of the world.

If anything made this self-evident, it was the cathedral, Gloucester's crowning glory. Following in their fathers' and grandfathers' skirret lines, local stonemasons had cut limestone blocks, carved glorious saints and hideous gargoyles with equanimity, built massive cylindrical piers and pioneered new forms of vaulting for ever higher ceilings and broader inner spaces. The walls and windows were inscribed with *memoria* and the floor paved with gravestones. I reveled in awe of the dead;[2] after all, the living were so troublesome.

My biggest problem with Gloucester was the regional accent—I didn't have it. Mum was determined that no rural "arr" would creep into our voices. "Don't speak like that," she'd say. "It sounds so *awful.*"

I spoke well, and paid the price on the streets.

"Whatcha staring at, kid?"

"Nothing," I'd say.

"You're staring at me, kid." The scenario hardly varied. A sneering boy approached while his accomplices loitered nearby. Smiling, he'd grab my shirt.

I'd swing at his face and he'd dodge. The others would grab me from behind.

They'd let me go just in time for me to receive a fist in the face. I'd see stars, and recover only to find my head cradled in the crook of his arm. I hated when they did that. They all did.

"Bloody bastard!" I'd mutter.

He'd twist my head. "Give up!"

"Go to Hell."

"You can't beat me, toffee-nosed wop snot." He'd twist again.

I'd push, we'd fall to the ground; but he wouldn't lose his grip. My knees were always either bleeding or scabbed.

All of a sudden they'd be gone, and adults would appear as the running footsteps and laughter faded around the nearest corner.

"Disgraceful," a woman said on one occasion. "Look at you, fighting in the street like a common hooligan!" She had a high-pitched voice and her face was encrusted with make-up. I wanted to kick her in the shins. Her husband gave me a look of silent sympathy.

I'd return dishevelled to the café, much to Mum's embarrassment. Dad was trying to run a business and couldn't have scruffs like me wandering in and out. The café in front wasn't so posh, but the extension Dad had built on the back, a fine dining room named Don Pasquale after himself and Donizetti's opera,[3] was sacrosanct. I was barred from its portals unless previously tidied and vetted by Mum; even then, Dad scowled.

Why was Dad so bloody difficult? I knew nothing of his past, nor of psychology for that matter, but it seemed from the smiling black and white photographs that he'd been happy before the war, so I blamed it on his present—the restaurant, the sweat of his brow.

I recall him endlessly stamping into the restaurant kitchen and shouting at Frankie the chef or rolling up his sleeves to do the dirty work himself: washing dishes, sweeping the yard, cleaning out the drains, all the while muttering mild obscenities in English and nasty blasphemies in Italian. In his more communicative moments, he'd complain that he slaved long hours with poor produce, hopeless staff and unappreciative customers and still managed to produce the best restaurant in the West Country. His pride was genuine, but it didn't seem to bring him any lasting satisfaction.

"Nevertheless, customers entering the Don Pasquale on a busy evening were greeted in continental elegance by the patron and his wife. Dad's Italian charm and Mum's English refinement worked in gentle counterpoint. This was very satisfying to the customers and extremely good for business. The excellent dining was enhanced by their mutual experience of working a crowd. Waiters appeared magically when required and evaporated into thin air when not. The twitch of an eyebrow or slightest turn of a head set in motion a chain of events that attended each client's every need. And if there were any doubts about Dad's foreign origins,

THE DON PASQUALE: fine dining; continental elegance

Mum's impeccable accent soothed and reassured them. She spoke the Queen's English, and when the need arose she put just the right edge on her voice to hob-nob with the gentry.

In her high heels and elegant dresses, Mum was admired by others and jealously prized by Dad. If she spoke or laughed too easily with a male customer, Dad might remove her abruptly from the bar and demand to know what the hell was going on. Perplexed by his arbitrary suspicions and unable to calm his fears, she retreated to the Ladies to recompose her makeup and her nerves. Meanwhile, the abandoned customer was left to prop up the bar, picking at olives and gherkins, and wondering where his charming hostess had gone.

Dad complained about the staff. They were unreliable. They didn't respect him. They were lazy. They stole his wine. They wasted his food. One Sunday as we returned from church he called in at the restaurant and came back shaking his head in frustration.

"Staff problems?" I asked, repeating an oft-heard phrase.

He laughed at my precocity. "Yes, staff problems. I can't rely on anyone."

"When I grow up, Daddy," I said, "I'll come in the restaurant and work for you and you'll always be able to rely on me."

He shook his head, "I know you mean it son. I appreciate it. But you'll change your mind. When you grow up you won't want to work with me. You'll go off and do what you want to do. But that's okay. I won't try to stop you."

"No!" I protested. "I want to help. I'll stay."

"No you won't," he insisted.

"But I will." I was alarmed. "I *want* to."

He said. "No you won't, but it's okay."

By now we'd moved into a large house in Sandhurst Lane. Dad drove slowly through the empty Sunday streets and I cried all the way.

When the time came years later, Dad was true to his word and didn't lay even a sliver of guilt on my head, at least, not on that count. Instead, it landed mostly on my brother, Philip.

Dad stood in for God—patriarchal, all-powerful, silent and incomprehensible. He was selfish and unfair, generous and thoughtful.

As children do, I trusted that every beating was my fault; after all I'd been warned. Besides, there was nothing unusual about it in those days. From smacks on the bottom to public thrashings, tales of crime, punishment and bravado quickly buried the pain and humiliation. Phil was once chased through the house as Dad swung a broom at him, and got over it by joking afterwards about how funny he must have looked as he dodged the blows. We were old-school Catholics, and denial was an indispensable tool of our household.

Dad wouldn't lay a hand on the girls, however, and reserved special treatment for them. When he found Yolanda holding a boy's hand at age fourteen—he'd actually been following her suspiciously from a distance— he informed her that she was *a slut*. This expectation of betrayal hinted at something in his past, but all we ever turned up was a pale photo of a child with Dad's face, born out of wedlock years before he met Mum, and a fragmentary anecdote by his sister Evalina about a period when he lived in Trieste with a French woman called Marie.

Who was that man?

My younger sister, Maria, took me by surprise at his funeral when she echoed the very same question, and I realized for once that I wasn't alone. He was a mystery to all of us, apparently to himself as well.

I swore that would never happen to me.

2

HOLY, ROMAN & CATHOLIC

EVERY SUNDAY MORNING mum woke us early to dress up and traipse off to ten o'clock mass. There we'd join the crush of people surging through the heavy doors and vying for the best pews. The congregation greeted one another in reverential whispers. As we entered, the men made themselves respectful by removing their hats, the women by putting theirs on.

I took a smear of holy water from Mum's fingertips to cross myself, passed the Catholic Truth Society bookcase, genuflected in the aisle and knelt to say a prayer or two while waiting for the first shake of the bells. The priest led with a chalice full of yet-to-be consecrated hosts, altar boys in train.

For the next hour or so the passage of time slowed to an agonizing crawl. To this day, the smell of wood varnish, floor polish, body sweat and frankincense numbs me more effectively than any tranquilizer. The altar was decorated with beautiful, sometimes magnificent flowers, but no breath of natural freshness ever seemed to waft my way. More often, the blood drained into my feet and I had to sit down. Fortunately, the Latin mass required frequent changes of position.

The reading of the gospel stories offered a brief reprieve, for I liked Jesus tremendously. He made enemies in high places, upturned tables in the temple and outraged the pious. But then we had to listen to the Epistles, preachy entreaties to do what we *should*. Evidently, Christ was one thing, Christians were something else.

"Ite, Missa est," concluded the priest.[4]

"Deo Gratias," I sighed.[5]

As we left Mum and Dad always commented on how beautiful the mass had been, while I thought how wonderful the fresh air tasted.

Escape was an interim affair, for God's servants always lurked nearby, and even enlisted my unwitting brother. Philip came home from White-friars Priory School one day talking about a pupil who'd served mass one morning, taken communion, looked up at the clear blue sky and announced, "What a beautiful day to die." Then he got on his bike and rode straight down London road, through a red light and headfirst into an oncoming car. Father Walsh, the headmaster, announced to the assembly that he'd gone most definitely and directly to paradise.

ST. PETER'S: *no breath of natural freshness ever seemed to waft my way*

Contemplating this, I decided that if I were to cycle down London Road and into an oncoming car, even under the same gracious circumstances, I didn't fancy my chances in the afterlife. Nevertheless, I grasped from this story that religion's function was to relieve death's sting. As long as you avoided mortal sin since your last communion you were safe. However, this soul-saving sacrament wasn't just a wafer of bread, it was a very slippery state of mind.

I practiced assiduously for my First Communion, but when the body of Christ was finally placed on my tongue, I felt only disappointment. I was awarded a glow-in-the-dark statue of the Madonna and a brand new red missal, but felt I'd cheated my way into the Assembly of God.

Sister Teresa said, "If you can't feel the Holy Spirit it's because you haven't yet opened yourself to him. You must be pure of heart."

Judging by results I obviously wasn't, but on the other hand I didn't feel *that* impure. I asked what Heaven was like.

"Heaven? Why, it's a wonderful place where everybody is pure."

There was that word again. "Yes, Sister; but what do they *do?*"

Sister looked perplexed. "Why, they adore God of course."

"Like in church? For all eternity?"

She smiled. "Exactly."

And that was the alternative to Hell?

Mass was just the first of the Sabbath rituals; the next was embracing the brethren. A sizable proportion of Saint Peter's congregation was as Irish as Canon Roach, and it was a short walk from the backyard of the church to the social club, where on Sunday mornings the stout flowed like water.

We Catholics were a minority in Protestant England, and Dad's nationality was an added liability. I didn't know it at the time but now I understand how Dad took refuge from his insecurities in the company of fellow outsiders. English xenophobia was always tempered by humor, but it was xenophobia nonetheless, and to many Englishmen he was a "bloody foreigner" while the Irish were "bloody navvies."[6] Here, however, they were all Catholics together, *tanks be ter God*!

Afterwards, we headed home for the sacred Sunday roast, the third ritual of the Lord's Day.

At home, with a schooner of Amontillado sherry in hand, Mum was queen of the fragrant Sunday lunch. She turned out roasted joints, batter puddings, carrots, peas, potatoes roasted, boiled and mashed, gravies, trifles, meringues with fruit, whipped double cream, cheesecakes and pies, all as if by magic. Cheeses stood on the sideboard with bread, biscuits and celery. A tray of mint chocolates awaited after-dinner coffee and brandy. Sunday was the day our family feasted and became English. In fact, it was the day it became a family.

If mass was boring, lunch was anything but. Dad opened the wine, carved the meat and was determined that we respect his sacrifices and Mum's. We'd bloody well enjoy it, or else. Sometimes he'd remind us how he'd stared hollow-eyed and hungry into prewar Paris restaurants, and once been chased off by a fuming maître-d'. "That night," he'd say proudly, "I swore I'd have my own restaurant one day and eat whenever I was hungry. I'll never forget what it's like to have nothing." He smiled grimly. This was as close as he got to letting on about the past.

This day and this meal had to be perfect. Knowing it all too well, I hung on tenterhooks, fearing the confrontation I knew was coming. My brother had fun by goading me to the point of fury, then standing back to watch the outcome. Known from an early age as the bad-tempered one, I never had a leg to stand on. In later years Dad would thump the table so hard that every plate, dish and utensil jumped. "Eat like a bloody Christian," he'd say. I could rarely figure out what had upset him, nor exactly how Christians ate.

Dad's constant eruptions left me increasingly inured to him, more scornful than fearful. Meanwhile, he chomped noisily on his food, pried detritus from his teeth with his extra-long Calabrian little-fingernail and ferreted out larger morsels with his tongue. He apparently considered himself subject to a different set of table manners than the ones Mum instilled in us. That we lived under his roof and within his realm was never in doubt.

I resented being there with all my might, hardly tasting the food and wishing I could be anywhere else. As knives and forks were placed side-by-side on cleared plates, and serviettes removed from shirt-collars and laps, the thanking began.

"Wonderful, darling. God bless you," said Dad.

Philip said, "Thanks Mum. This was really great."

Yolanda added, "Yes indeed," with a satisfied sigh.

Little Maria licked her lips and hummed contentedly, "Mmm . . . ."

They probably weren't staring, waiting for me to trip over my own words, but that's how it felt. I smiled wanly, "Thanks Mum, it was very nice." I never quite believed that such half-baked lies would go uncontested, but all I received were blank looks on which I projected my own reproach. Mum gazed on me with mingled love and sadness, and I felt guilty for being an alien in the bosom of my family.

However, by this time I was more angry than anything. I ran upstairs, buried my face in a pillow and screamed, "Bastard, bastard, goddamn bastard." My feelings remained long after Dad was asleep in front of the TV, and in the following hours and days, at the oddest times, they burst in shards of spite like buttons from a bulging waistcoat. I was as baffled as my victims.

My freedom was short-lived, however, and I had to go down to clear the table, take my place before the telly and watch old Pinewood and Hollywood films. These, I presumed, were the edgy, prewar, black-and-white days when Dad and Mum had been young and happy. The world we lived in was different, and as I tried to compare its shapes and textures I fantasized about time travel into the past or future—anything to escape the present.

I was eleven when I stole my first box of Maltesers[7] from Mister Meadow's sweet shop. I was caught, not red-handed but after leaving a trail of evidence that culminated in an empty box hidden conspicuously among the flowerpots.

Dad approached me with unusual subtlety and extracted my confession without violence. Then he whisked me over to Mister Meadows to apologize, to Canon Roach to confess, and a few days later to Doctor Doherty, to repair the psychiatric anomaly. Mister Meadows was more embarrassed by the baring of family secrets than upset by his loss. Canon Roach was strict and gave me penance, but absolved me. The child psychiatrist was another matter.

For several weeks I visited his offices regularly to complete intelligence tests and answer his questions. I enjoyed the attention. Dad had picked him because he was a fellow Catholic, but he was also a detached professional who advised Dad that my shoplifting was a cry for help, and that he should spend more time with me. Dad in turn gave the good doctor his own opinion—that doctors were all quacks and bloody fools and that he knew perfectly well how to raise his own children thank you, and to mind his own damn business.

In the end, I was left with no sense that I'd been forgiven, redeemed or cured. Life hadn't budged. Had God punished me? It didn't seem so. Still, I didn't steal again for years. Only when I was once and for all beyond the long arm of Dad and the church did I become an expert shoplifter and helpless kleptomaniac.

For the time being, however, I feared eternal Hell and prayed every night to Jesus who, with a twitch of his eyebrows, could mend my ways and free me from the evil within. But Catholic logic worked against me. If He answered all sincere calls for help, but was deaf to me, I must be insincere. Self-loathing proved at least that I didn't condone myself, but the question remained—how was I to connect life itself to my fate as a Roman Catholic? The answers were supposedly provided by the Catechism of Christian (i.e., Roman Catholic) Doctrine.

—Who made you?

—God made me.

—Why did God make you?

—God made me to know Him, love Him and serve Him in this world, and be happy with Him forever in the next.[8]

I was used to being disregarded by grown-ups; who wasn't? What was more troubling was that my peers appeared to be perfectly untroubled by the spiritual doubts that tortured me. Some professed to believe, "just in case," shrugging off the untenability of their position with an ease I found inconceivable. They were no more use than my teachers, my family and their ever-silent God.

3

EDUCATION

Shortly before my eleventh birthday and my entry into senior school, Dad announced that he would take me with him to Italy. Philip had gone the year before and now it was my turn. Mum, staying behind to look after the restaurant, waved as we drove off early one morning in his Jaguar Mark Two. This was a status symbol that merely elevated him in England but glorified him in his homeland and among his family, both of which he'd abandoned as a young man.

As the powerful motor ate up the miles, Dad explained the Highway Code and road signs of each country we passed through. It was his way of bridging an uncomfortable gap. I'd hoped, perhaps expected, that this trip would bring what I'd always longed for—a real connection, stories about his life and predictions about what awaited me in the big wide world. After all, wasn't I just like him?

Oblivious to my hopes, he shied away from my childish questions with the same old excuse, that the past was gone and the future was unknown. During that trip I realized he was never going to share his personal life. Worse still, when his beloved sister Evalina discovered my ignorance of Italian customs and language, she scolded him and he scowled at me. I was a source, or at least a reminder, of his shame.

One particularly hot afternoon, however, we left a small café and came upon a woman in rags, crouched on the ground, one arm spread-eagled against a wall, the other clasping a squirming infant. I watched her as she targeted Dad by twisting her face into a grimace of misery, whining histrionically and grasping at his clothes. His reaction astonished me. With a kind word and not a second thought, he fished in his pocked and dropped a few coins into her palm. She thanked him with great sighs, as if he'd saved her from certain doom.

I was thinking hard. "She was a beggar, wasn't she?"

"Yes," He glanced at me.

"But, wasn't she acting?"

He smiled. "Yes."

"So why'd you give her money?"

"Because she wouldn't be acting if she didn't need it."

For a few days we got along unusually well.

That winter I joined Philip at Whitefriars Priory School for Boys. The Carmelite monks, in brown robes and scapulae, always had a stick of chalk in hand. This versatile tool could just as easily write on the blackboard as regain a wavering pupil's attention when, out of the blue, a flung nub would sting your head or neck. The masters found satisfaction in a good shot, and a suitably wry comment might even raise a laugh from the class. We were as merciless with each other as the teachers were with us.

We expected nothing but the most stringent discipline. Once, waiting for an overdue teacher, our boisterousness was escalating into bedlam when a sudden cry went up, "McGuire! McGuire!"

There was a mad scramble as each boy tried to get back to his desk, straighten his tie, don his blazer and tidy up. Dark robes billowed outside the window and within moments the full six-foot-six frame of Father McGuire, senior dean of discipline, filled the doorway. He was a master of intimidation, corpulent but not soft; the only teacher without a nickname.

Without raising his voice in the least he cut through the noise one syllable at a time, like a slow knife through butter.

"What is the meaning of this?"

McGuire: a brilliant interrogator

His eyes darted from face to face. We stood to attention, staring at the floor. When the last speck of dust had settled he evaporated from the doorway, reappeared at the master's desk and repeated in the barest whisper, "What is the meaning of this?" It wasn't a rhetorical question. He would provoke one of us to say something—anything—and then use it against us. He was a brilliant interrogator.

I felt the blood drain from my head. It became ice cold, as if it no longer belonged to me. McGuire walked right up to me. "You look pale, Schettini. Are you ill?"

I wondered how long I could stay standing. McGuire was well-known to pick on one boy and make an example of him. "Thank you Father. I'm a little ... I'll be all right." A cold sweat moistened my forehead.

His eyes bored into mine as if I might be mocking him. But he just said "Hmm," and carried on walking, up and down each aisle, stopping to scan each boy's face for signs of weakness.

Back at the master's desk he asked, as if he didn't know, "For whom are you waiting?"

Some brave soul said, "Mister Hayward, Father."

"Mister Hayward has been unexpectedly called away," he said. "I shall conduct this class."

For the first time he looked irritated, went to the window and scanned the grounds. He turned back to us and said, "Sit."

At last my blood flowed again, making me warm and dizzy.

His idea of conducting a class was harder on us than on himself. "You will all write one hundred lines," he said, picking up a piece of white

chalk and writing the line with unerring legibility on the blackboard:
"I shall wait quietly and patiently in between periods." With any other
teacher the word *period* would have provoked puerile schoolboy snig-
gering, but now there wasn't even a shared look of complicity. "I will read
each and every line, and they will all be legible. Do you understand me?"

We spoke in clear, strong unison, "Yes, Father."

He rubbed his hand on the front of his habit, leaving behind a dusting
of chalk. We took out exercise books and pens and got down to it.

"I shall return," he said ominously. On his way out he stopped in the
doorway, turned and added, "If this disgraceful behavior is repeated I
shall personally cane each and every one of you."

We stood up as one. "Yes, Father. Thank you, Father."

He left. We breathed.

Whitefriars was a private school with somewhat higher standards than
the state school system, and we were about as content with our lot as any
English schoolboy. We had no expectation of respect and would have
been surprised to learn that we had rights. United by our own unwritten
rules, we wrestled or boxed one another on matters of honor, generally without involving teachers. Strong and belligerent, I fought often,
winning and losing in equal measure.

I was also a good pick as a front-row prop in a rugby game, or so
everyone thought. Try as I might, however, I was unmoved by competi-
tive spirit and saw little point in exhausting myself to get a ball from one
end of a muddy pitch to the other. My disinterest raised the ire of my
teammates, whom I challenged to *not* pick me, but time and again I was
nominated on account of my size and srength to what was considered a
privileged position, and time and again I disappointed them.

The same disinterest affected my academic performance. Term reports
described me as lazy and untidy, careless and erratic, though more colloquial expressions were applied in class. It wasn't lost on us that the monks'
vow of celibacy was a perverse attempt to thwart nature, and we accepted
their periodic unpleasantness as a side-effect. I witnessed physical but
never sexual abuse, though I can't speak for others. The corporal punishment they inflicted on us seemed to sublimate their most twisted energy.

WHITEFRIARS SCHOOL
CHELTENHAM

SENIOR SCHOOL.

Name *Schettini, Stephen*   Age *11.6*

Form *S I A*   No. in Form *29*   Average Age of Form *11.11*

Term *Michaelmas / Hilary*   19 *64*

Pass Mark 45%

	Marks %	Position	
Religion	53	22	*Stephen can do better*
English Language	60	22=	*Lazy, careless and untidy*
English Literature	54	20	*Could do much better*
Latin	21	20	*Extremely weak.*
Greek *Essay*	48	27	*Careless and untidy work.*
French	58	17	*Exam shows recent effort. Until then, work well below standard*
German			
History			
Geography			
Arithmetic ⎫			
Geometry ⎬	67	7	*A good mark. Very lazy at times during term.*
Algebra ⎭			
General Science	50	23	*Work rather erratic.*
Physics			
Chemistry			
Biology			
Art			*Fair. Must concentrate much harder.*
Craftwork			
Music	28	25	*Must learn to pay attention.*
P.E. and Games			*Quite good effort*
Speech			

Conduct *Satisfactory*

Times Absent *3*   Punctuality *Satisfactory*

General Remarks *Stephen seems to have settled well but he must also work well. So far we have been easy on him but we shall not be so next term*

Next Term Begins *16th April*

Next Term ends *17th July*

Half-Term *18th – 21st May.*

[signature] Head Master.

SCHOOL REPORT: *lazy and untidy, careless and erratic*

One never admitted to being intimidated by a forthcoming caning, nor in retrospect to having been truly hurt. Nevertheless, a prolonged wait outside Father McGuire's door after school could elevate the punishment into a minor torture. The cold-blooded canings were best because they were quick and businesslike. He was certainly the most professional. I experienced the following scenario so often that even these four-and-a-half decades later only the present tense rings true.

"Offence?"

"Fighting, Father."

"With whom?"

"Tuohy, Father."

He opens the door and calls Tuohy in.

"Offence?"

"Fighting, Father"

"With whom?"

"Schettini, Father."

"Cause of this conflict?"

"Can't remember Father," (in unison).

"Hmm," (not without satisfaction).

We're standing at attention, trying to look impassive, trying not to tremble. Father levers my left arm into a horizontal position with the tip of the cane, takes a couple of practice shots through the air and then slashes down on the very tips of my fingers. They turn icy-cold, then red hot, tingling and throbbing. He slashes again and misses, and again and misses. He understands pain and isn't interested in the easy target of the palm. When inflicted with precision the pain creeps slowly from the extremities up the entire length of the arm. On the forth try he makes contact once more, and then a third time. With a twitch of the head he indicates that I'm to change arms. I hold my right arm at seventy-five degrees to my body and he lifts it the remaining fifteen degrees with the cane, into a fully horizontal position. The first stroke makes a loud thud. "That," he says, "doesn't count." He knows it doesn't hurt. It takes him six slashes to connect three good hits. The pain's climbing in overlapping throbs. Meanwhile, the feelings in my left arm have receded, leaving a tingling memory of ice and fire.

I watch as Tuohy is subjected to the same treatment and notice that he cringes and twitches between strokes. I pray I didn't; I'm not sure.

We learned history and geography, maths and science, art and rugby. We were even methodically instructed on the dangers of smoking, but the facts of life were *off* the curriculum.

Mum introduced me to sex with a glossy, unillustrated pamphlet from The Catholic Truth Society, called "Coming of Age (Boys' Edition)." The author warned against touching one's penis, just in case it proved enjoyable, and successfully armed the guilt crucifix in my groin.

I was terrified of the opposite sex anyway, and my contact with them was limited to the girls of Charlton Park Convent School, who shared our school bus. One or two sometimes smiled shyly at me, but for some unfathomable reason I fixated on Melissa Godfrey, whose chief attraction was her stentorious self-possession. After months of longing and inner struggle I finally summoned up the courage to ask her out and was rewarded with a decisive reply that rang like a bell throughout the bus, "Stephen Schettini, I wouldn't go out with you if you were the last boy on Earth." My self-esteem crashed through the floor and lay like an indelible blot on the asphalt. From then on, as we passed that unmentionable shrine each morning and evening, I sank a little deeper into my seat and my shell.

Mum told me, "You're just like your father." Dad said it too, but it still made no sense. He was a ladies man, and I was scared stiff of girls. I'd have loved to be the glittering Pascal in the photographs, to brim with confidence, travel the world and not be like other men. As school days drew to a close I was excited but also apprehensive about my forthcoming freedom.

I'd never experienced the pleasure of work well done, of writing a good essay, conducting a successful lab experiment or playing a satisfying game of rugby. I'd half-consciously developed a self-image that rejected the qualities held in esteem by others and told myself that consensus was just form of control. I wouldn't give in. My term reports had accurately described me as unmotivated. "Doesn't apply himself. Lazy. Slovenly." Their most convincing words rang in my ears for years—"You're stupid,

Schettini. Stupid," though they never put that in writing. In fact, my laziness was all the worse for wasting my mind. Still, they rejected me. I rejected them back.

As my sixteenth birthday approached I felt like an oddball, an outsider in my family and in my country. Dad had created a business for his children to inherit but complained about it incessantly. Why would I follow him down that road? Everything about him that I liked was packed away in that suitcase under the stairs.

It all hit me at once. I'd never go into the restaurant. I had no academic prospects and was as hopeless with girls as I was with God, but independence was bearing down on me like an express train. I actually pulled up my socks sufficiently to scrape together a dozen O levels. With a vague sense of relief, I took a job as a laboratory technician in a chemical plant. My attempts to escape mediocrity had led me to a dead end.

Mum commented, "What a shame you can't do better." It was nice that she cared, but Dad, astonishingly, took the time to sit down and say, "Son, this job won't satisfy you for long. Why don't you think about going to university? Wouldn't you like that?"

His confidence in me was like a thunderbolt from a clear blue sky. All I'd wanted for the last five years was to get as far away as possible from school—and from Dad—but that single gesture turned me around in an instant.

"If you want, we'll look into it. You can take your A levels here in Gloucester and live at home. You won't starve."

What made Dad think of higher education? As far as I knew he had no intellectual interests, though I later discovered that he'd memorized large chunks of Dante's writings, and once adored opera. He'd repeatedly run away as a boy and ended up at the Tivoli "residential school," an Italian epithet for "secure." He never could make head or tail of my homework, which was heavily laden with maths and science, and the only books I ever saw him read were the lives of Saint Francis and Padre Pio. In fact, I'd often find him at my Superman and Batman comics because, he claimed, they put him to sleep. He watched TV westerns, crime shows and courtroom dramas for the same reason. He was street-wise and smart, and though his family values might have been a little medieval he had a broad view of the world. He could make me as furious as ever, but he was the only man I knew whose life was enviable, or at least had once been.

In any case, I'd now received an injection of moral support, and my imagination began to weave grandiose visions of academic glory. Perhaps I'd get somewhere after all.

4

TURBULENCE

MY GENERATION GREW UP RESPECTFUL and squeaky-clean; boys sported short-backs-and-sides and girls wore demure frocks. By our late teens, however, we'd become raucous, unkempt and apparently senseless. The sixties were upon us.

Our parents were perplexed. They'd learned the hard way about the ups and downs of life and were thankful to not be at war—or *were* they? They glorified peace and prosperity, tut-tutting the distressing images from Vietnam, but they couldn't stop talking about *their* war; with God on their side they'd destroyed Hitler and the Nazis. It wasn't just pride that kept them talking. It was *nostalgia*, of all things. The 1939–45 War had been a glorious bonding experience. It transcended the generations who lived through it and even bridged the gaping chasms of English society. Mum loved that class barriers fell and the nobs mucked in with the rest. In those xenophobic, belt-tightening years it seemed the English invented a new society, only to see it trashed by their spoiled offspring.

Our generation saw reality in a different light. The multiple hydrogen bombs mounted on thousands of missiles around the world terrified and disgusted us. The strategy of the day, *Mutually Assured Destruction* (MAD), demolished any residual respect for authority. The triumphant march of materialism brought not a shred of relief to the starving millions in Africa, and the flood of labor-saving appliances and industrial food were like a conspiracy to extinguish the human spirit. Raised on tales of righteousness and brotherhood, we felt betrayed.

My hair grew over my ears and I sported a shadow of soft fuzz on my upper lip. Philip, the respectable son, worked side by side with Dad in the restaurant. I was barred, lest I scare off the customers. Content to avoid them both, I took jobs by turns as a milkman, a farmhand, a chain boy,[9] a plasterer's mate, an electrician's assistant and a general laborer. The restlessness had barely begun, and my earnings melted away instantly on short-term relief.

My regular drinking companion and best friend was Stuart James, who lived just a few dozen yards from our new home on the edge of Gloucester's surrounding farmlands. We'd grown into adolescence together. His stepfather, a successful solicitor whose practice wasn't slowed in the least by profound alcoholism, was even more forbidding than Dad. Our mothers brought Stu and me together, but it was the two incomprehensible men in our respective homes that bound us. We spent hours escaping them, hoping for adventure and wondering what our seemingly eternal futures held in store. His passion was music, and he assumed that mine must be too. My ambition was less specific; I just wanted out. Still, we were boyhood friends. We grew up together, listened to the Beatles, recited *Monty Python's Flying Circus* skits, roamed the fields and ponds around Gloucester and fantasized about our approaching adulthood.

My bad temper was by now a part of my identity, though not an issue with Stu. With him and others I might be grumpy or fretful, but it was my immediate family that triggered the real tantrums. Years of trying to suppress them left me hardly knowing what I felt, and I developed a stony persona. Perhaps I'd steeped too long in the tannic brew of unreflective Catholicism. Stu tried valiantly to shake me up and put me in touch with the currents of the time. In spite of my lengthening hair, restlessness and changing self-image, I remained as rigid as a brick wall. His mission, for which I'm eternally thankful, was to make me bend. He spoon-fed me the momentous music of the day as the new *de facto* reality.

He played me Bob Dylan. While the needle scratched its way around the vinyl albums we smoked his stepfather's untipped Senior Service, sipped beer and contemplated the unapproachable charms of the neighborhood girls.

One summer night as we loitered by a large iron-bar farm gate and looked up at the starry sky, I asked, "What's out there, d'you think?"

"Dunno."

"Don't you ever think about it?"

"Like what?"

"Like life, other people out there?"

"Dunno," he said.

I shrugged. "Maybe they're staring in this direction and wondering if anybody's out here."

His eyes opened wide. "D'you think they are?"

We speculated until we didn't make any more sense. But as I walked home I realized that such thoughts lent me freedom. I loved the silence that followed those unanswerable questions.

As clear as it might have been to Stu that inflexibility was a feature of second-rate Catholicism, I could never quite put my finger on exactly how. Perhaps I was too close to it. Pope John XXIII tried to lighten things up by translating the Latin mass into the vernacular, much to Mum and Dad's chagrin. But the new English service was even drearier than the old one, for removing the ancient language only made it more banal. I was ready to give it all up, but Dad was vehement that as long as I lived in his house, I'd attend mass every Sunday.

At about this time John Lennon said of his band, "The Beatles are more popular than Jesus." If he'd been wrong the fury would have been less, but it was a moot point anyway and just proved that we really were free to think, say and do what we wanted. Popular music had turned a new corner, the word *psychedelic* entered the vernacular, girls went on the pill, a new breed of protestors stuck flowers in gun barrels and the Age of Aquarius was proclaimed. Aldous Huxley's *Doors of Perception*, was republished as college professors took hallucinogenic drugs and urged their students to "turn on, tune in and drop out."[10] This wasn't mere recreational drug use; it was a serious, if misguided, attempt to expand consciousness and rediscover an authenticity that was quite lost on the establishment.

My beard thickened and Mum and Dad's influence waned. I remained an annoyance, accepted nonetheless because I was my father's son; but the world into which I was heading had changed beyond their recognition. One of the few things we still did together was to watch television, but this too was transformed. Quite apart from John Cleese's bizarre humor and the sickening daily images of the first televised war (in Vietnam) the moral shift from closed-mouth kisses to on-screen nudity was dizzyingly rapid. The usual silence in our living room became positively eerie as we gazed upon the unspeakable. If ever there was a time for God to break his silence, this was it.

Unlike Whitefriars, Gloucester Technical College was well populated by girls, but it was a year and a half before I found the courage to ask one out. I was as shallow as most teenage boys and had a single requirement—long blond hair, which Gloria had in abundance. I took a chance and she said yes. Overcoming my own fears was such a stroke of daring that I didn't even consider her personality or the potential of a meaningful relationship. Much to Philip's delight the poor girl was a cold fish. He poked fun at me and even got Mum to laugh along.

Gloria and I were locked in my room one day when Mum knocked on the door and it failed to open. She was halfway down the stairs and in tears by the time we'd sorted out our tangled socks and underwear. All I felt was guilt, whether for my lost innocence or my lost soul I'm not sure.

If Mum and I had been more open at the time, I might have told her the truth—that my virginity was perfectly intact, that even though we were naked, Gloria had kept her knees doggedly together and I didn't know what to do next anyway. But never under any circumstances would the subject be brought openly to our family's table. Quite apart from the inconceivability of talking about sex, Mum hated to contemplate anything painful, and nothing pained her more than my failings. I hid my feelings as best I could, mostly from myself.

Each Sunday, dragged in Dad's tow, I stood in the pews, stared warily at the altar and wondered what to think. When I tried to discuss it, I discovered that most Catholics, even of my age, preferred to believe without the burden of independent thought.

By contrast, the air at college was fresh and secular. Teachers spoke to students with respect for their personal opinions, and religiously avoided all mention of God. Rather than questioning my willingness to believe, however, I merely questioned the beliefs themselves. My dependence on some sort of faith wasn't abated; if anything, it became more urgent.

Tom Butler, raised as an Irish Catholic, was now a proud apostate and committed communist. He plied his ideology on me and took delight in crushing the remnants of my belief. I liked him for his convictions, but it was his personality that sealed the deal. He was confident, forthright and cheerful even about the filthy capitalists. Above all, he walked around seemingly free of guilt and untouched by the wrath of God. Tom's influence was instrumental without being fundamental. He helped me stray from Catholicism, although I did it in a sublimely Catholic way.

My academic performance improved modestly at college. I studied science, and became fixated on a degree program at Oxford in maths and philosophy, though my marks never approached Oxbridge standards. Still shy and sometimes sullen, I landed instead at the far less illustrious Woolwich Polytechnic to read maths and computer science.

Leaving home was a strangely unceremonious affair. Phil drove me up and dropped me off in Woolwich, and I spent a miserable week trying to become enthusiastic about punch cards[11] and statistics. The independence I'd craved for so long turned out to be a new lesson in loneliness, though I became adept at denying the humiliating fact.

In search of diversion, I went for a pint with Tom, who'd begun a Social Science degree at Enfield Polytechnic. He waxed enthusiastic about his classes, his teachers and especially the college itself. It was a still a hotbed of sixties radicalism, even though we were now in the early seventies. Half the social science faculty teachers were communists of one stripe or another, and Tom was in seventh heaven. Over a few glasses of bitter I determined to switch course and college. Next morning, I ensconced myself at Enfield in the office of the chief administrator, who protested that the course was full, and didn't budge until he relented. That morning I discovered the combined power of desperation and persistence, and was rewarded by the taste of success.

On my first morning, Tom and I walked together into the corridors of knowledge at Ponders End.[12] We were accosted by a tall, wispy-bearded fellow standing guard over a large trestle table. It was neatly laid with a variety of pale yellow books, each embossed with heavily bearded busts of Karl Marx and Frederick Engels.

He nodded severely to Tom and said, "Morning comrade."

Tom nodded back, "Comrade."

The tall one turned to me, "And who have we here?"

Tom introduced us and held out a sixpenny bit. "For a manifesto please . . . ."

I was handed a thin booklet, *The Communist Manifesto*.

"I've heard of that," I said, "but I never knew what it was. So, it's a book."

The two exchanged a glance.

"You've really no idea have you? Go and read it," Tom admonished.

"Welcome to Enfield," added his friend, with just a trace of sarcasm.

Much to my surprise, I read the booklet twice. With carefully selected facts and relentlessly involuted historicism, it explained why things weren't as they should be and insisted that change was both inevitable and imminent. The world was splitting into two camps and everyone had to take sides. Which would I choose?

I accompanied Tom to political meetings, where bearded men in leather-elbowed jackets dug into heavy satchels and assaulted one another with doctrinaire catchphrases. They thumped their tomes in biblical style, spoke in exaggerated non-BBC accents, drank massive quantities of beer and constantly voiced their disgust for the middle classes. I was a "snot-nosed, shit-arsed petit bourgeois fuck," but I might marginally redeem myself by flogging copies of the tabloid *Socialist Worker* at factory gates.

I'd decided when leaving home that it was unfair to give up on God just because I'd finally broken free of Dad, and thought my new freedom might bring me closer to what I'd always wanted to believe. I meant to keep going to church on my own terms, but Sunday mornings came and went and I never raised myself. My good intentions continued for a few more months before I finally accepted that I'd no longer the slightest inclination to revisit the scenes of my spiritual disappointment. Besides, I now realized that the church was an instrument of class oppression. This was no reflection on Jesus, who remained a hero and true revolutionary in my heart. The church was the villain. Tom didn't challenge this subtle distinction, but did suggest I keep it to myself.

I had no idea who I was, what I wanted to do with my life, or even why I was on the planet. The lonelier I felt, the more I tried to make myself likable, my temper notwithstanding. But many of the people I was now mixing with exhibited an anger light years beyond mine, reveling in images of violent political change. Tom wasn't the least bit like that, but neither did it disturb him. His working-class roots and his fluency in the political idiom enabled him to mingle freely. My lack of both left me on my accustomed marginal perch.

I turned to the actual writings of Marx and Lenin, rather than the interpretations of what they "really" meant. I tinkered with them and even wrote a leftist diatribe to the *Gloucester Citizen*, much to Mum, Dad and Philip's consternation. But rather than drawing me in, these ideas ultimately led me backwards, from dialectical materialism to idealism, to Hegel and Kant. Then I leapfrogged forward to Freud. The comrades spat out all these names, with unvarying contempt, as indulgent and bourgeois. I left communism further and further behind, turned off more by its followers than by its creed. They were an unsavory lot who'd never in a million years create a brave new world.

They even resorted to guilt as I withdrew. "We missed you last night, comrade. Sick, were you? Came down with a case of middle-class apathy?"

I shuddered. It was dawning on me that there'd never be a political solution to misery, especially if this lot fixed the world.

Tom, however disappointed he might have been by my decision, wasn't petty. We were still friends sharing a flat in Palmer's Green. After a late-night party one cold, sunny Sunday we trudged through Highgate Cemetery looking for Karl Marx's tomb. What we found was a monument to rigidity. The gravestones were dusted with snow and the unkempt gardens felt comfortingly haunted. We sat on a bench, rolled cigarettes and talked about life and death.

"What's the point?" I asked.

"Of life, or of death?" Tom inveterately cracked one-liners, funny or not.

"Of existence," I was earnest. "Whatever we do is reduced to this." I indicated the dead, all around. "What's the point?"

"History," said Tom. "We do our bit."

"History comes to an end. Then what?"

"You remember the other day you asked me what a nihilist was?"

"Yes."

"It's what you're going to be if you keep thinking like that. You'll never get anywhere with questions like 'What's the point of it all.' It's not even a real question."

"What d'you mean?"

"It's got no answer. There's more to dialectical thought than just stringing words together and sticking a question mark at the end."

KARL MARX'S MONUMENT: *to rigidity*

He had me there, or so I thought at the time. Still, the revolution was just a theory, especially in complacent old Blighty. Apart from the few occasions when an issue came to life, the Vietnam War, for example, the radical left was ignored so completely by the establishment that the various factions could only maintain the sense of struggle by arguing viciously with one another. Besides, their smug certainty was the symptom of just another belief system.

More important to me, I was still relentlessly ignored by women, at least as a sexual object. It's the nature of those without self-confidence to have no hope of ever acquiring it, and I was stuck in this vicious circle, sex-starved and stymied. I blamed the crucifix in my groin. I blamed Dad. I blamed myself, though not in any constructive way. I watched friends and acquaintances pairing off as if it were the most natural thing in the world. It was the seventies and the sexual revolution was in full swing. I couldn't speak to a living soul about it.

Actually I should be more specific. Women *did* appear to be attracted to me at first, until I opened my mouth. Loni, a Scandinavian fellow student, approached me one day after class. "I'm having a party this weekend. I'd love it if you could come, and Tom."

"Great!" I said. "Thanks."

"That's wonderful." She smiled radiantly.

I was terrified.

As we entered their flat, she introduced us to her husband. So hungry and unrealistic had my hopes grown in the intervening days that the only man I'd imagined in her life was me. Although I'd told myself over and again that she couldn't possibly be interested in me, it had been all I wanted and was really willing to believe. My stupidity now washed over me. I was a sham and disappointment to myself. I can't imagine what my fake smile must have looked like to them.

He talked about his job while Loni leaned on his shoulder, looking intently at me. Then she asked, "Steve, why are you so unsure of yourself?"

I looked around. There was nowhere to retreat. "What do you mean?" I mumbled.

"Well, you're so big, so good-looking and so intelligent. It's just . . . strange."

I opened my mouth and closed it again, took a swig of beer and smiled awkwardly.

Loni said, "You have an inferiority complex, don't you?"

I went as stiff as a board.

She put her hand on my shoulder and said, "You know, there's no need."

I escaped at the first opportunity and walked for hours through the night streets of London, stung by my own absurdity. By the time I finally got home and crawled into bed, however, I knew I'd been handed a gift, a cool snapshot of myself from someone with no stake in the matter. I fell asleep and dreamt of Dad's voice echoing all around. "You can't change human nature."

I kept trying to shout, "Yes you can. You can!" but no sound emerged.

My humiliation at Loni's party wasn't lost on Tom, who'd been saying for some time that I should loosen up. He dragged me over to the flat of a friend—John Barber, whose hair and clothing hung from him like outgrown skin. John stood in the doorway like an emaciated bear and pointed at me. "He's the one?"

"He's the one." Tom confirmed.

"What one?" I asked apprehensively.

Neither one bothered to answer.

John led us into his threadbare apartment and sat at a table. He stuck three cigarette papers together, laid out a bed of tobacco and crumbled some heated resin into it. The room filled with a pungent aroma. He rolled it up with a makeshift cardboard tube at one end and licked the whole thing pornographically. While I stared, too intimidated to ask questions, Tom rocked back and forth in silent amusement.

"So," John turned to me. "Wanna get high?"

"Sure," I said, quite unsure.

Tom laughed out loud.

We passed the smoke around, the room grew cloudy and the joint became black and foul. I went to the bathroom to rinse my mouth, and when I returned the floor had grown spongy. Tom and John were grinning like a pair of Cheshire cats.

"Well, Steve," asked John. "How're you doing?"

"Fine, fine. I feel great."

"Are you stoned yet, man?"

I shrugged. "I don't know."

He put on a Beatles' album. This was music I thought I knew. My ears popped open and the sounds seemed utterly new, somehow more tangible, as if they'd taken on shape and color. It was an experience that needed no explanation.

John put fresh grapes on the table. "Here."

They too produced a unique sensory experience, as if I'd never tasted before. I flashed back to the cradle, and stared into a swirling mass of indecipherable sensory impressions. I wanted to laugh and cry. The room felt embryonic. I snuggled into it.

Next morning as the No. 149 jostled us to and fro through North London, I sat silently beside Tom, staring out at the shabby streets and thinking that something momentous lurked beneath the surface of the streets, or perhaps of my own mind. I felt like Dylan's Mister Jones.[13]

Second year began and I was scanning the notice board at college looking for lodging. I read, "Four girls looking for fifth person to share house in Ponders End.

The door was opened by a pretty brunette wearing a muslin smock and a broad smile. For once, my nice middle-class English was an advantage. "Ye seem like a decent fella," she said ushering me in. "I'm sure the others'll agree." She said she was a Geordie and added proudly, "Me da's a miner."

The girls took me in as a brother. Discovering that I was likable after all, I became silently infatuated with first one, then another. Every evening we lit candles and incense, smoked, drank endless mugs of tea, talked about the momentous changes of our times. We listened all night long to the songs of Carole King, Joni Mitchell and Bob Dylan, all of whom gave shape to our generation's disaffection—Dylan particularly. He was a master of the idiom, and made far more sense than the communists.

The excitement of these broadening horizons only accentuated the agonies of my thwarted libido. Each of my four flatmates brought their boyfriends home and, moaning through the thin walls, drove me crazy with frustration. With each passing night the thought that I'd ever have a girlfriend became a little less believable. I could only bide my time.

I wanted to study freely, and not just toe the line. I knew that if I could read and understand Karl Marx, history's most turgid author, I couldn't be as stupid or lazy as they'd said at Whitefriars. But preparing for exams became supernaturally difficult as words detached themselves from textbook pages and focus eluded me. Off-topic books interested me far more than curriculum studies, and provided beautifully circular arguments to justify my disdain. Ludwig Wittgenstein validated my suspicion that much of what passed as philosophy was just semantics. I read what I wanted to read and saw what I wanted to see.

Nevertheless, I craved a world of reality, not of ideas. Marx had said that philosophers only interpret the world, and that the point was to change it. Already convinced of this, I found my suspicion of academia deepening. I had a thirst for knowledge, but distrusted most of what was being spoon-fed to me. I felt education circling like a vulture, waiting for me zombie-like to conform to the curriculum, be shunted from college into the workforce and end up as the brainwashed servant of a faceless system. This was even worse than Dad's predicament. Mired in his work, with a family he didn't appear to enjoy, with nothing to look forward to but retirement—it seemed a fate worse than death. The specter of a pointless life loomed large. It was no passing depression but a lasting feature of my mental landscape that not only withstood the test of time but fuelled my restlessness for *real* life.

If all this sounds unbearably ponderous, then perhaps I've properly conveyed my state of mind at the time.

I admired Jesus Christ, but didn't trust religion. I respected Newton and Einstein, but suspected the scientific community. These men had founded new ways of seeing based on their own experience, but for most people truth is a matter of consensus, not evidence. My question was, what could I know for myself? To find my own way, I'd have to reject whatever I didn't understand. Both religion and science were too sophisticated.

Turning to the marginal old systems of astrology, numerology and tarot, I learned to cast horoscopes and dabble in arcane rules. I compared my flatmates' birth charts with their characters and judged for myself— or tried to. The trouble is, people are so complex that I couldn't tell whether I was describing what I saw or seeing what I described. Still, I had intriguing conversations with my fellow students and my imagination soared on speculation about the meaning of life, the nature of right and wrong and matters of cosmic significance.

From these subjects I acquired a rudimentary vocabulary of psychology and human motivation, truth and illusion. They gave me a context in which to see my own strengths and weaknesses and the wish to find inner balance. I sought it in dowsing and the geometry of ancient ley lines, standing stones and earthworks. I read the half-crazed theories of Wilhelm Reich and tried to collect orgone energy. I was now shopping regularly at any bookshop with shelves on alternative and occult sciences, and consuming every crackpot theory I could lay my hands on.

Well actually, I wasn't shopping; I was shoplifting.

I'd turned away from God and towards Communism, then from materialism to spiritualism and from good sense to convenient sense. I rejected the bourgeois drugs of alcohol and religion in favour of consciousness-expanding marijuana and hashish. I even rejected my generation's sacred new counterculture, cut off my long hair to protest the counter-establishment and wore it short-back-and-sides thereafter. I manufactured my own world. Right and wrong weren't absolute but relative truths, conscience a lubricant on the conveyor belt that carried us from school to work to family to grave. I'd do better on my own, I decided.

Gradually, I lost touch with school, Tom—even the girls at Ponders End. I approached drugs like a sacrament, music as a neo-religious experience and contrarianism as a dogma. Morality was evil. I wanted true freedom. My unfounded self-doubt flipped into rootless self-worth.

Perhaps shoplifting was just a way to get things for free, but such unflattering truths were lost on me. Flying high on daring, I fashioned all the convenient elements of Christianity, communism, science, necromancy, counter culture and spiritualism into bricks in my wall of self-serving justification. Successful theft was exhilarating.

It began with books but soon turned to food, kitchenware and electronics. I got clever at it. Ever cockier, I invited friends to witness my skills and even stole for them, handing over the booty as selflessly as Robin Hood. Those who expressed concern for my soul were excluded. I stuck with the loyal, who admired my skills, envied my daring and liked the stuff. Their unbounded gratitude drowned out my whimpering inner voices. I labeled every twinge of conscience as capitalist indoctrination. I felt cheated when I actually paid for something with hard-earned cash.

The whimpering inner voices wouldn't go away. The harder I tried to deny them, the more I felt the pull of the vortex. I willed myself to stop, but my thieving hands had a life of their own.

Desperately wanting to be somewhere and someone else, I escaped into the magical books of Don Juan[14] the Yaqui Indian sorcerer, reading the stories over and over until I had them virtually memorized. The writer Carlos Castaneda claimed to be Don Juan's apprentice. He painted him with luminous imagery, and his lessons were concise, profound and eloquent. They had the weight of universal truth, and the raging debate as to whether or not he really existed was irrelevant to me. An archetypal father figure, Don Juan taught young Carlos to erase personal history, to lose self-importance and above all to practice the subtle art of *not doing*. He was demanding, funny, intimate, trustworthy, frightening and extraordinary. Castaneda's life was turned upside down as he grappled with a reality that was off the map. Behind all the theatrics and outlandish stories he spoke to me too. I understood that I wasn't an entity unto myself and I couldn't keep on rejecting everything and everyone else. I was heading for an implosion. I needed guidance.

For my twenty-first birthday, Christine, one of my Ponder's End flatmates, gave me a copy of the I Ching.[15] She and her boyfriend, Mick, had shown me how to ask a silent question, throw three coins six times to build a hexagram and then look up the answer. The sixty-four possible outcomes are cryptic and seminal, obliging you to think things through for yourself. The mere fact that it had survived almost five millennia was a testament to its fluidity. The more I consulted it the more clearly I understood how murky my own mind and motives were, but my behavior had a momentum of its own, and still nothing changed.

Alan Watts had compared the I Ching's hexagrams to Rorschach inkblots. I scoured his writings in search of solutions. The son of a missionary, Watts had grown up in Asia and gave many of my generation their first glimpses of Buddhism and Vedanta. His field of study was religion, but he wasn't religious. In fact he urged his readers to "resist every temptation to join the organization." But he also thought that despite the allegiance of many Westerners to scientific rationalism, we actually build our lives on purely metaphysical assumptions. Even Albert Einstein, who saw space as curved and time as bendable, professed that, "The only real valuable thing is intuition." I was primed to doubt everything I knew and understood.

Christine and Mick had invited me to take LSD with them in a way that made me feel privileged. "It's not like grass or hash," Chris warned. "It's much stronger, and it lasts longer." Mick chuckled at her rhyme, shaking his straggly beard and long hair.

It was a quiet Monday morning in May and promised blue skies. Mick cut into a piece of blotting paper, dividing the two translucent dots into three pieces. Like a first communion, I put the wafer on my tongue, tasted only paper and waited to feel special. This time, however, I was pretty sure that something would happen.

We washed it down with eggs, bacon, toast and tea. "Fill up while you have an appetite," Mick said.

It was warm and sunny, and the streets were quiet. We walked up Silver Street to Hillyfields Park on the very edge of London. It was like open country.

"Feel anything yet?" Mick asked.

Christine shook her head.

"No," I said.

I placed one foot on a stile and was just about to cross when a lone flower in the footpath stopped me in my tracks. I bent right down and found it the most beautiful thing I'd ever seen. Without realizing, I was on my hands and knees.

The flower inflamed my heart; it was a gift from God, its finery only inches from my nose. I'd never seen such nuance, nor traced the lines of

LSD: I'd never seen such nuance,
nor traced the lines of growth of any
living thing with such attention

growth of any living thing with such attention. I whispered my thanks. The longer I stared, the more it revealed. I was sure that if I were patient enough its very cells would become visible. It seemed to stare back at me and I was rapt, in direct contact with it. I thanked the universe for existing, for providing me with a body and sustenance to see and feel. Life was as miraculous as this flower's momentary brilliance. We were on a par. "Thank you," I said, speaking to everything. "Thank you, thank you, thank you."

Mick said, "Steve?"

I looked up. I'd entirely forgotten his existence.

"Mick?" I was incredibly happy to see him.

He smiled, "It's working."

Christine and he exchanged a look. I grinned so widely I thought my mouth would tear open.

"Come on," Christine said, holding out her hand.

We walked out of the woods at the top of a grassy hillock and lay under the sky. Just as staring into the flower had let me into its microscopic world, the billowing of the clouds put me on speaking terms with the entire planet. I felt an ineffable sense of love, and kept mumbling inanities about Mother Earth.

I saw none of the visions of Heaven and Hell that I'd heard so much about, and was well aware that only one thing had changed, my brain chemistry. These miracles weren't unusual at all; only my noticing them was different. I was paying a different sort of attention, like a newborn who perceives colors and shapes without identifying them as named objects. I saw that meaning itself was concocted, and that our everyday interpretations hid the infinite from view.

The sun moved across the sky but I felt no passage of time. By the time we got back home the horizon was thickening with red, gold and yellow streaks, and now I had a sense of something precious slipping through my fingers. As time returned my feet became concrete ballast; my brain churned with mechanical reckonings. We sat in the large room and tears streamed down my face as I resisted the return.

Christine embraced me. "It's all right," she said. "We know."

Hours later, exhaustion finally overwhelmed me. I fell asleep with an acute pang that over the following days grew from a sense of loss into an indeterminate promise. My need for the world to accommodate some sort of rational explanation had been uprooted. I now knew experience with no agenda. Life could be more excitingly and terrifyingly spacious than I'd ever imagined.

5

BIG WIDE WORLD

IN MY FOURTH AND FINAL YEAR, I enrolled in a philosophy class, hoping that I'd learn to put my thoughts in order—in short, to philosophize. I'd patiently studied the thoughts of others for three years and was ready for the real thing, but the white-bearded professor couldn't have been less interested. He presented us with a catalog of mostly dead thinkers and prepared us to be examined on the names, dates and trends of Western thought.

I was scandalized that only Western philosophers mattered and "the world" meant *Europe*. Even American and Australasian thinkers were only grudgingly admitted. What of Islamic art and science? Indian thought and culture? China was an empire when Europeans were still scavenging for roots and berries. The sole mainstream Western figure to really interest me wasn't even considered a philosopher. This was Albert Einstein. The theory of relativity caught my imagination, and so did his ability to explain it. He even made God worth believing in. Most of the scientists and academics I'd read expressed themselves so poorly that if they'd actually found out something to help me peel away the walls of my skull, I was none the wiser. In a few deft paragraphs, using examples from everyday life, Einstein showed that there was no independent truth in the physical world, and that each observer's experience depended on where he or she stood. Meanwhile, Kurt Gödel[16] demonstrated that every logical system is built on assumptions that can never be proven.

So what could I know? Did knowledge have any point? While my philosophy professor droned on I turned these questions over in my head. The one thing that concerned me was overcoming my own compulsions—shoplifting and drugs, guilt and inadequacy.

Enfield College was strange to me now. I decided to use my final examinations to express my protest. Instead of cramming my head with the facts, figures and quotations that would earn my degree, I immersed myself more deeply than ever in the ideas and stories that truly gripped my imagination, few of which even registered on academic radar. I had the time of my life writing every exam and project on my own terms, and paid the price.

I'd been the first of my family to pursue a "higher education," and no doubt they believed I'd squandered an opportunity, but I'd decided to resist becoming a unit of skill made to fit a predefined social function. I'd read *1984* and watched *Modern Times*. I didn't belong, or I didn't wish to. It didn't really matter which.

To all appearances I'd lost my marbles, but in retrospect I see that I was just trying to be true to myself. Had things gone "right," I would have crashed later, in more narrow corridors of life than those described here.

I told myself I'd done my best. I'd even half expected to convince the authorities that I knew what I was talking about—that they were wrong and I was right. Without compunction, I took my place in the examination room and pointed out the invalidity of the questions and the limitations of Western knowledge. I quoted Karl Marx, Bob Dylan, Jesus Christ, Wilhelm Reich and Gotama Buddha. I handed in my completed papers with a sense of enormous satisfaction. My classmates were impressed by my cheerful confidence. They hadn't seen me in class for months.

Results were posted two weeks later, 151 names accompanied by the pass grade A, B or C, and two names with an F for Fail. One was mine.

"I don't care," I lied to myself as I walked away. "It doesn't matter." At the campus gates I turned around for one last look. I'd broken the rules and paid the price, but I'd also stuck to my unrefined beliefs. For all the disruption that followed, that was something I never regretted.

I left my London digs, hitchhiked home and walked into the Don Pasquale in an army surplus jacket. I couldn't have looked more out of place. Dad left his customers and came to embrace me. Mum gazed from behind the bar with a glass in one hand and a linen serviette motionless in the other. For once, I felt the safety of family, and hugged him back.

"It's okay," he said.

I knew that, but it was nice he said so.

I had no idea what to do next. I was given a single chance to re-sit the exams, but I let the deadline come and go with little interest. No occupation called to me. I was intent on remaining free, but willing to work, and happily subsisted on £3-a-day archaeological digs in North Wales. After four years of student life in London, the slow-paced physical labor and fresh air were a welcome change.

About a dozen and a half people, mostly my age, worked on a partly excavated Roman villa in Dolgellau.[17] A party atmosphere prevailed from the very first night and every evening we gathered in the village pub to laugh the hours away. There were even some pretty girls.

One afternoon, one of them slipped her hand into mine. Things moved quickly. In my room, she undressed quickly and lay impatiently in bed. She aroused me cold-bloodedly and to my horror I ejaculated prematurely and shrivelled in an instant. Disgusted, she grabbed her clothes and left. I ran to the door. Gone. I paced. Hours of restlessness gave way to uneasy sleep. Laughter and pointed fingers filled my dreams.

Next evening, a bottle of wine in my hand, I knocked on her door.

"Who is it?"

I said my name.

"Come in."

I stopped in the open doorway. She was on the bed in coitus with one of the other diggers. "What do you want?" she asked casually.

I reeled.

A few days later word arrived of a remote site on the Isle of Anglesey, and I volunteered. A Neolithic cairn[18] was perched on the edge of eroding coastline, about to crumble into the Irish Sea. For six months I worked with three others in the bluster of winter winds and icy rain. The elements chastised and strengthened me.

That winter was unremittingly cold and damp. It was occasionally beautiful to stand where the fine sands of the river ran into the friendly sea, but such days were rare. More often the water chopped menacingly, dragging skirts of rain from the dark clouds and shaking them out where we stood. I bit down on the hardship, putting aside every penny and waiting for opportunity to tap me on the shoulder.

Even while paying my penance, however, I continued to sin. In Holyhead, where we went home each evening, I spied a fluffy eiderdown on a department store shelf and stood on my toes to take down the large box from the topmost shelf, hoisting it conspicuously onto my shoulder. I approached an assistant near the exit, smiled, and asked, "Would you mind?"

She held the door open helpfully as I managed the awkward load.

"Thanks so much," I said, feeling at last a twinge of guilt. I was no longer just relieving an anonymous corporation of its ill-gotten gains. I was lying right to the face of a friendly, shyly smiling girl.

At home, as I opened the box and spread out the luxurious queen-size down-filled quilt, all my feelings of bravery and cleverness wavered. I was overcome by remorse. The theft must have been discovered by now, and the poor girl probably felt responsible, was perhaps even being held responsible. I'd hurt an innocent bystander. My sense of grandeur evaporated.

Filled with guilt I went out for a walk, saw a beautiful saucepan in the window of a kitchenware shop, and went in without a second thought. Two minutes later, it was under my RAF surplus greatcoat and I was striding down the street with something for which I had absolutely no need. My clever skill had become a compulsion, operating in spite of my better judgement.

Fear was now lodged in my heart, and self-loathing.

One of my favorite people on the dig was Tim, a young American twisted by polio. With indomitable spirit he'd trekked overland to India and back.

He was the very caricature of a hippy—long, wispy hair and beard, a care-free laugh and tasselled suede jacket. He was misshapen, but walked with a gait that both served him in moving one leg in front of the other and gave him the air of one at ease with life. As we strolled on the windswept beach of Barmouth one day, I asked, "So how's India?"

Tim stopped in his tracks, looked into the distance and seemed at a loss for words. "India's . . . amazing. It's like nowhere else. You have to go."

"I do?"

He laughed. "Sure. Go on now," he said playfully. "Off you go."

My heart flew open. "Okay."

Tim cocked his head, stared for a moment and said, "You're serious aren't you?"

"My God, I think I am!" I said. "Wow! I'm going to India."

We laughed.

"So how do I do it?" I asked.

"Head east," he said. "You can't miss it."

"Hitchhiking?" I asked.

"Just through Europe. From Istanbul it's best to take buses. They're not expensive."

"Istanbul . . . ?" The minarets towered in my mind.

"Then Turkey, Iran and into Afghanistan. Maybe I'll see you there."

"You're going back?"

"Yep. Don't know when, but I'll be heading out again. By the way . . . ."

"Yes?"

"Travel light."

By the next day it was all decided. I felt free, all ties were cut. I had neither personal ties nor career—no responsibilities. All I'd leave behind was disappointment. A single decision had transformed my afflictions into blessings.

I bought a small army-surplus canvas rucksack and vowed to take no more than would fit in it. A lightweight sleeping bag took up half the space and I added a water flask, a six-by-six-foot square of tent canvas and some twine. My biggest item was a pair of size twelve infantry boots, which fortunately didn't have to go in the bag. They were hard as wood, capped with steel and tough as a Churchill Tank. The British Army, I reflected, had won the war in these things.

I returned to Gloucester for the final preparations and got my vaccinations, a new passport and some spare photos for the visas I'd need en route. The pictures from an instant photo booth at the bus station showed a shifty-looking character, unshaven and sneering.

Biding my time at home, I felt confined and restless. I wandered up Worcester Street and into Sainsbury's, the local supermarket. I picked up a piece of cheese and slipped it into my pocket. A woman stood at the end of the aisle. Had she seen me? It was impossible, I was brilliantly unremarkable. I strolled past the checkouts and into Northgate Street thinking how silly I'd been, since the Don Pasquale was fully stocked with finer cheeses than this, when a pair of arms encircled me. I struggled. It was the woman from the aisle. I couldn't shake her off. A male colleague appeared and I was carted quickly away from the wide-eyed onlookers and locked into a storeroom.

I sat on a box, held my head in my hands and tried to shut out the voices in my skull. A policeman arrived, very matter-of-fact and incongruously friendly.

"I'm going to ask you a few questions and then we'll go down to the station," he said. "Then we'll fingerprint you, take your statement and charge you. D'you understand?"

I nodded.

I spelled my name for him and he looked up quizzically. "'Ere, don't your dad own the Don Pasquale down Worcester Street?" He had a Gloucester accent. "What's a lad like you doin' in a predicament like this then?"

"I don't know," I said. "I . . . I just wanted to see what would happen, whether I could just take things and get away with it. I s'pose I'm not very good at it."

"Of course not," he smiled sympathetically. "You're an intelligent lad. A student, are you?"

I nodded.

"Well, I've seen stranger things in my time, I can tell you." He shook his head. "Come on then."

He didn't rub my face in it as he drove me to the station, nor even ask sarcastically whether Dad's restaurant had run out of cheese. This officer of the establishment was taking a personal interest in me. He was likable.

"It's a first offence, small item, and you come from a good family; maybe fifty, a 'undred quid."

He apologized as he locked me in a cell, "Now, it won't be long." It was a small vault lit by cached fluorescent light. In the silence of it's massive walls I felt temporarily dead to the world, and when the door opened I sprang to my feet in relief.

The policeman fingerprinted me, made me sign some document and offered me a lift home.

"I'll walk, thanks."

He nodded. "Well, good luck, son."

At home, Mum asked where I'd been for so long.

"At the library," I answered.

The charge of petty larceny hanging over my head didn't really bother me. If anything, I was grateful for the wake-up call, for my compulsive behavior suddenly seemed far less compulsive. Besides, I was headed for India. Nothing could hold me back. I told Mum and Dad my traveling plans as if they was the best of news. Mum gripped the arm of her chair and asked whether I'd *really* considered it. How long would I be gone? What would I do there? How would I manage for money?

Dad sighed, took Mum's hand and squeezed it. "It's okay, Gwenda."

"But . . . ," Mum tried.

Dad gazed at her as if he was remembering something. "He'll be fine."

She turned to me with a forced smile and said, "You'll write then, will you?"

"Of course, Mum," I nodded.

"Really?

"I promise."

I learned years later what Dad had told her in private. "If we try to stop him, he may never come back. If we let him go, he might."

At a much younger age than I, he'd left home himself, bitter and confused. Conveniently separated from his family at first by the Atlantic Ocean and then by the war, he finally returned to find his mother impoverished, blind and at death's door. This was one source of guilt he carried knowingly, regretfully and ponderously to his grave. He didn't wish that burden on anyone, least of all me.

In the following days I caught Mum glancing constantly at me, biting her tongue. While waiting for my travel documents and court hearing I spent hours in Gloucester City Library scouring atlases and journals in preparation for my route through Turkey, Iran, Afghanistan and Pakistan. Picture books stirred my imagination and settled any remaining doubts.

One picture, I never forgot. On an ancient, crumbling parapet stood a group of young Tibetan monks, wrapped against the cold in red woolen robes. Their heads were smoothly shaven, their unblemished skin bronzed by the slanting light. Crystal-clear eyes gazed into the camera with ineffable calm. The Himalayan valley floor stretched behind them to a distant, white-capped massif which, halfway up, surrendered a narrow ledge to a monastery perched like an eyrie. It was hard to tell whether the impression of calm emanated from the group of young men or from the vast space around them.

When I saw this picture again years later I knew at once that these weren't ordinary monks but *tulkus*, officially certified reincarnations of dead masters. Fine clothes, well-nourished skin and clear eyes told of their privileged upbringing. At the time, however, I saw them as the most fortunate people on the planet, either fully awakened[19] or on their way.

What did that mean to me? Freedom from and control over myself—a sort of personal perfection and, since it was often described as "blissful," a permanent high. I wanted that.

It was almost time to leave. I was waiting for my shots and, even though I imagined I might never return, my court hearing. Why bother? Soon I'd be hacking my way through jungle undergrowth, strolling the streets of crumbling cities or even crossing this very Himalayan valley to apprentice myself to some inscrutable guru. How unimportant would my past life be? I'd be free from myself, perhaps even acquire unnatural powers. As preposterous as this might seem in little England, it was the sort of thing that happened all the time in Asia, surely.

I knew that spontaneity was the key. I'd search without looking. I carefully skipped over the library's section of practical guide books and avoided charting an itinerary, preferring instead simply to motivate myself with the inchoate inspiration of images like these young lamas. My trip would open me to the new, change me beyond recognition and leave behind my demons forever. That couldn't be prepared for. Planning was the enemy of the spiritual quest.

Yes, not just a trip but a quest! I'd pay any price. So far, I'd amassed £250. I added to it by selling off my complete set of Beatles albums and my envied Dylan bootlegs. Truth be told, if music had been half as portable in those days as it is today I'd have taken it all with me, but I wanted to leave nothing behind. I emptied my bookshelves, cupboards, drawers and wardrobe too, selling and giving away everything I couldn't take except, at Mum's pleading, a handful of "smart" clothes.

All I'd need were two jean shirts and two pairs of jeans, one to wear and one for spare, and four pairs each of underwear and socks. My bag was almost full.

On the day of my court appearance I sneaked out to avoid questions about why I was dressed up in the very clothing I abhorred so much. I told the lady judge I'd been experimenting with lawlessness and had obviously failed miserably. I'd never steal again. I meant it, even if I doubted it. Nobody spoke against me, and she commented that the case was unusual, my being a well-bred boy—as my accent clearly attested.

Still, she declared me guilty and levied a fine of £20. As I turned to leave I noticed a young man taking notes.

I'd anticipated being exposed in the pages of *The Gloucester Citizen* and had already explained the facts to Phil. He sighed, shook his head and said he'd do what he could to protect Mum and Dad. The editor-in-chief was a customer of the Don Pasquale. He'd told Phil that although the story couldn't be suppressed, he'd keep it off the front page.

Close on the heels of the paper delivery boy, I snatched it out of the letter box almost before the ink was dry. The headline was tucked discreetly away on page six, but the unpronounceable Italian name stood out like a neon sign. I was described as "the son of a well-known local restaurateur." It soon lay safely shredded at the bottom of a deep rubbish bin.

Back at home Dad asked, "Have you seen the paper?"

I looked mystified and shrugged. Clearly, I'd overestimated my talent for lying, for Dad went straight to Mister Meadows the newsagent and bought one, returning to his wingback chair and scanning page after page with particular thoroughness. I looked on, resigned. Finally, he stopped turning pages, read attentively and finally looked up.

"Your mother mustn't see this," he said, rolling up the paper and handing it to me.

When I came back he was gone.

Dad's nonreaction devastated me. I sat in the empty room and all my defiance crumbled. Remorse flowed through me at the realization that I'd hurt more innocent bystanders. Thank God at least that I'd be gone soon. Now there really was nothing left to stay for.

I prepared some unleavened bread to last the first week or ten days. I had in mind a long-lasting concoction of wheat, rye and buckwheat flour kneaded into a thick dough, with nuts and dried fruit. It baked slowly on a low shelf for eight hours, firm when it went in and rock-hard when it came out. I had a dense, three-kilo demi-baguette.

Mum asked incredulously, "How are you going to *eat* that?"

"Look," I showed her my latest acquisition, a sturdy hunting knife. "I can chip off a piece with this knife and hold it in my mouth until it softens up. Or I can soften it in water."

Her eyes welled up as she watched in silence.

My final preparations were four hand-sewn denim pouches—one went around my neck for money and documents, and the others neatly enclosed my I Ching, its casting sticks[20] and my forty-year ephemerides.[21] I was ready.

Next morning I stood in the doorway, the small bag at my feet. Mum cried. Dad hugged me tightly. I felt guilty.

Mum said, "You will write won't you?"

"Of course," I said. "Don't worry."

"Don't worry?" She smiled bleakly as tears streamed down her face.

My eyes watered dangerously. It was time.

"Well," I said. "Goodbye Dad. 'Bye Mum."

"God bless you son," said Dad.

Mum held a handkerchief to her face.

I threw the bag on my back and promised again to write. They followed me to the doorway. I kissed Mum, walked up to the traffic lights and turned the corner. I waited for the tears to dry before turning to face the traffic and putting out my thumb. The sky was grey and threatened rain. It was chilly.

PART TWO

AWAY

Apart he stalk'd in joyless reverie,
And from his native land resolved to go,
And visit scorching climes beyond the sea;
With pleasure drugg'd, he almost long'd for woe,
And e'en for change of scene would seek the shades below.

—GEORGE GORDON LORD BYRON
Childe Harold's Pilgrimage
Canto the First, verse VI

6

ON THE ROAD

THE LAST FERRY FROM DOVER left at midnight. I stood in the soft English rain outside Canterbury and thought of my empty bed in Gloucester. A mossy bus shelter was beginning to look welcoming when headlights approached. "One last try," I thought, sticking out my thumb.

The car stopped and the window opened. "Where to?"

"Dover," I said.

"Sorry mate. I'm 'eaded for Ramsgate."

"Ramsgate's fine. Any ferry'll do." I climbed in.

"Where you off to then? An 'oliday in the sun?"

"Not a holiday," I said. "I'm heading for India."

"India? 'Itchhiking?" He was incredulous.

"Yes," I said.

"You can't get there 'itchhiking."

"Why not?"

"Well," he groped, "S'too far, init?"

It was my turn to laugh. "It doesn't matter how far it is, does it? As long as there are roads."

"But wotcha wanna go *there* for?"

"To see it," I said.

"Oh! Looking for adventure are ya?"

"S'pose so. Always wanted to be an explorer."

He laughed, more freely now.

The only remaining ferry was headed for Zeebrugge. I'd never heard of the place.

"Uvverwise," said the clerk, "you'll 'ave to wait 'til morning."

"All right then. A single, please."

"The return's only six poun.' Might as well get it now. Gotta come back sooner or later, 'aven't ya?"

"A single will do thank you."

"All right then," he shrugged. "S'your money."

I woke up in Belgium at the crack of dawn, England behind me.

I headed north, to Amsterdam and the Van Gogh museum. I'd just watched the film[22] with Kirk Douglas and Anthony Quinn and took comfort in the thought that if this unhinged artist could produce master-pieces, surely I could rise above my weaknesses. It was my one and only planned diversion.

On Antwerp's outer ring road, hemmed into a narrow shoulder by a concrete wall, I choked as a huge lorry thundered by, trailing clouds of dust. It cleared to reveal the door of a Volkswagen microbus sliding open. "Come on man. Hey run!" The voice was American.

The three couples inside all wore Goulimine beads and the reek of patchouli oil filled my nostrils as the bus whirred up to its full forty mph. I thought we'd connect, but it turned out they weren't fellow travelers at all. With their long, pretty hair and Michelin guidebooks, these were sightseers, not truth-seekers; here was evidence of the transformation of naïve hippy authenticity into just another trend.

Still, they took me to Amsterdam. I thanked them and climbed out.

Immersion in Van Gogh's swirling paintings left me feeling that, for a few hours at least, I could see through his eyes. Hippy tourists and fashionable users may have imbibed drugs for recreation, but for me they were just a brief reminder of the perceptions that lay beyond the rational mind—a perspective I hoped to rediscover without chemicals.

The experience was nevertheless exhausting, and I strolled afterwards through the Amsterdam night before picking a café and ordering a sandwich, some coffee and a piece of Moroccan hashish. It was a treat to sit in the cobbled streets and smoke in peace. The lights of the city rippled like Vincent's paintings.

Next day I breezed through Cologne, Frankfurt and Stuttgart. At a service station near Austria I stretched my fly sheet over a small clump of bushes to form a barely concealed shelter. The sandy ground adapted cozily to my bones. I popped a wedge of rock bread in my mouth, waited for it to soften and stared happily at the night sky.

The morning sun filtered blue and cheerful through the translucent fly sheet. There was a police car nearby, and a couple of officers wandering in my direction. It took just a minute to roll over, stuff the makeshift camp into my pack and walk past their suspicious stares.

A young couple picked me up.

"Where?" They asked.

I said "India?"

"Indien?"

"Ja, I guess so," I said. "Indien."

"Gott!" The man's eyes widened in the rearview mirror. "Indien?"

They took me home, pulled out a bilingual dictionary and made it clear they wished they could be part of the trip, vicariously or otherwise. Next morning they dropped me off on the autobahn with a packed lunch, their address in my notebook and their imaginations stirred. That day saw me through Austria and Italy. By evening I was walking along snowy Alpine roads into communist Yugoslavia.

Poor, rural Slovenia was a contrast to the tourist Alps of Switzerland, Italy and France. Crops were sparse and the small towns sulked in an industrial pall. It seemed that the anti-communist propaganda I'd been scorning for years might actually have some truth to it.

At a country crossroads, I bought cheese, bread and fruit from an unsmiling woman in a monochrome shop. The two female customers stepped back from their over-the-counter conversation without removing their eyes, and my smile only deepened their frowns.

At a busy ring road outside Belgrade a traffic policeman looked me in the eye, blew his whistle and held up his hand. I and the traffic halted. He beckoned with a white-gloved hand and I warily obeyed. He gestured at an untidy signpost pointing out a dozen or more directions and questioned me with raised eyebrows.

I said, "India."

"Indija?" His eyebrows moved up slightly.

I nodded.

He pointed firmly to the side of the road to make me wait. I was tired and he made me nervous as he stopped one driver after another. Finally he beckoned me to a multitrailer cruiser.

The policeman turned to me. "Iran? Va'i?"

What could I say? "Yes, okay. Thanks."

His triumphant smile was a relief, but as I clambered into the passenger side of the cab I faced a scowling driver who clearly resented the intrusion. We were well away from Belgrade when he pulled into a truck stop, gestured me out and locked the door behind me.

I walked on, waited a little and watched the late sun approach the horizon. The moon's first quarter rippled from the surface of a stream, and I decided to call it quits for the day. Following a wooded tract between two fields, the stream led me to a grove of young willows. I collapsed gratefully, drank from cupped hands and pulled out my bread, It was now as hard as rock. I stabbed at it, but the hunting knife glanced off dangerously, almost piercing my thigh. Instead, I smashed off some fragments between two river rocks, soaked them for a few minutes and chewed them with my leftover plums.

Here was some privacy, a cool green world that held me comfortably in its palm. The birds quietened down, the crickets stirred and the spring continued to bubble as evening's mantle fell. An ant negotiated the jungle of grass, climbing a tall blade in the long shadows of last light. Reaching the tip, it groped into the void for a few moments, then marched back down undeterred, to explore the next. On its behalf, I took stock of the expanse of grass, a veritable infinity. The ant never lost heart, and I resolved to be equally single pointed. But to what purpose? The ant knew its place. My cleverness, my sophistication, and worst of all my freedom, placed me at a profound disadvantage. I had miles to go and no colony to report to.

I slept in short fits, waking to turn or to listen to a passing night animal.

Up at first light, I left the bruised grass with a little nostalgia. But for my memory, there'd soon be no sign of my stay.

The local traffic was meager, overshadowed by the procession of European freight liners thundering towards the Middle East. They spat stones and gravel in all directions and I gritted my teeth.

A tiny café offered coarse bread and bean stew. I paid first, was given my plate and thereafter ignored. Smiles were few and far between. I felt Europe slipping away.

At a bend in the road I put down my bag. A small BMW pulled up, its roof rack piled high, the rear seat filled to the ceiling. The driver got out and locked the door before approaching me.

"What country?"

"India," I said.

"No, no, no. Where *from*? America? England? Deutschland?"

"Oh, I'm English."

"British-English?" He seemed suspicious.

"Yes." I pulled out my passport.

"We will speak English," he instructed.

I shrugged. "It's the only language I know."

He unlocked the passenger door and broke into a formal smile. "Please to enter."

The car strained under its load.

"I am Mehdi," he said. "Means 'Guide,'" he said. "To be guide by God."

"Guided," I said.

"'Guided? Yes, yes," He nodded enthusiastically. "You teach me correct English."

· I got the picture. "Fair enough."

"What is 'fair?'" He asked.

I explained. He asked my name.

"My name's Steve."

"Steepf," he said. "Is good? Steepf?"

"Well, not quite."

He stiffened and he made me repeat his name.

"No, no, Mehdi, *Mehdi*," he said vehemently, exaggerating the aspiration and throaty rhythm.

I responded, I thought, rather well.

He shook his head triumphantly, "You see! My language too is difficult."

"Well, yes," I said. "I expect it is."

His home was Teheran, and he smugly described his job in the oil industry. He was a proud "modern," but also a Haj who'd completed his obligatory pilgrimage. Mehdi and his lot were determined to "Westernize" old Persia without it becoming godless, but for all their money there was nothing to buy. The trip to Europe was no less a rite of passage than the one to Mecca. Like so many others before him, he flew one-way, bought a car and loaded it up. Despite the toll of en route duties, taxes and bribes, some people actually made a living like this. Mehdi had kept back two-thirds of his investment, he told me, just to get his precious cargo safely home.

He joked, "Easterners go west for goods and Westerners go East for God."

If Mehdi was going all the way to Teheran and didn't tire of my company, we'd cover some fifteen hundred miles, half-way to India. That morning, however, our focus was the Bulgarian border.

The guard gestured Medhi into a squat concrete building while I sat in the car. It was dry, dusty, hot and bleak—far more claustrophobic than Yugoslavia. The women wore dark clothes and identical headscarves. Men rode bicycles, all with panniers bearing the same bottles of red wine and loaves of bread. Monotony ran wild.

Half an hour later, Mehdi stepped gingerly into the car and drove us stiffly away. Only when the border post was out of sight did he breathe again.

"Bureaucracy?" I asked, and explained the word.

He nodded wearily. "He was bureaucrat." Mehdi patted his wallet.

We parked in Sophia and passed soldiers at the doors of grey buildings to buy bread and apples. Outside town he pulled up beyond a tiny hotel. "I will pass here at six-thirty tomorrow morning. Good night." He looked expectantly at the door handle.

I ducked quickly into a small vineyard. Unlike the sandy borders of the autobahn and last night's soft grass, the surface was dry and flinty. In a trench between vine rows, I ate my bread and fruit and adjusted my groundsheet restlessly. Still, the sky sparkled comfortingly and I fell into a fitful sleep, dreaming of other skies until sleep and wakefulness merged. The stars turned.

At sunrise I watched the sparse traffic pass and wondered what would happen if I stuck out my thumb, but at the appointed hour I made out the unmistakable silhouette of Mehdi's overloaded BMW.

"How did you sleep," he was bleary eyed.

"Okay thanks," I answered. "You?"

"Very, very bad," he said miserably. "The bed was bumpy, and the hotel was not clean."

"You mean lumpy," I said, "Sorry to hear that."

So the dirt I'd slept in was cleaner than the human soil of hotel bed sheets; plus, I'd had the stars for company. Poor Mehdi was hooked on the promises of progress. Imperial, wealthy England had looked down on the rest of the world for so long that those under its gaze, anxious to prove themselves its equal, had fallen for it themselves. Seeing Mehdi succumb to materialistic allure strengthened my resolve to resist it.

Over coffee and fresh bread, we planned the day's drive into Turkey.

The Bulgaria-Turkey customs post was a legendary feature of the Hippy Trail. Turkey's drug laws were draconian, and more than one Westerner had been put away for thirty unremitting years. The senior officer here was known to be a human lie detector. Fortunately, I was clean.

Mehdi didn't know that for sure, and insisted we split up. I was happy to distance myself from all his cash. On the road more than anywhere else, money was trouble.

The crush of human bodies inside took me off guard. I waited politely behind, only to see newcomers push past. It was frustration that ultimately propelled me into the garlic-smelling, sweat-reeking scrum. Although smallness was the greater advantage, I made full use of my size and strength, insinuating a limb here, a foot there until the crowd deposited me at the counter, my English manners in tatters. The morning sun beat on the uninsulated roof.

The uniformed official finished with the man beside me and fixed his eyes upon me.

"Passport?" he demanded perfunctorily.

I tried to look as innocent as I actually was.

He wrote in a ledger and muttered impassively, "Ingiliz."

With a frank gaze he asked, "Where are you going?"

"India," I answered.

His smile broadened, revealing a full set of magnificent white teeth. "To smoke hashish?"

"Certainly not."

He leaned toward the counter. "You don't like drugs?"

I smiled. "Not at all."

He looked through half closed eyes. "Show me your money."

I hesitated for only a second, then retrieved the thin book of travelers checks from inside my shirt. He made a note and stamped my passport. "Have a good trip."

"Thank you," I said.

From the ferry over the Bosphorus I spied the minarets of Istanbul, Europe at my back like a defunct civilization. Here was a new reality.

7

FURTHER

I was tempted to explore Istanbul, but Mehdi showed no interest in pausing. For three days I corrected his English, watched unfamiliar scenes through the car windows and reminded myself that my goal was India. On the third night, in pitch black, Mehdi woke me. "We are at the Iranian crossing. The border will open in the morning."

He battened himself down for the night while I left the car and found a spot among the motley crowd of waiting migrants. They rustled to life well before dawn, positioning bullock carts, cars and buses around the still-closed gates and doorways. Among the pedestrians was a back-packer with a London accent, "Got a spare camel or two for the officers?" he guffawed. "Might speed fings up a bit, ay?" His humor wasn't as contagious as he expected, and I thought of Eric Idle's parody of the British loudmouth. A girlfriend clung sullenly to his side, yawning vacantly.

"This'll take a coupla years, I should think," he went on, waving *Asia on a Dollar a Day* in my face.

I raised my eyebrows. "May I?"

"'Elp yerself, mate."

It sprang open to a page about the Crossing from Turkey into Iran.

"They open at seven," I read.

The girl looked at her watch and mumbled, "S'only aaf-six."

I looked around. "So where's Iran?"

"Maybe they lost it," he said. "Ay? Lost it! Ha-har! Get it?"

The girl smiled wanly.

He jerked his thumb over his shoulder, towards a narrow road swallowed by blowing sand. "It's bloody miles. Once we get through here, we gotta queue up again on the uvva bloody side."

The book confirmed his story.

A freight liner pulled up in a hiss of air brakes. "It's them wiv money what gets there first, init?" he yelled over the din.

I joined the people cramming into the customs shed. At seven o'clock the crowd surged, and by eight I was gripping my stamped passport.

Iranian officials were condescending to their Turkish neighbors. On the wall hung a gilt-framed photo of the straight-backed Shah, a brocade collar and chest of medals adorning his perfectly white uniform. I'd learned from Tom Butler to consider him an American lackey. Meanwhile, Ruhollah Musavi Khomeini[23] bided his time in Parisian exile, embodying both the medieval hopes of his people and the empire-bashing aspirations of the Western Left. Their common foe was SAVAK, the Shah's secret police.

My interrogator sighed. "Name?"

I told him.

"Destination?"

"India."

The corners of his mouth rose almost imperceptibly. "We do not tolerate the possession or trafficking of illegal substances in Iran. If you are caught with drugs of any sort you will be severely punished. Do you understand?"

I blurted out, "Yes sir."

He stamped my passport and sent me on my way with a flick of his eyebrows.

While waiting for my ride, I sat in the dust and wrote to Mum and Dad, fretting over the fact that I'd already spent ten pounds, complaining of

Mehdi's tourist attitude but remarking on my good luck so far. I also wrote with feigned disinterest, "I think I'm getting an attack of diarrhea." It would be the first of many. My note concluded, "I'm a bit suspicious of how easy it's all been so far but I'm sure that something will happen to shake my trust in my good fortune."

Meanwhile, Mehdi had drawn alongside with a relaxed smile. "Welcome to Iran."

"Well thank you. That's a better welcome than I got back there."

"Just a bureaucrat," he rolled the long word on his tongue. "It is his job." We laughed.

Mehdi waxed prosaic about his beloved country, forgetting his new English skills and becoming more pompous by the minute. Through the window, the barren flatness gradually gave way to signs of habitation. I asked about the people and the low mounds from which they emerged.

"These are poor people. Ignorant."

"They're your people, aren't they?"

"My people," he said disdainfully, "are in Teheran."

"Who are they, then?"

He shrugged indifferently.

Years later I saw *National Geographic* photos of the interior of these homes—long and tubular, clean and airy, with natural climate control. But that morning I saw only children staring, arms hanging motionless. Their static world and our moving one graphically out of sync. I'd have loved to have stood with them, and to shock Mehdi, but it was still a long way to India.

"Soon you will see the great city of Teheran," Mehdi announced. I imagined a vast, ancient mass of natural homes radiating outwards from picturesque squares and mosques.

However, Teheran grew from a murky outline on the horizon into a cityscape of concrete high-rises. Soon Mehdi was switching lanes gleefully on a multi-lane urban highway. The only traces of ancient Persia were handbarrows, bullock carts and the shabby Middle Eastern poor.

"This," said Mehdi proudly, "is the new Iran."

I forced a smile, inwardly agape at the concrete sprawl and polluted air.

He insisted on a response, "So, how do you like it?"

"It's very . . . Western." I said.

"Yes, yes!" He gripped the wheel and shouted excitedly, "Thank you."

I was groping for a more honest expression of my feelings when he pulled up. "You must write to me," he said abruptly. "Yes? Goodbye."

Taken off guard I gathered my things and said, "Oh! Goodbye then. I . . . ."

He signaled me to close the door.

"Thanks," I mouthed, but he'd already disappeared into the melee. I felt discarded—and free.

I found the Freak Hotel in a narrow entrance wedged between two shops. It was the place to stay in Teheran, a Gormenghast-like warren of rooms linked by improvised walkways and common balconies. Long-haired Westerners were everywhere, but the smell of marijuana was noticeably absent. The Hippy Trail was well mapped.

"'Ello-'ello then," said a familiar voice. "Look 'oo the cat's dragged in."

"Oh, hello," I said. The unfunny couple from the frontier had come up the stairs behind me.

"You must've caught the early bus?" he prattled.

"Lift, actually."

"In a lorry?"

"Car—a BMW." I was smug.

He didn't notice. "All the way from the border?"

"From Belgrade."

"Gor!" he exclaimed. "You mean . . . ?"

I nodded.

A young Iranian approached. "One room?" he asked amiably.

"One for me, please," I said.

"Only one room. Two beds. Nothing else available tonight. Sorry."

I turned to the couple.

His hand was stuck out. "Tony," he said. "Me friends call me Tone. And this 'ere's Mavis." She forced a smile.

I pronounced my name. A frown passed over his face.

"Italian," I explained.

He looked baffled.

We handed over our passports and paid for the night. They went out; I fell instantly asleep. Horns honked, lorries rumbled, scooters buzzed and motorbikes zoomed through my dreams. Dad's restaurant was strangely transposed into Persia. The tinny, amplified call of the muezzin issued from the cathedral. I heard a bullock cart clatter down Worcester Street.

Waking up in a sweat and with a pang of isolation, I went to the communal bathroom and stood under a stream of cold water. Back in the room I tidied my things and sat cross-legged to cast the I Ching. I was counting sticks for the fifth line when Tone and Mavis walked in.

His looked at me with dismay. "What the 'ell's going on?" he demanded.

"I Ching." I said.

"That there's weird," he said. "Looks like praying."

"So?" I asked rhetorically. What self-respecting Hippy Trailer hadn't heard of the I Ching?

They ignored me, storming around the room manically and arranging things from their huge backpacks in little piles. Mavis read from a list— "compass, multifunction knife, tin opener, torch," then several changes of clothing, toilet paper, traveling clock, detergent, boxes of candles and matches, aluminium pots and dishes, first-aid kits, whistles, packets of dried soup and instant meals. On their bed lay a tent, a lantern, a stove, short-wave radio, a folding axe and a coil of rope. I was jealous of their Swiss Army knife; I'd made a serious miscalculation by not bringing one. My hunting knife was great for chopping wood and fighting bears, but useless for peeling apples, and there'd been a noticeable absence of quality steel since leaving Europe.

They threw me several dirty looks until Tone finally stated, "We're goin' to the bathroom."

What was their problem? Were they religious? Atheists? At that moment my own countrymen seemed stranger to me than Mehdi, with all his peculiar notions.

I returned to the oracle. I'd cast hexagram 56 – *The Wanderer*. "Strange lands and separation," it said, "are the wanderer's lot." I read it through three times, reflecting on how it might illuminate my circumstances.

Tone and Mavis reappeared, dirty looks and all, and I headed out by myself, eating at a small café and wandering the uninteresting streets.

Back in bed, I listened to my roommates' breathing; watching my illusions evaporate, on the road at least, I'd thought I could count on people of like mind.

Next morning they left with a curt, "Bye, then." I nodded in reply.

I spent my day at the Afghan embassy waiting for a visa. "Afghanistan," mused the clerk back at the Freak Hotel, "Cheap hashish. Everybody love Afghanistan."

8

HERAT

I CLIMBED ATOP A FULLY LOADED, painted afghan lorry. The driver smiled.

"Herat?" I asked. "How long?"

He continued to smile.

A voice came from inside. "About two hours."

The driver beckoned me in and squeezed by to shut the door.

An old man smiled toothlessly and invited me to sit by patting his sack on the floor. I smiled back, and sat, wondering if he'd been the speaker.

"It's the best seat in the house," said the same lightly accented voice from behind me. A bearded young man held out his hand, "I'm Erik."

"Steve," I said, and guessed, "Dutch?"

"Yes," he said. "English?"

I nodded. "So this is Afghanistan."

He turned out to know a lot about where we were and what was going on. In those two hours I made a friend.

Herat was a town of pale red dust, not only underfoot but in its crumbling walls and houses, as though it had just emerged from ancient times.

Through open doorways I glimpsed the verdant luxury of hidden court-yards. Every nook and cranny begged to be explored.

Erik guided me to the Pelican Hotel, a large plot surrounded by irrigated grass and tropical flowers. The sign was hand-carved in shaky Roman letters and on the grass a live pelican preened itself incongruously.

Our room contained just three naked cots, but the low windows extended the living space welcomingly into the cool green shade of over-hanging palms. While Erik found the bathroom, I filled an aerogramme from margin to margin with tiny writing, trying to impress on Mum and Dad how very serious I was. I assured them I had enough money, pointed out that I'd traversed half a continent in just ten days and promised to share my insights with them.

After showering, Erik and I explored the dozens of shops for hippy tourists. Poorly tanned leather goods flowed from every storefront. There were hats, belts, bags and pouches, all handmade from unpliant leather with no variation of style. The stink of rawhide was at times overwhelming.

Shopkeepers smiled ingratiatingly as we passed, tempting us with cool interiors. All attempted to guide us to raised cushions where we were served plates of boiled sugar lumps and glasses of piping hot tea. We sipped and were entertained by our hosts, who were always ready to discuss any conceivable topic but the merchandise. Only after a long, discreet delay did the proprietor snap his fingers to initiate the parade of goods. Any expression of interest caused him to name a price, and although objections instantly lowered it, they were powerless to halt the bargaining process. Eventually the figure fell so low that further refusal became insulting, and the deal was struck. The whole affair was genial, subtle and based entirely on guilt. Erik bought a hat and I some purpose-less trinket. I left in a peevish mood, vowing in future to feign complete disinterest.

Erik said, "It's their country, you know."

"Yeah. It's just . . . ?"

"Exhausting?"

"Exactly."

"It's up to us to learn their customs. Isn't that why we're here?"

"I suppose so."

Herat was a small, mostly ancient city with a smattering of modern infrastructure. As we approached a crossroad, a young policeman on a central dais signaled us to stop, then to proceed. He continued waving to imaginary traffic, and then to an approaching colleague. The two chatted for a minute before sauntering off hand in hand.

Erik looked puzzled and asked, "They're policemen, right?"

A man approached us from behind. "Good day," he said, "You are Americans, correct?"

"English," I pointed to myself, "And Dutch," I indicated Erik.

"England . . . ," he hesitated, "Dutchland. Very good."

We smiled helpfully.

"You are looking for hashish? I have far out hashish."

He pulled out a cake the size of his hand. "Ten dollars," he said.

It was hard and odorless.

"A little old," I said.

He dug in his other pocket. "Opium? Very fresh."

He held up a much smaller lump, sticky and as pliable as Plasticine. Erik looked interested.

HERAT: a small, mostly ancient city

"Five dollars," the man said, eyes pleading in his wizened face. He described the difficulty of feeding a young family, for which he looked too old. I asked his age.

"Thirty-one," he replied.

"*Thirty*-one?" I asked.

He lifted three fingers in sequence. "Ten, twenty, thirty-one."

My mind flooded with guilt. How could I be so healthy when a man just a few years my senior had virtually exhausted his span? This was no lie; a lifetime was etched in his face. We bought his wares.

We were soon approached by a twelve-year-old boy, a far more canny businessman. He explained that he had five younger brothers in his charge, for the parents were dead. He was cheerfully undeterred by fate and also the first to offer us a quality product. "Zero-zero," he assured us.

Back at The Pelican Hotel we sat down for a smoke with Hank and Pete, a couple of Americans. I rubbed a mixture of marijuana and hashish together until a pile of fine dust lay before me. I poured it gently into the fist-size bowl of a hookah and crowned it with a burning coal. The reservoir was packed with crushed ice.

A translucent blue flame hovered over the surface as the mixture ignited. It went down evenly, rapidly and painlessly.

I inhaled to the bottom of my lungs and I passed it on. When I could hold my breath no longer, I exhaled a thick stream of still-dense smoke.

We stared for a moment in silent astonishment before the Americans erupted into clapping and whooping. Their noise receded rapidly into the distance as the room tipped sideways. I was looking at the ceiling, but my head was pointing downwards, or was it? I tried to regain balance, but my perspective was spinning out of control. I lay on my back to breathe alone, promising myself I'd never do it again.

Hours later, Erik brought me fresh fruit and bread, and I fell on it gratefully. He seemed relieved by my good appetite.

The two Americans' Peugeot hurtled towards Kandahar with Hank at the wheel. Shifting sands washed over the baking asphalt, obscuring the road. Periodically, an Afghan lorry passed, passengers perched on the roof and gripping the wrought-iron lattice. The cabs and sides were always brightly painted, in contrast to the monochrome landscape.

As night fell, the way grew indistinct. Despite the speed, a sense of stillness and monotony permeated the car until, from a great distance, a glow grew into a smattering of campfires. A dozen kerosene lamps grew distinct, and against them silhouettes of tents, camels and people.

"Lookit!" said Pete loudly, leaning against the steering wheel. "D'you think these guys live out here?"

"These are Azeri," said Erik. "Nomads. Like the Bedu of Arabia."

"Bedouin? Real Arabs?" Hank was now leaning forward too, and the car was slowing down.

"It's Bedu, not Bedouin. And they're not Arabs. They're Bedu, I mean, the ones in Arabia. These are Azeri." His tone was reverential.

"Uh-huh." Pete wasn't interested in the fine points of Erik's discourse, but pulled up anyway. He hung out of the driver's window while Hank got out and draped himself across the roof to stare.

Children scampered about, alerting everyone to our presence. We looked at one another apprehensively, ready to flee at the first sign of trouble. But three men came forward smiling, beckoning to us.

"*Melmastia*," said Erik. "It's their obligation to offer hospitality."

"You know all about these guys? Speak the lingo too?"

"No," Erik said regretfully.

"But whadda we do now?" asked Hank. "Take off?"

"Not me," Erik stepped forward decidedly. "If you don't want to stay, just toss my bag out."

I went with him towards the welcoming committee. The others followed warily.

The camp was now a flurry of activity. Tent flaps opened, children ran about excitedly and old women bustled about. We were led to a fire on the periphery and, as the men stoked it I noted revolvers in every belt. Rice and camel meat arrived on a large dish, and Erik began to eat with his right hand, forming small bullets of food and popping them in his mouth. Our hosts plied us to keep eating until with some difficulty we convinced them we were full.

After-dinner conversation began.

I touched my chest and said "England."

The men nodded and smiled. "England!"

The Americans followed suit, saying, "U.S., U.S.A."

The Azeri looked blank.

I pointed at them and said, "America."

There were looks of relief. "America. Very good." The children had been ordered away from the fire and craned their necks to see and hear.

Erik pointed to them. "You?"

An older one touched his own chest, opened his arms to encircle the camp, and then wider still to include the mountains and beyond. He pointed to the camels. Their coats were tattered, and strips peeled off in places. Firelight flickered in miniature through their sad eyes.

The exchange went on for half an hour or so, until Pete jumped up and said, "Okay, time to spice things up a little."

Erik was alarmed. "What? How?"

"Let's fire up the old hubbly-bubbly!"

"Oh no," pleaded Erik. "Please no."

"Aw shaddap," said Pete.

Hank squirmed, but made no effort to rein in his friend.

The men watched him saunter to the car and return with the pipe, which he set in the sand. "Wanna smoke?"

"Please don't do this," said Erik, almost whispering.

"Stay out of it, man."

Erik got up and moved away from the pipe, keeping the same distance from the Azeri men. Hank gestured for water, which was brought with great care. Pete sloshed it into the pipe, spilling half into the sand.

The men watched impassively for a few moments, but the eldest stood up and the others drifted away. Hank lit the pipe with coals from the edge of the fire. It was soon smoking like a mighty steam engine.

Hank coughed violently as he passed the mouthpiece to Pete. "Man," he spluttered. "Sure do miss the ice!"

Pete laughed uproariously. Erik was staring at the ground with his head in his hands. The Azeri had turned their backs on us and were closing down for the night.

Pete passed the mouthpiece to me. "C'mon man. Toke!"

"Oh, I . . . ."

"Don't be such a fuckin' wimp man." He glared at Erik.

The mere touch of the pipe threw me into confusion. I didn't want it, I didn't need it, but a little voice said it would silence my racing thoughts, and I sucked on the mouthpiece. In the intake of breath I heard the flutter of returning demons.

Hank and Pete bustled about trying to get comfortable in the car. I lay near Erik and stared at the cold sky. Camels snorted. Stillness was everywhere but in my heart.

I hoped with all my might that I would thenceforth quit smoking.

9

KABUL

RAYS OF SUN SWEPT DOWN from a high ridge throwing a sheet of light across the land. The camp rose to life, and as we rubbed our eyes a wide bowl of camel milk was placed before us. Steam rose from it in the cold morning air and I sipped at it cautiously, but it was unexpectedly delicious. The Americans wouldn't touch it, so it was left to Erik and me.

Our hosts struck camp. Tents, belongings and people were rapidly loaded onto the backs of camels and spirited away into the cool air of morning. We sped away over the wide, flat road keeping the mountains to our left.

In the backseat Erik and I pored over his map, comparing the two routes into Pakistan. "This way," he said, explaining his plan. "South from Kandahar across the desert, through the border to Quetta." He looked up.

"Or," I traced an alternative line "North through Kabul and over the Khyber Pass to Peshawar."

"My way," he said, "We'd meet more people like last night. And imagine, right across the desert . . . ."

"It'll be grueling," I said.

He nodded enthusiastically. "These people are resilient. We have so much to learn."

I pointed. "But look, from Kabul across to Bamiyan, the giant Buddha statues."

He shrugged indifferently and said, "The desert."

"The mountains," I replied.

We looked at each other.

"You'll go over the Khyber Pass," he added regretfully.

Erik described the campaigns of Alexander the Great and then the Persian, Mongol, and Tartar armies. "The Pathans weren't conquered by the British, either," he added admiringly. "Just suppressed for a few years."

By midmorning we reached the outskirts of Kandahar, buildings scattered across the parched desert like litter. We stopped for fresh fruit, but it was costly, so we settled for dried dates. We ate rice with raisins and greasy bones of camel meat with okra before returning to the car, wrenching misshapen dates from the clump as we went, and spitting damp seeds onto the hot ground.

Pete said, "This place is a fuckin' wasteland. Nothin' but freakin' desert."

Hank appeared nervous.

"Actually," said Erik, "It's an oasis."

"Oh yeah right," echoed Pete sarcastically. "A fuckin' oasis," and turned away.

Hank looked frustrated. He opened his door and asked as invitingly as possible, "Coming?"

Erik said, "No thanks. I'm heading for Quetta." He turned to me. "Sure you don't want to come?"

"I'm sure."

Erik slung on his backpack and grinned. "Good luck, man. See you later." He waved at the others and stuck his hand out towards me.

"Safe trip, Erik," I said, a lump rising in my throat. Funny, we'd only met a few days earlier.

"Gonna miss yer buddy?" Pete cajoled.

Hank looked thoroughly fed up. I hoped that when the two finally came to blows I'd be out of the picture.

"We going to Kabul or not?" I asked.

Pete drove all the way while Hank stared at the windswept sands. There was silence for an hour, before Pete abruptly sighed, and announced, "Know what I need? A fuck. I need a good fuck. I haven't had a fucking woman in weeks."

I had the curious sense he was reaching out, trying to get past his boorish behavior, and that this was as close as he'd get to apologizing. He glanced at his companion, then glared at me in the mirror. I held his gaze impassively. The silence hardened again. We'd soon be there.

Kabul in 1974 was a mishmash of a town, half crumbling from neglect and half dragged into the twentieth century. Beggars crouched in doorways on busy, paved streets, arms outstretched and pleas drowned out by honking traffic. Women walked by, some in burkas, others in high heels and styled hair. Kabul was experimenting with personal freedom.

With a sense of relief, I left the two Americans to each other and walked blindly until I came to a quiet street with a restful hotel and its sign, The Golden Temple.

A man in a Sikh turban greeted me cheerfully.

"Come. Please come in. You are most welcome."

Within the courtyard a fountain trickled water into a small pool. There were no Westerners. I paid three nights in advance.

I luxuriated in the privacy of my own room for a little while, filling the empty blue page of another aerogramme. I recall believing that I was putting Mum's mind at rest, but I also took pains to describe the rifles and revolvers to be seen everywhere. Was I also trying to punish her?

I went in search of a post office. Some of Kabul's streets were lined by glass-fronted shops and filled with plastic-wrapped goods. One of them even had a sign announcing, 'Supermarket', to which I was drawn like a moth to a flame. A large man at the entrance eyed me mistrustfully, but let me pass. My gaze fell at once on the home comforts of Cadbury's chocolate and Cheddar cheese.

Another burly man stood at the other end of the supermarket, arms folded across a menacingly barrel chest. A shopper reaching for an item hid me from sight for a split second, and I watched in horror as my hand slipped a one-pound chocolate bar into my shirt.

My heart was beating like a pneumatic hammer. A biblical phrase ran through my head—"Cut off the hand that steals." From the opposite pavement I glanced back to see the doorman as stationary and as menacing as before. I gulped, made my way to the street and returned to The Golden Temple.

The elation that used to surge from the success of my petty crimes had become a haunting combination of self-loathing and detachment from my own senses, as if I'd watched a lousy thief, not me, at work. I took out the booty, slid off its dark blue wrapper and unfolded the foil. Row upon row of symmetrical squares looked up at me impassively, each one etched with the familiar logo—a symbol deeply rooted in my own spoiled childhood. I broke off a piece and placed it on my tongue to melt luxuriously, but instead of a dopamine surge, all I experienced was a gluey, sickly taste. After just a few weeks, my palate had adapted to the simple fare of rice, light pan breads and vegetables.

How could it be so easy for my body to adapt and yet so hard for my mind? The risk I'd taken was stupid beyond words, and for what? Like the superstitious child I was supposed to have grow into, I beat a spineless mea culpa on my breast. This journey wouldn't free me from anything. I'd dragged along all I hated and feared about myself like a ball and chain.

While searching for cleansing, astringent tea, I retraced the memory of Dad leading me from sweetshop owner to priest to psychiatrist. It had seemed so easy to just take what I wanted, but now that what I really wanted lay legitimately within reach—putting an end to my compulsions—it wasn't easy at all.

The main streets were lit only dimly, but still too much so for me. I turned into dark laneways and the moon shone in eerie silence, full and accusing. Thick tobacco smoke and male conversation wafted from an open window. In a corner outside, a girl's voice crouched in a shapeless burka, whispering protectively over a bundle in her arms. The embroidery around her face rustled. A bubbling sound from within made me look up, and I watched a refilled narghile being set down amid a circle of men. One of them glanced in my direction and turned away. The girl's hand brushed my ankle and her voice pleaded. I dropped some coins in her hands.

I imagined Don Juan at my side, whispering urgently, "This is no time for self-indulgence, you fool! Look. Look! Your life is passing you by."[24]

10

BAMIYAN & BAND-I-AMIR

To return, to stay or to continue? All options led to stalemate. The I Ching told me, "Nothing that would further."

I stood restlessly at the front desk.

"Are you going somewhere?" asked the proprietor of the Golden Temple.

"Somewhere," I stated. "Where?"

"Goodness, so many places."

"Such as?"

"Bamiyan," he said thoughtfully, "and nearby, Band-i-Amir. High in the mountains. Beautiful lakes in the desert." He smiled.

"Lakes in the desert in the mountains?" It sounded like a riddle, but fine. More than fine, actually. I stared at him.

"Go and see. You will be happy." His smile was infectious.

"Okay then, Band-i-Amir it is."

Bamiyan was about a hundred miles from Kabul. There were tourist buses, ten-to-fourteen-seaters with high-backed chairs and secure harnesses, but behind the bus station, drivers of small cars and vans offered less comfortable rides for bargain prices. Even among them, however, Bamiyan proved to be an unusually expensive destination. One driver named what I thought was an extortionate price. "Eight hour ride," he replied to my protests.

Every driver had the same story; it was equivalent to a four-hundred-mile trip. Eventually I gave in. The driver took my money and jerked his thumb towards the back of his Toyota pick-up. The flatbed was about six feet by ten, piled with sacks of dry goods. Three men were already sprawled on top. I took the only available position, half-reclining, with my back propped up against the edge. A minute later, another man joined us, and then another. I was surprised to see a woman, burka and all, helped on by her husband and wedged protectively into a corner. Soon there were fourteen of us in the back, squeezed against one another like sardines. My leg was already cramping and I was reconsidering my decision when the powerful little engine sprang to life and the driver slipped the clutch against the highly revved motor. The pickup groaned into motion.

We accelerated slowly to forty miles an hour as assorted arms and legs shifted to find tolerable positions. Except for the strategically isolated woman, everybody was intertwined. At first I resented the overlapping of private space, and shrank away in an effort to maintain my little privacy. Every inch I ceded, however, was immediately claimed. Eventually I did the same right back to them, and my neighbors immediately accommodated me. In time, a camaraderie emerged from this pragmatic adjustment.

We left the asphalt just a few miles outside town and headed for the interior. The road became a track, and the track little more than a route lined with assorted buildings and villages. One corner of the vehicle rose precipitously while another sank into a pothole, then the whole leaned sideways or fell suddenly into a cavity. We were driving up a dry water-course that in the spring would be a raging runoff from the mountain snows. There was no road surface, not even gravel. Carefully negotiating one pothole after another, the driver only rarely shifted up from first gear, and never beyond second. We stopped frequently. Passengers got in and out and business was transacted. Afraid of losing my place, I stayed put. Every joint ached.

The saving grace was the scenery, not so much the vegetation as the spectacular play of light and shade on the desert mountains. They rose and fell in nearby sandy golds and distant ethereal blues. As we rose to greater heights, the turn of a corner or rise of a hill revealed landscapes of unimaginable depth. The country stretched into pure space.

My traveling companions and I swatted at clouds of flies in the heat and munched on fresh fruit. They joked with one another, trying to let me in as much as possible with sign language. I was happy to be with ordinary Afghans. I'd been disappointed too often in my search for adventure and hated the predictable hippy trail. Here were "real" people at last.

The day passed in this tedium of bone-jarring thuds, nonverbal companionship, sea-sickening lurches and biblical scenery, until at last we found ourselves gazing down upon a perfectly verdant valley. The young man opposite me sniffed the air and thumped his chest tearfully, saying, "Bamiyan, Bamiyan," like a child. If he was homesick, I envied him his return.

All day long, we'd seen one barren mountain ridge give way to another until the desert was as smooth as pastry dough, each fold radiating its

BAMIYAN: in a flash of sunlight, the ancient standing Buddha was revealed

own shade of light to create a vista of vast proximity. Now at our feet, set within vertical cliff walls like Shangri-la, was a valley floor riddled with irrigation canals. Blankets of bright green crops were divided by lines of dark trees. We drove along the foot of the northern cliff.

Beyond the open space an enormous shadow dominated a sheer rock face at the western end. It was surrounded by several hundred smaller shadows—caves, most of them impossibly high. The lorry brought us into a direct line of sight, and the large shadow resolved into a niche in the vertical cliff. It contained something of immense bulk. In a flash of sunlight, the sandstone features were set in sharp relief and the ancient standing Buddha was revealed.

It wasn't placed in the cliff but carved out of it, and where I expected a face there was an empty shelf; a vertical slice from the forehead met a horizontal section at the upper lip. I decided immediately and mistakenly that it had been defaced by Islam's prohibition of graven images. In fact, the face had always been a separate, delicate plaster construction on a wooden framework, its gilt periodically renewed to maintain the *sugata*'s[25] enlightened complexion. The eroded remains had survived the ravages of eighteen hundred years, but were to last only another twenty-five, for the Taliban blasted them into rubble in 2001, teaching the world a shocking lesson in impermanence.

As my attention returned to the banal I noticed with familiar disappointment that Bamiyan's pastoral valley had been hastily cobbled into a tourist outpost. Buildings of every sort were drafted into the hotel and restaurant business and menus proudly offered local attempts at Western fare. I upset the waiter by insisting on rice and vegetables.

Nevertheless, the dining room was a traditional arrangement of low tables and plentiful cushions. My belly filled, my limbs pleasantly extended, I strolled along the base of the cliff to the smaller giant statue and explored the surrounding caves. Carved from the living rock, they were beautifully finished, interconnected chambers with domed or vaulted ceilings. Some were accessible from outside paths that snaked up the face, and a few eventually connected to inner passageways leading to outlooks around the head itself, 175 feet up. Two hours later, tired out, I'd barely scratched the surface.

West from the main statue and temples, the caves grew less refined until they were just natural fissures in the soft rock, and yet inhabited. Wretched families crouched outside watching over a few pungent goats. I advanced cautiously, alms at the ready, but the men cowered and the women called nervously to their children. No hands reached out. I backed off guiltily. They had the air of a pariah community. I never discovered why.

The decayed wall carvings, empty alcoves and pottery shards back at the larger statue bespoke a heyday of Buddhist culture, and I visualized Marco Polo crossing paths with Chinese and Indian travelers in what was once an important silk road City, commercial center and a place of study, meditation and art. Bamiyan's statues and caves had maintained their full glory for centuries, though now the entire valley was under the plow.

I stopped for tea. Leaning back on the restaurant cushions, I reflected that I might spend days or weeks exploring the caves, but for what? I was in search of experience, not archaeology.

THE BUDDHA: *where I expected a face there was an empty shelf*

At the next table four Americans, one of them a girl, were talking excitedly about Band-i-Amir.

I leaned over. "Are you going to Band-i-Amir?"

"You bet," one of them replied. They shifted to include me. "You?"

"I dunno," I remembered the hotel keeper's enthusiasm. "How far is it?"

"Fifty miles."

I hesitated. "I'm not sure I could face another trip like the one up here."

"They say it's not so bad. We're leaving in an hour."

"Oh well, count me in."

We pushed our tables together and ordered more tea.

The painted lorry was rimmed with lattice and wrought iron. We got there early and steeled ourselves for the usual crush of passengers, but the driver simply collected our money, climbed into the cab and lurched off. It was a luxury to sit or stand as we pleased but, once underway, sitting turned out to be impossible. The road, wider, less pitted and rock strewn than the narrow road from Kabul, enabled us to maintain a good twenty-five miles an hour, at which speed even shallow potholes produced a spine-compressing thud that shot from coccyx to skull and left the brain vibrating like a bell. We hung on to the overhead rail that normally secured the tarpaulin cover, and flexed our knees to absorb the shocks.

With the canvas rolled up there was a 360° view. We climbed higher into a sky that rolled like an ocean as we reached out to touch it. At the crest of a rounded mountaintop we came to a dead stop and the driver pointed ahead, urging us to look. I was dazzled by a thing of incredible simplicity, alone in all the surrounding miles of colorless terrain; a single bright yellow flower grew from a crack in the rocks, surrounded by drab cacti, open like a delicate saucer. In an alpine meadow it would be just another wildflower, but here it stood out gloriously.

But the driver still waved me on impatiently. Peeking over the very brow of the hill I gazed into the most startlingly deep, blue water I'd ever seen. In a perfectly vertical hole that sank hundreds of feet below the desert surface lay a profound lake, as still as the sky it reflected, its color fantastic. I glanced back. The driver nodded with satisfaction. The stillness of the water was uncanny. I struggled to believe what I was seeing.

As I moved around the rim, a whole vista of lakes came into view, flowing over a series of natural dams and cascading from higher to lower, a divine landscaping.

My companions were running to the rise of the hill. One stared at another lake that rose from the valley floor like a giant bowl, its containing walls sublimated from the mineral-rich water itself. They reached improbably upwards, holding back an immense mass of water that flowed over one edge into a gentle stream lined with limestone overgrowths.

We wandered the hilltop until our driver called us back and carted us into the valley, where two large canvas tents stood ready for us. We sat on sturdy Afghan rugs, and sipped tea, then spent the remaining daylight hours exploring.

Alongside one of the lakes was a long flat strip of stone, a sort of natural sidewalk, at the end of which a ragged old man stuck fish on a stick and grilled them for a few coins. The water was icy cold, the air crisp and dry. It was as deserted as Eden after the fall. We walked and gawked until we were exhausted, slept like logs and gawked again the next morning.

BAND-I-AMIR: a lake rose from the valley floor like a giant bowl

By late afternoon, the driver was back with another load of tourists, and soon we stood on the flatbed looking backwards, unwilling to tear our eyes away.

Band-i-Amir has remained a crystal clear memory ever since, overshadowing many a lesser wonder. It certainly made Bamiyan feel crowded and contrived. I spent some days exploring the caves and the surrounding area, telling everyone to go to the lakes. Those who'd been spoke of nothing else. The beauty was heartrending, for it made you want to grasp the ungraspable. I hated even to leave Bamiyan, for it took me further from the lakes.

The descent to Kabul was mercifully shorter than the ascent, but the grimy city was anything but welcome. Back at the Golden Temple hotel in Kabul, the owner eyed me without a word. I thanked him, and he just smiled. My time here was over. I looked eastwards now, to the Khyber Pass and Pakistan.

11

THE KHYBER PASS

N O OUTPOST OF OLD BLIGHTY[26] was more infamous than the North West Frontier. As we approached Landi Kotal, I looked out for remnants of ancient battles. But even the great weight of history was overshadowed by the extraordinary bazaar, devoted almost entirely to the twin commerces of armaments and black market currency. Burly guards filled doorways, bullet-filled bandoleers criss-crossed over their chests—stereotypes, but no joke. The authorities were conspicuous for their absence. Since the times of the Raj, governments had picked their battles strategically on this heavenly perch, or avoided them altogether.

A shopkeeper invited me in with a cheerful smile, eager to practice his English and in vague hopes of selling me a gun. His regulars were Pushtuns from the surrounding mountains. Tabletops, floors and walls were strewn with a motley assortment of weapons. The only firearms I'd ever encountered before were the shotguns of Gloucestershire, where flat-capped men in tweed jackets shot ducks and pheasant as a pastime. Here in Landi Kotal, military ordnance filled one building after another. Kalashnikovs held pride of place, but close at hand lay grenades, rocket launchers, mortars, mines and devices I couldn't even name. There were Brownings and Enfields from the first and second world wars, and tattered pieces from earlier centuries; even a blunderbuss. Some pieces were handmade replicas, others repaired and patched with scraps of bicycle parts and biscuit tins. My host invited me to fire one, but I had no confidence that one end of the gun was any less lethal than the other.

Buses were few, but a staging post on the outskirts of town offered transport down to Peshawar and the rest of Pakistan in fifties and sixties vintage American station wagons—what the English called "shag-wagons" because they were as large as bedrooms. The Pushtun drivers prized their great capacity and uncomplicated V-8 engines. None of them got underway until at least twelve people were crammed inside and another handful installed on the roof rack, complete with baggage and livestock.

I paid my fare, climbed up and hung on as we headed down the snaking road. My bearded fellow passengers stared at me unabashedly as I lurched from side to side on each hairpin bend, hanging on for dear life while they swayed gently with no apparent discomfort. The road fell to the east like a meandering river amidst spectacular scenery. Jamrud, our destination, grew slowly like a target in a gun sight. It was a terrifying, exhilarating ride of a lifetime.

As relieved as I was when the car came to a halt, I got off reluctantly and squeezed my limbs into the narrow seat of the waiting Peshawar bus, musing that I could have spent my remaining years on the roof of that ancient Chevrolet and counted my life worthwhile.

But now here was Pakistan—humid, populous and chaotic.

The newly minted Muslim nation had been independent from India for less than thirty years. Its billboards and packaged products still bore the decaying marks of the British Raj, reminding me of home and stirring up waves of ennui. I'd thought when leaving that it would be a great adventure to live without plans or ambitions, but the point of my wanderings was very much in question. I was in Pakistan simply because it was the next place. Moving on kept the specter of pointlessness at arm's length—barely.

Dizzy with all this mental diarrhea, I hardly noticed something more ominous gurgling in my gut. Raised on English tuck shops and the rich

fare of the Don Pasquale, I'd been helpless against the sweet temptations
of Kabul and the deep-fried treats of snack vendors at every bus station.
I'd even eaten fresh fruits and vegetables, the greatest risk of all given the
water in which they were rinsed. My innards felt frail, evincing the vague
sensation of broken glass in flow.

Wandering the city streets, I was disoriented by the heat and crowds,
unable to distinguish one street from the next. Suddenly overcome by a
wave of liquidity, I entered the nearest restaurant, stepped into its dank
toilet and crouched gratefully over the hole in the floor. I was riveted by
cramps and when I creaked to my feet and washed my face and hands, I
found that standing and walking were a mighty effort.

Back in the dining room the proprietor sat at the counter on a high
stool, staring at me with a faint look of disgust as the waiter approached.
I ordered lassi—yogurt whisked with salt and crushed ice—but just
couldn't get it down. In a moment of clarity I saw myself sitting at a
grimy table in a gloomy restaurant, flies crawling over me, my alimentary

KHYBER PASS: the road fell to the east like a meandering river

canal awash with bacteria, facing the prospect of endless hours in filthy urban toilets. I craved to be back in the cool of the mountains.

Outside, I hailed a cycle rickshaw.

"Bus station," I mumbled.

The man at the ticket counter responded instantly to my request for a mountainous resort. "Swat."

The cooler air revived me, and I noticed the people had changed from lowland Aryans to tall, blue-eyed Pushtuns once again. Swat was the name of the valley and also the river that turned from a meandering snake into a ferocious torrent as it climbed into the Hindu Kush.

At Madyan, the surrounding hills were stretched apart and the sky widened. I had the distinct impression of entering a Wild West frontier town. At first deserted, the streets suddenly filled with men as the mosque emptied and I stepped down from the lorry. Revolvers and rifles were ubiquitous. Shopfront shutters clattered open to reveal threadbare merchandise—plum tomatoes, onions, garlic, okra and dark, shrivelled apricots. At one end a group of Westerners stood munching. I went over.

Bent over a wok, a diminutive, bespectacled man peered up at me through thick lenses, stated in a broad Australian accent that his name was Ali, and asked, "Falafel?" His black hair was clipped, his beard long. He wore a Pushtun outfit.

"Thanks," I munched. They were excellent, though spicy.

A French girl asked, "You look for a place to stay?"

"Yes."

"Come. We show you." She introduced herself as Annick and her companion as Jacques.

"Thanks," I said. "I need to rest for a few days." My eyes ached.

"The Dutchman's house," suggested Annick.

"See you again, brother," called out the Australian as we turned away. "Allahu akbar."

From the main street I followed a path to a watery grove of tiny islands networked by charming footbridges. Thatched mills and water wheels crowded the canals, creaking rhythmically as white-dusted, dark-skinned boys stacked flour sacks on waiting carts.

The house of Annick and Jacques was just beyond the busy grove. They busied themselves, and soon had a stew bubbling gently on the rude clay stove. The house consisted of lattice poles for uprights and straw mats for walls and roof, so they fed the fire cautiously; any misplaced spark might spell disaster. After dinner, Jacques led me uphill to the Dutchman's house; he pointed to a corner where I could bed down for a few rupees.

"See you tomorrow," said Jacques as I laid out my roll.

I fell immediately into a profound sleep, but in the night sharp cramps shook me roughly awake. I had to dash into the bushes.

The Dutchman was sitting on the veranda when I woke, his arm bound with a tourniquet. He squirted a drop of clear liquid from a syringe.

"Insulin?" I asked.

He laughed. "Smack, man." He pressed the needle into a bulging vein with a grim face and sucked a small amount of blood into the syringe.

"Aren't you worried about getting hooked?" I asked.

He shook his head. "The trick is to never increase the dose."

He pushed the plunger down, and in a heartbeat every muscle in his body relaxed. Sitting erect, he closed his eyes. Insects buzzed. Two birds of paradise danced from branch to branch, long, ornate tails waving playfully. For a few minutes, the Dutchman was immobile against the scenery.

Abruptly, he sprang to his feet, called out, "See you," and bounded away.

Ali sat on his haunches at the falafel shop. With knit eyebrows and bulging cheeks, he ejected an expert line of spittle into the gutter.

"Aliekum," he said.

"Hello," I replied.

Behind him was a tall, proud Arab in pristine sky-blue baggy-pants and shirt, carefully mixing batter. "The response," he said, "is, 'wa aliekum al salam.'"

"Omar," said Ali, "thish is Shteve, the bloke I told you about . . . ?"

Ignoring Ali, Omar prompted me: "Wa aliekum al salam."

I mimicked the sound as best I could.

Omar returned to his batter. "Perhaps you'd like to help out in the shop?" he asked. "You need money, no?"

"Um," I said.

He showed me how to grind chickpeas with garlic, onion, green mangos, salt and spices and deep fry the balls in mustard oil. As we worked he talked about Islam, quoting the Koran and interspersing his sentences with praise of Allah and the Prophet and asking me to repeat Arabic syllables after him.

I asked no questions as he spoke; he wrapped up every pronouncement tidily, leaving no room for doubt. In an effort to change the subject I mentioned, "I've never cooked with mangos before."

Omar's lecturing turned to mangos—green, yellow, red and otherwise. He spoke with unshakable confidence, neatly maneuvering the topic back to Islam. Ali nodded mechanically and spat periodically into the gutter.

"What *is* that?" I finally asked.

"Nashwaar," said Ali, regrouping the bulge in his mouth. "Want to try?" He flicked open a small tin of dark brown resin.

"Which is . . . ?" I prompted.

"Pounded tobacco paste." He extracted a fingerful and plugged it inside his cheek.

"That's all?"

"Thatsh's it. The Indiansh mixsh it with betel nut and lime, all rolled up in a leaf, but it'sh the tobacco that doesh the trick."

Omar's stirring of the wok slowed impatiently.

Ali spat and proffered the tin once more.

"I don't think so," I said.

"An unpleasant habit," confirmed Omar.

Crestfallen, Ali spat the black lump into the open gutter where it was nudged downstream by the trickling water. At a loss for words, he was rescued by the tinny chant of the muezzin. He looked up, "The adhan!"

"Come," enjoined Omar. "Pray with us."

I followed before I even realized I'd rather not. He possessed an impressive, discomforting power.

Even white-bearded men deferred to this charismatic man. Ali told me as we walked behind that Omar's first language was Arabic, not Pushto, for he was Saudi. It was as if we walked in the train of royalty.

Outside the mosque I copied the others, rinsing my mouth, eyes, ears, nose, hands and feet. Inside, we lined up barefoot and knelt. Prayer began quickly, and the men moved in unison. We leaned forward, looked into the palms of outspread hands, burying faces in them and looking awed. The ritual felt more familiar than I would have expected, but was mercifully brief. Nevertheless, like the more long-winded Catholic ritual, it left me feeling as godforsaken as ever.

"Come," said Omar.

"Omar's speaking at the madrassa," Ali enthused.

The small room overflowed with cross-legged, turbaned men. Omar spoke for an hour, directing the occasional English phrase at Ali and me.

As the meeting broke up, Omar put his arm around my shoulder, led me back to the bazaar and made a gesture of handing me over to Ali. "Here. Learn to operate the restaurant."

Ali and I worked and chatted all afternoon, but he responded to my questions about his past in the most perfunctory way. When Ali pulled down the shutters in midafternoon I slipped away like a truant, thinking up excuses.

With packages of walnuts and rice under my arm, I passed a butcher's shop. I hadn't eaten meat in years, and was now reminded why. A goat's head lay on its side on the floor, its neck red and moist. Its body was still on the block, where the butcher tore hide from flesh. The discarded head looked in horror upon its own fate. Another goat, small, brown and very alive, was tethered nearby, bleating and trembling uncontrollably on one side of the shop. Its gaze turned momentarily towards me, and back to the carnage. I was rooted to the spot. The butcher leaned back to take a breath and glared at me. I stepped away hesitatingly, unwilling to leave the goat to its grisly end. My feet felt like lead. My mind swirled. Shouldn't I buy the poor creature to free it, even to my last penny? And then what? Milk it each morning? I looked again. It was a male. What was I to do?

A customer arrived. The butcher sliced deeply into the carcass and dropped the thigh joint onto several layers of newspaper spread in the pan of a hanging scale. A cloud of flies buzzed and settled. Thousands more ripped and microscopically chewed the moist flesh, morsel by morsel. How many eggs, I thought, how long before the maggots crawled?

The buyer walked away jauntily, the package reddening in patches under his arm.

The remaining goat glanced at me again. With a couple of words and an unmistakable gesture the owner bluntly suggested I buy meat or leave. I left them to their grisly business.

My agitation faded slowly as I walked through the cool and damp of the mill grove and up the hill. Over the Dutchman's kerosene stove I fried walnuts in mustard oil with garlic, rice and tomatoes, and ate pensively. My intestines gurgled uneasily.

Stretched out on a large boulder, I enjoyed the accumulated heat of the day as night fell and the air grew cold. The Milky Way emerged like a gash in the firmament, its stars emerging one by one. There was no moon and the mountain snow caps, the pale, warm rock and my own white skin were cast in a ghostly starlit hue. The symbols of time broke through the dark. My heart was still, my mind quiet, for once. The eternal chatter had ceased, if only for a moment. I let go and tumbled into the sky like a ripened fetus hurtling down an oversize birth canal.

12

GOING DOWN

I WAS ON A FLINTY DESERT, the wind howling at my back. The cathedral spires of Gloucester were near, I was sure, but the sand stung my eyes. No matter which way I turned, sharp fragments struck my face. My clothes were shredded, my skin scorched and torn. The night went still for the merest fraction of a second, and then the grit tore through my gut. I awoke in a cold sweat, gasping in pain.

In the scrub that served as a garden, I squatted in a half-conscious doze, too feverish to think, too exhausted to move. My knees grew stiff and locked in place. I was riveted. As the light rose in the eastern sky I staggered to my feet, leaving behind something green and vile. I rummaged in my bag for some tetracycline pills and washed them down with cold tea. The pills churned in my stomach. The air itself tasted bitter. I crawled back into my sleeping bag and shivered.

The Dutchman was preparing his morning shot. Like a knife, the sunlight poured through the door and into my eyes.

"I don't feel so well," I said.

"Sorry to hear that," he replied indifferently. I glimpsed his silhouette in motion as he arranged the tourniquet, pushed in the needle and fell still. A few minutes later, he sprang to his feet. "See ya," he called over his shoulder.

My mind went back to the ridiculous sense of indestructible glee as I careened down the Khyber Pass on the roof of a shag-wagon. I'd need a doctor now, perhaps a hospital, but was oppressed by the thought of a cramped bus journey back to stifling Peshawar. Sleep overtook me.

I was awoken by Jacques and Annick. The sun was high behind them and it was an effort to make out their troubled looks.

"Man," said Jacques. "Look at you."

"I'll be fine," I gasped involuntarily.

"You're yellow," said Annick.

"What?"

She said, "Your skin is yellow. Your eyes are yellow. You've got hepatitis." Jacques nodded.

My head fell back. "Bloody marvelous. Must've picked it up in Kabul."

"Okay," said Annick, "let's get you to the hospital."

"A hospital, *here?*"

"A little one, yes," said Jacques hesitantly.

I muttered. "Thank God."

"Doctor first, God later," Jacques said.

My energy depleted, I let them gather my stuff.

My legs were like rubber. Jacques propped me on his shoulder and Annick carried my bag. We paused periodically so I could catch my breath and swig water.

"It's boiled," said Annick.

"Bit late for that," I mumbled. I was wasted, but not in pain. Across the main street we took a steep laneway down through a grove of trees. The shade was as invigorating as a cool spring. Annick knocked on a wooden door as Jacques propped me against a tree.

The door opened to reveal a beaming young man dressed Pushtun-style in baggy trousers and shirt tails to his knees. "Please to enter." Tall and stringy, he flapped his arms with artless self-importance.

The dark-shuttered room was lined with glass-paneled wooden cupboards. Behind their grubby panes were jars of colored liquids and torn cardboard boxes.

I faced the man's grin, bare inches from my eyes. "You have hepatitis, yes?"

"That's what I'd like to know," I said. "Is there a doctor here?"

"This is hospital. We have doctor. Of course."

I aroused what wits I could. "Where is he? The doctor?"

He smiled at nobody in particular.

"Are *you* the doctor?"

He moved his head from side to side in a gesture that could have been agreement, denial or uncertainty.

"Yes?" I nodded to prompt a clear answer. "No?" I shook.

He bobbed his head around, "Call me Doctor Amin."

I glanced at Annick. She shrugged doubtfully.

He pulled down the skin under my eye and tut-tutted. "Hmm. Yellow in color."

"So is it hepatitis?" I asked.

"We will verify," he smiled. "Please to give sample." He took a beaker from the cupboard, held it out me and pointed to a side door. The beaker obviously wasn't sterilized but it seemed a moot point.

He cocked his head to one side saying, "Thank you, thank you," and sat down to wait.

Annick had fed me a full liter of water as we came over, but it now produced barely a trickle of urine. Back inside, I put the beaker on the table and stumbled back to the chair.

"The test will be taking one hour," said Doctor Amin brightly. "Please to return." He held open the door. I was about to protest when Jacques grabbed my arm and put it over his shoulder.

"Let's wait outside."

We sat under a tree in the grove.

"Is he really a doctor?" I asked.

Jacques shrugged. "And if he isn't . . . ?"

"How are you feeling?" asked Annick.

"Actually, not bad. Just weak." It was true, I'd had no pain or discomfort for some hours, although my eyes shrank from sunlight.

Annick said, "The pain comes from eating. Your liver can't do its work."

I fell asleep.

The doctor roused me, beaming from ear to ear. "The test is positive. You have hepatitis."

I was relieved to put a name to it. I asked, "Do you have medicine?"

"No, no, no," he shook his head. "No medicine."

"Well, where do I get it?"

"Medicine no good." He smiled broadly.

Jacques affirmed, "He's right. There's nothing for hepatitis."

Annick added, "Rest. No fat. No spice."

"You two seem to know more about it than the doctor."

"So many people with hepatitis," said Jacques.

"What about antibiotics?" I asked.

He shook his head. "Bad for the liver."

I wondered about the tetracycline I'd taken.

Doctor Amin said, "Hepatitis, inflammation of liver," and drew his hand diagonally across his belly. "Very large," he frowned. "Liver cleans blood. Inflamed liver means dirty blood." He shook his head. "Dirty, dirty, dirty." After a moment's silence his face brightened up. "Glucose. Very good energy. Pure." He shook his head again and said, "Glucose, glucose, glucose."

I looked at my friends. Jacques said, "We'll get some for you at the pharmacy."

"There's a pharmacy here too?"

He nodded. "Sort of."

"You will get better," said the doctor. "No fat. No butter, oil, spice. Fruit, and glucose, glucose, glucose. Easy." He laughed. "Difficult to forget. We will look after you. You will get better. Come. We have bed."

"Here?"

"In the ward."

"You have a ward?"

"Of course!" He beamed proudly as we followed him in.

There were a dozen or so patients. One was coughing and hacking over the edge of his bed into a tin can. A young man moaned quietly. There was no nurse, no equipment. "This is the only ward, I suppose."

"Intense care," the doctor pointed to a small room. Inside, an old man gasped for air while his family sat around.

Doctor Amin pointed to an empty cot next to the coughing man and said, "This is available."

"I couldn't take a bed when others are so much in need," I said, considering a return to the Dutchman's hut.

"You are depressed in here, isn't it?" The doctor was more perceptive than I'd thought. "There also is veranda." He pointed outside.

A double door led out to a recessed concrete deck. Walls extended outwards to the left and right, extending the roof against sun and rain. It was so private, I wondered why anyone would remain inside.

"In case of bad weather, we will bring the bed inside."

Within minutes my six-foot frame lay prone, ankles dangling uncomfortably over the end of a five-foot-six cot. I'd grown inured to these things since Istanbul; a cradle of jute rope strung in a rectangular frame, guaranteeing bruised ankles to anyone above average height.

"How long will I be here?" I asked the doctor.

He smiled happily. "Several weeks or months."

I tried unsuccessfully to sit up. "Months?"

"Rest and diet," he said. "We bring food every day, thrice. I return."

Jacques rearranged my rucksack into a bolster and put it behind me. Instead of dismay, relief dawned on me—I didn't have to vacate my bed in the morning, nor catch any bus, nor even go in search of food.

Annick returned with a dish, mug and spoon, some powdered glucose and bedding. She sat beside Jacques and my eyes closed.

In my dreams Mum reached towards me, but my fingers wouldn't close on hers. Dad stood outside the restaurant looking fretfully up and down Worcester Street. I called to him but my voice was soundless. I had to pay a bus fare, but my legs wouldn't bring me to the ticket counter. In railway stations and airports, I asked strangers the way to Gloucester. They shrugged.

The doctor stood by my bed; in one hand was a tall beaker and in the other a flask of fluorescent red liquid. "Drink," he proffered.

I tipped it into my mouth. Each sticky, bitter-sweet gulp woke me a little more until a brown stain came into focus. It ran along a crack from base to blunted edge of the broken rim. I pushed it back into his hand.

"This is filthy!" I thought I'd shouted, but heard only a whisper.

His smiling teeth gleamed in the twilight. "Not to worry; antiseptic."

The taste of disinfectant lingered in my mouth as he made his rounds and gave each patient a swig from the same beaker. I wanted to get up and storm out in protest, but I was already falling back into delirium.

The good doctor returned later with a steaming pot of dal and a basket of bread. He filled my enamel dish with the murky yellow liquid and handed it over with a kindly smile, placing a large round of bread on my bed. I watched him dispense food touchingly to his other patients. My body thrived on the bland meal. I lay back and looked over the scene before me. The sun rose to the left, sprinkling golden flecks on the mountain peaks. Beyond the foot of my bed an empty field was stubbled with the dry, crumpled stalks of last season's maize.

A farmer and ox worked the land. The man used clicking sounds and the beast brute strength to maneuver the crude plow through the flinty ground. In a loincloth and a pair of sturdy leather sandals the farmer stopped only to wipe the sweat from his face, fling an old root or rock to one side or pat the animal's flanks in appreciation. Dust flew up in little clouds, sticking to the sweat of his body. Gleaming rivulets dribbled over the grime, creating patterns, drying in the heat and cracking open so that his skin looked like the baked earth itself. Unwavering, he turned over one furrow after another.

I watched in awe. Small, wiry and worn by life, he seemed twice the man I'd ever be. I'd never need anything as he needed this. I'd never known real determination. It had all been too easy, my life.

I slept intermittently. The doctor returned with more dal and bread and inquired after my health. I ate mechanically, set down my dish and spoon and sank onto my back. Genesis 1:5 came to mind: "And the evening and the morning were the first day."

A suppressed whine rose steadily to a wail, and then a heartrending shriek. Shocked into full consciousness I listened to a cacophony of lamentation from the intensive care room.

It went on for an hour or so before moving away from the compound, a procession shouldering a flimsy stretcher along a high ridge and into the hills. I dipped in and out of sleep as the procession wound its way behind a eucalyptus grove and marched again into view, now at a considerable distance.

I asked the doctor next morning, "The old man died last night?"

He nodded, then held up his grimy beaker of red liquid questioningly. I shook my head.

"As you prefer," he shrugged.

For weeks I lay in my cot and watched the farmer wring his crop from the hard earth. He turned up each morning and evening with a hoe over his shoulder to open the mud dam, divert water from the nearby stream into his irrigation channels, carefully clear the waterway and saturate each plant before plugging the breech. He never wasted a gesture, and I took his attitude as a model for my new life. I'd decided the hepatitis was a watershed, and I'd been blessed with a new lease.

I was happy to receive visitors, usually. Omar arrived one day with Ali. I stared at the sky as he lectured me. It was an easy matter to flutter my eyes and feign exhaustion. I heard the swish of Omar's fine clothing as he strode away, and the patter of Ali's feet.

Jacques and Annick came every day, always bringing something to eat. A notable visitor was Annemette, a Danish girl who'd lived for several years in the valley, eking out a living from her charms. Some local men had become both benefactors and confidants of sorts. She'd run out of money years before and claimed she wanted to go home, but whatever her reasons, was resigned to her ignominy.

"There's never quite enough money," she complained unconvincingly. She didn't seem to care about her life and preferred to talk about me. "So how'd you end up here?"

"I dunno. Just traveling. Same as you."

"No, not the same as me. I got stuck. I have nothing to go back to and nothing to look forward to. You're not like the others who come here. You've got a light in your eyes."

I looked up. Was she mocking me?

"I'm serious," she said dryly.

Was she reading my thoughts?

"No, I'm not reading your thoughts."

"You're freaking me out," I said.

"It's all in your expression. I can read people. My life depends on it."

She was guileless, not stupid.

I asked her about the archaeological ruins in the area, the remnants of the same Buddhist culture that had thrived in Bamiyan. She told me what to look for, and where.

"But if you're interested in Buddhism," she said, "Why aren't you in Dharamsala?"

"Where?"

"You haven't heard of Dharamsala? In India, just across the border. There's a Tibetan colony there, and the Tibetan Library. I thought everyone knew about it."

I gestured her to go on.

"The Dalai Lama went there after the Chinese invaded Tibet and set up a Tibetan government in exile. You can study there. They have classes every day. It's *living* Buddhism." She swept her arm around her. "All you've got here is Buddhist ruins."

"Why aren't *you* there?" I asked.

She shrugged. "It's not my thing."

"What's here?"

"I'm more interested in what *you're* doing here," she evaded.

"I wanted to get away from the heat, and it's an opportunity to learn a bit about Islam . . . ."

"You've been hanging out with Omar and that Ali guy."

"Yes. I . . . ."

"They're bad news," said Annemette bluntly, "especially Omar. Keep away from him."

"You're *ordering* me?" I asked.

"Sure I'm ordering you," she laughed. "For your own good." She cocked her head. "He's a control freak."

I nodded. "Islam's not for me anyway."

"Whether it is or not, you won't find out from him."

"He seems to know a lot," I said defensively.

"You're right. He seems to."

"You think he doesn't?"

"He's one of those who makes the Koran say what he wants it to." She hesitated. "You know, there are good men around here. They keep to themselves, but some of them tell me things they don't even tell each other. I'm safe, an outsider. The fact that I've survived here for so long is proof enough that I'm discreet. Anyway, their opinions are worth more than all his big speeches and fancy ways. They keep their sons away from him." She stood up. "This valley can be a dangerous place. Be careful."

"Thanks," I said.

"So you're looking for something, are you?"

I smiled. "Something. I dunno what."

"I'll see you again."

I watched her leave.

By now I was on the mend, though my appetite was a shadow of its former self. I was content with the thrice-daily ration of dal and bread, supplemented with spoonfuls of glucose. Each day I slept a little less; my skin lost its yellow hue, though it was now stretched tautly over my bones.

One morning Jacques and Annick announced that they were off to India. "Perhaps we'll see you there," said Annick sentimentally.

I smiled. "Yeah. Perhaps." I felt sad too, and tried to express the gratitude I felt. I ended up sounding silly, and we all laughed.

Jacques said, "It was nothing, man. Pass it on."

Annick bent down to kiss me on the cheek, and they left. As I watched them walk around the corner of the building I knew it would soon be time to move on, perhaps for Dharamsala.

13

AT THE BOTTOM

ON JULY THE FIRST, I bid a warm farewell to Doctor Amin, walked gingerly to the bazaar and climbed aboard a bus. With rubbery legs and a woozy head, I was unready for the trip through the plains, and so headed North instead, for a change of scenery. It was good to be under my own steam again.

Kalam was end of the line. For the last few miles the road had been little more than a rock-strewn track; it now petered out altogether. Beyond, a wide plain spread out to the feet of the snow-capped mountains to the north and east, and a swathe of smooth pebbles on each side of the river suggested the swell of the spring run-off. The river poured torrentially down towards the lower valley, hemmed in from east and west by a procession of dark hills. I'd craved immersion long enough. Here was a perfect opportunity in a place rarely frequented by other Westerners.

The bazaar consisted of half a dozen tiny shops with a few baskets of tomatoes, onions and okra. Scrawny chickens had the run of the street. The truck pulled up at a two-story restaurant that stood grandly apart from the neighboring buildings. Along the lower level open shutters revealed an open fire on a raised brick grate. Men sipped tea and ate at long benches, rifles propped up within easy reach. Flat rounds of bread browned on an iron slab and a cauldron of water simmered. There was no chimney, and the walls, benches and tables were uniformly blackened.

Two men sat across a table from one another, each straddling a bench. One of them stared at me and, without breaking off his gaze, ejected a stream of naswaar spittle into the straw covering the floor. His companion's elbow hung loosely on the edge of the table between them, fingers restlessly tapping the breech of his rifle. Their revolvers were holstered. The proprietor wore a rag over his shoulder and a holstered sidearm.

I smiled, pointed to the sign and asked, "Hotel?"

The owner showed his stained teeth. "Room?"

I nodded. "Yes, room."

He raised an outstretched palm. "Five rupee."

"No," I said. "Two rupee."

He grimaced and said. "Here one hotel, no two. My hotel." His swept the barren landscape with his arm. "My hotel, one hotel, five rupee."

I said. "Three rupees?"

He shook his head flatly, turned and walked away.

"Okay, okay," I said. "Five."

He smiled, and as I handed him the money he led me to the upper landing. There were four rooms on one side and three opposite, the remaining space being taken up by the stairwell and, luxury of luxuries, a toilet. Five-rupees didn't seem so bad after all.

He showed me a plain concrete room with a single cot and two shuttered windows overlooking the landing. There was no view outside.

"How about these?" I pointed to the two rooms overlooking the front.

"Eight rupee," he said.

The rooms were no different except for a barred, unglazed window overlooking the street. Both were unoccupied and I convinced him with elaborate hand gestures, smiles and a smattering of Pushto to let me have one for five rupees, on condition that I'd forfeit it if other guests showed up. He smiled. Perhaps he liked me after all.

I settled in. The toilet consisted of a hole in the ground, but it had a concrete floor with two raised foot imprints and was clean. It also had a tap with a dependable trickle of water. I filled a battered enamelled tin

KALAM: the river poured torrentially down towards the lower valley, hemmed in from east and west by a procession of dark hills

basin and washed my hands and face in my room. Exhausted, I opened the shutters, threw myself back on the bed and fell into a dreamless sleep.

By midafternoon, the tiles over my head were burning under the midday sun; my body was covered in sweat and flies. Diesel engines and the shouts of men drew me to the window, and in the open road before the hotel boys and men poured from a lorry, all dressed in roll-down woolen caps and waistcoats, baggy pants and shirts, all bearing side-arms. Kalam seemed small and insignificant, and yet it was a staging post for people in and out of the surrounding hills.

At the head of the valley, the snowcapped heights of Mount Falakser melted into the rushing river Swat. I planned to follow it upstream once my strength had returned. In the restaurant I washed some bread and cream down with hot tea and was feeling restless when the scraping of a bench and table across the floor behind me made me turn.

The two men who'd stared at me when I arrived were back. One of them, blue-eyed and sandy-haired, stared intently, while the other watched him nervously. His gaze alone was intimidating, but he also had a few inches on me. His eyes wandered in their sockets like loose marbles.

"You are English?" He picked up his rifle and approached.

I stood up hastily and forced a smile. "Yes, I'm English."

He said, deliberately, "English kill my grandfather."

"Oh," I said. "I'm sorry."

"You are sorry?" he was incredulous.

"To hear that. Sorry to hear that. It's terrible."

"Why are you here?" His rifle muzzle wavered towards me.

His companion, dark-haired and shorter by a head, now scrambled to his feet and put his hand on the other's shoulder. "My friend was liking his grandfather."

With a light and reassuring voice, the shorter one guided the other slowly but surely away from me.

The tall one reluctantly allowed the other to lead him away. I sat down as they left. His companion glanced at me with obvious relief as they went down the steps. Finally I took my eyes off them and found the proprietor at my side, shaking his head apologetically.

Why *was* I here again—cultural immersion? I wondered if the long-term consequences of hepatitis included poor judgment, but I was too exhausted to think it through.

Lunch was a complicated affair of meat and okra in an oily sauce, garnished with green chili. I tried to explain that my digestive system couldn't cope with it.

I picked up a chili, held my belly and grimaced.

"No chili?" he was puzzled.

I nodded. "And no oil."

"Oil?"

"Mustard oil. Ghee. No," I said.

He nodded uncomprehendingly, took the plate, removed the chili peppers and put it back in front of me.

I picked it up again and shook my head.

He looked exasperated.

I peered around the kitchen. "Perhaps . . . I cook?" I asked, not very hopefully.

"You making food?" He made stirring motions.

I nodded.

He rummaged in an alcove under the stairs and dug out a wick-fired stove and battered aluminum pot.

My eyes lit up.

I pointed. Could I take it upstairs? He nodded. I was delighted. He looked relieved.

In the bazaar I bought a set of wicks and a bottle of kerosene. Back in my room I reduced some tomatoes with garlic and simmered potatoes in the juice.

I was still recovering and slept a lot. The days passed dreamily. Still, I felt the isolation creeping up on me. When, one day, I heard an English speaker downstairs trying to make himself understood, I jumped up. It was a Danish fellow I'd met in Madyan.

"I though I'd run into you," he said.

"You came to visit?" I asked.

He shrugged, "Sure," looked around and asked, "What do you *do* up here?"

"Not much. It's quiet."

"That it is," he nodded. "Aren't you lonely?"

I shrugged. "I'm still recovering my strength."

"Who do you speak to?" We walked to the hotel kitchen.

"Oh, people." I ordered a pot of tea and carried it up to my room.

He rolled a joint.

"I haven't smoked in ages," I said. "Hard on the liver."

"You look okay," he said firming it up and passing it to me.

"Really?" I drew on it carefully and coughed.

He took it back and drew huge lungs full of the smoke.

"No more for me, thanks."

"This is easier for the throat," he said, patting his shoulder bag.

"What?"

He withdrew a syringe and a couple of phials.

I raised my eyebrows.

"German morphine," he grinned. "Pharmaceutical quality."

"You brought that from Europe?"

"Naw. Got it at the pharmacy in Madyan."

"How?"

His eyes widened in amazement. "Just asked for it."

"You don't have to be a doctor?"

He laughed. "What do they care? They just sell it."

"Must cost a fortune."

"Medical aid. Subsidized."

He tied a tourniquet, opened the phial, filled the syringe and pressed the needle against his skin.

"That's a huge needle," I commented.

"Yeah," he grimaced. "They only have the Chinese ones here."

Finally, he drew a few drops of blood, pushed the plunger home and closed his eyes. His features took on a look of grim satisfaction as he slumped back, the needle and syringe dangling from his arm.

I was relieved when he stirred again.

"Wanna try?" he asked.

"Dunno," I said. "What's it like?"

"It's like . . . nothing matters," he grinned. "No pain, no worry."

"Oh," I said. "Like heroin?"

"Pretty well," he shrugged.

"I've smoked heroin," I said. "And snorted it."

"Never shot up?"

"No," I said doubtfully.

"What a waste!"

"Isn't it more addictive?"

"It's more fun." He dangled another phial between two fingers. "You buy me another one, okay?"

"Okay," I said. "Let's boil up the syringe first, though."

"Whatever," he replied.

I submerged the syringe in water in the cooking pot and lit the kerosene. As we waited I watched my companion. He hardly moved or spoke.

"Okay now?" he asked.

"Let's give it twenty minutes," I said.

"Twenty minutes?"

"They say to boil water that long, don't they?"

He grunted, "Whatever."

Eventually I said, "It's ready," and held it up to cool.

He tied the tourniquet at the very top of my arm and knotted it tightly.

"Perfect," he said picking out a purple vein in the crook of my arm.

Then he broke the phial and told me what to do. "Close the plunger and suck up the stuff."

I did as he said.

"Squeeze the air out of the syringe. Now shoot."

I couldn't get the right angle.

"Like this," he motioned with his hand.

I just couldn't hold the needle steady against the vein.

"Do you want me to do it?"

"Well . . . ," I said doubtfully. "Okay."

He grabbed it and pressed it against my skin. His hand was trembling.

"I . . . I don't know," I said.

"Aw, don't worry," he pushed it roughly through my skin, sucked up a little blood and fumbled it. The needle came out of my arm, leaving a large bleeding puncture. Blood tricked down my arm.

"Look," I said. "I think I can . . . ."

"Hold still," he gripped my arm and pushed the needle in again. Blood spouted around the needle and he worked it around inside until it was deep inside the vein. "Okay, got it," he said. "Now hold the syringe."

I took it from him.

"Draw out a little blood. Now press in slowly."

The blood and morphine slid in easily. Even before the plunger was completely depressed I felt a warmth coursing through my veins.

"D'you feel it?" he grinned.

"Yes." My unease gave way to a sense of detachment as the drug rushed through me. "It's like a hot bath."

He smiled.

The rush settled into a sense of muffled indifference.

After ten minutes I asked, "Now what?"

"What?" he asked.

"Is this it?" There was no euphoria, no laughter, no insight, or even illusions of it.

"That's it," he said. "Whaddya expect?"

"I dunno. I didn't expect anything. I just wanted to see."

The Dane left the next morning. "I don't know why you're hanging around here," he said. "There's nothing to do. You can come too, you know."

"I like it here." I didn't know why I was lying.

"S'up to you."

"If you know anyone heading this way," I said, "I could use a good book."

"Here." He opened a side pocket of his backpack and pulled out a thick, dog-eared paperback with no cover. "I finished this last week."

The title page read, "The Fellowship of the Ring."

"It's a good read," he yelled from the back of the pickup as it bounced over the brow of the hill and out of sight.

I planned to trek into the Chitral Valley, which ran parallel to the Swat, but my energy was still low. For today, however, I'd head for the foot of Mount Falakser. I wrapped some dates in a piece of cloth, tied it to my belt and set out.

It was early, and the steep crag behind the hotel cast a long, cool shadow. I walked easily in it for a couple of hundred yards, but the sun fell on me like a sack of stones. My body ignored my commands and fell to its knees.

I'd made a gross miscalculation. Not only was Mount Falakser beyond reach, even the short walk back would be an ordeal. I hauled myself along five or ten yards at a time until I was once more in the shade. It took half an hour to cross the two hundred yards back to the hotel. I crashed onto the cot, awoke that evening barely able to move, ate what food I had, lay back again and slept until morning.

Thankful of the book, I consumed it in two days. Time dragged on like a lead weight. What energy I could muster I spent on brief walks, keeping always to the shade of the hills. There were dozens of tiny communities in the surrounding hills. One of them had a small pharmacy, a house with a shuttered opening, manned by an English-speaking woman. It was from here, or somewhere like this, that the Dane had bought his phials of morphine.

"What may I do for you?" she asked politely. Her head was uncovered and she wore her hair in a tidy, demure bun.

"Um," I was embarrassed, not just because of what I was about to ask for but because it had been so long since I'd addressed a woman directly.

She cocked her head to one side questioningly. "Can you explain the problem?"

"Um, no, no," I said. "I just wanted to . . . um . . . buy some morphine."

"German or Chinese?" she asked matter-of-factly.

"German, please. And syringes? Do you have any?"

"Of course. What size?"

I couldn't believe it. Did she think I was a doctor? "Um, appropriate size for the er . . . ?"

"For one dose of morphine, of course. How is this?" She showed me a bulky glass syringe.

I nodded.

"You will need needles." The ones she took out were almost as thick as matchsticks, stainless steel tubes cut diagonally at one end and sharpened.

"Nothing finer?"

She shook her head, smiling regretfully. "Will that be all?"

"Some glucose please. Five packets."

"Very well. Here you are." She added up the total.

Thank you. I paid and left quickly.

Over the next couple of weeks I injected myself sporadically, forgetting my emptiness, refusing to acknowledge my loneliness, falling back on the cot, oblivious to pain. I stared at the ceiling and recalled health and strength in the cool green of England, dreamed of clean water, fresh fruit and damp fields. Would I ever go back? I longed for the distraction of books, music and company thousands of miles away; lifetimes too. I might as well have been on the moon.

I walked often to the pharmacy and back. The pharmacist saw me coming up the steep path and had my order ready by the time I arrived. The transaction was always surreal, and as I carried the poison back to my sickbed I felt the moral vortex tugging at my heels. But as soon as the morphine coursed through my veins any urgency for my wellbeing receded. It became routine. The opiate rush was psychologically feature-less, and even disdain couldn't dislodge it. It was just a relief to be shielded from my own judgment.

And yet it wasn't lost. A voice inside protested steadily. I woke at night with Mum's tender voice in my ear, clear as a bell, "Stevie, oh Stee-vie," she called. "You will look after yourself, won't you? Promise?"

This was the one thing that could bring me to tears. As they poured down my cheeks I savored their reality.

One afternoon I was just reaching for my paraphernalia, a little earlier than usual, when there was a knock on my door.

"Yar," I answered dozily.

The door was nudged open and there stood Annemette, the girl who'd warned me about Omar.

"Oh, hello," I said, taken off guard. "You're in town?"

"I came to see you," she smiled, businesslike.

"Okay, yeah," I laughed. "I was expecting you."

"I'm serious," she said pushing open the door. She glanced around the room. There was nothing but four walls, a window, a kerosene and cooking pot. The gear was in my bag.

"Really?" I straightened myself up.

"Yes," she peered again into every nook and cranny, making me nervous. "Aren't you going to offer me some tea?"

"Sure," I went to the landing for water and I stopped for a moment in the toilet to rinse my face and comb my hair.

"So . . . how are you?" I asked.

"Fine thank you," she seemed preoccupied.

I busied myself. She scrutinized me.

"There's not much to do up here." I spoke for the sake of speaking. "Still, there're no tourists."

"So, what do *you* do?" She held me eye-to-eye.

"Oh, you know. I cook for myself. I'm picking up some Pushto," I said.

"That's good. Pushto. Useful."

I narrowed my eyes apprehensively. Reaching down for the boiling pot my arm protruded for a moment, and she yelled, "What the *fuck* are you doing?"

"What? I'm making . . . ?"

She pointed at my arm. "You know what I mean. You're shooting up."

"No. Well. No, not really."

"D'you think I'm stupid? What the *fuck* are you doing?" she demanded again, rising to her feet. "You're recovering from hepatitis and shooting up? Are you trying to kill yourself? You'll destroy your liver. You're so *stupid* . . . so fucking stupid." She actually sobbed.

Why did she care? Why was I defending myself? "I'm . . . ?"

She looked at me ferociously. My lies evaporated.

"It's true. I got morphine at the pharmacy. It's German, clean and safe."

"Clean and *safe*?" She shot me a withering look. "Of all people," she said quietly, shaking her head. A tear stained her cheek. "I thought you'd be different. *Please* be different."

"I . . . Jeez, I'm sorry."

We sat in silence for a minute. I asked, "Why are you doing this?"

"I don't know," she whispered. "Because you have dreams."

"I—"

"Please," she implored. "Get out of here. Go away."

"Well," I began a speech I rehearsed on myself each day. "I'm just waiting for the monsoon to break in the plains and—"

"Screw the monsoon. Go away."

I stared.

"Are you waiting to overdose?"

"Of course not."

"So go."

Was it that simple? I groped. "I don't know."

"What's to know? Go!"

"All right, all right"

"Go on then."

"What? *Now*?"

She tapped her toe impatiently

"Okay!"

She sat back and watched. "Well?"

In an instant it was clear. There was nothing to think about. I could fritter my life away one day at a time, or I could take it back—now.

"Okay," I said. "I'm leaving."

"You leave this valley and you leave the morphine here and you don't come back."

"Yes."

She looked hard at me but her voice was quiet. "All right." Triumph gave way to sadness. "I'm glad."

"Really . . . why are you doing this?" I asked again.

She paused a moment. "I don't know. One of us has to get out of this valley."

I packed to hide my awkwardness. "How's your tea?"

"Fine. I'm not thirsty."

"D'you want my cooking stuff?"

"Leave it there," she said. "I'll get it to someone who needs it."

I shouldered my pack. "Okay," I smiled lamely.

"Good luck," she said.

"Whyn't you come too?"

"I'd be a lead weight around your neck." She laughed bitterly. "Go."

"Good luck then," I said.

"Right."

Half way down the stairs I turned. "Thanks."

"I'll know if you come back."

"I know. You're right. It's right for me."

"Me too," she smiled. "You just needed a slap in the face."

We sat by the road until a Toyota pickup arrived. I climbed in.

She stepped up, grabbed my shoulder and kissed me on the cheek.

Each particle of dust seemed to stick mercilessly to her as she stood in the wake of the pickup. The hotel, the tiny bazaar of Kalam, the flood plain and finally the faintest hint of Annemette disappeared from view. Gradually, I awoke to the fact that I'd escaped by the skin of my teeth.

PART THREE

COMMUNITY

Nothing is so firmly believed as that which we least know.

—Michel Eyquem de Montaigne
"Of Divine Ordinances"

14

INDIA

DOWN IN THE PLAINS the monsoon was beginning its tortuous build-up of humid air. Inside the cramped bus, the mere act of breathing took all my concentration. By the time we'd reached Peshawar my clothes were stuck indistinguishably to my skin.

Lahore's skies were dark, and I stepped off the bus into flooded streets, wading knee-deep in murky waters and trying not to imagine what lay underfoot. Its citizens accepted with matter-of-fact fatality the syrupy air and water, the stench and the floating detritus, treating each other with city-folk indifference. Privacy was not an issue, however. Through wide open shutters and doors I glimpsed dark, unimaginable hovels.

In no mood to search for a cheap room, I arrived at the YMCA guilt-ridden over the cycle-rickshaw driver who'd strained to get me to the drab modern building. Its only guest, I had the entire dormitory to myself. Poorly laminated wardrobes, tables and chairs were swollen with damp. An electric lamp emitted dim yellow light and an eerie silence completed the mood. I bathed and headed out for the museum.

From a distance the building was a great example of colonial architecture, but the interior was a shambles. The electricity was off. Monsoon rains dripped haphazardly from the ceiling and dribbled down the walls. Security guards hung around aimlessly.

I searched for the fasting Buddha, an example of Gandhara[27] art. It wasn't art history I was interested in; I was looking for inspiration. The image is of Siddhartha Gotama, later The Buddha, during his ascetic phase. The story goes that his meditation really started to bear fruit only after this phase of self-denial. He'd learned to survive on a single grain of rice a day, but one morning accepted a bowl of milk-rice from a shepherd girl and, with renewed energy, reached full Awakening.

I stumbled upon the statue in a grimy, fogged-up display case, and peered in. It depicted a small man in meditation posture, cheeks sunken, collar, ribs and blood vessels protruding. The bronze skin somehow conveyed the translucence of undernourished skin, and the face such an extraordinary expression of hope that I held my breath. This man, I thought, wasn't stopped by his fears.

I reflected on the confusion of my life—my infamous anger, my agonized love life, my incongruous political goals and the sordid people from whom I'd adopted them, kleptomania, drug abuse. How many reminders did I need? Would my debt to Annemette motivate me? With no life of her own, she'd handed me mine with no strings attached.

The India-bound bus approached the unfriendly border. The Grand Trunk road had twenty-five years earlier connected the two Indian cities of Lahore and Amritsar, but now it was intercepted by the border separating proud young Pakistan from complicated old India.

The situation wasn't without comedy. Pakistani officers were puffed up with waxed, twirled handlebar moustaches. They slashed the air with swagger sticks, itching to open fire. Enlisted men were well-fed and steely-eyed. A long line of trucks, buses, pedestrians and officials nonchalantly awaited the opening hour.

The gates eventually swung apart and the crowd pressed into the border post. With my papers stamped and in order, I walked through the dust to India, reflecting that few Pakistani or Indian citizens had that freedom. The mood on the opposing side couldn't have been less bombastic, the men smaller or more shabbily dressed, relaxed perhaps

GOLDEN TEMPLE: *a huge compound encircles the lake that in turn surrounds the temple itself*

by the knowledge that they outnumbered their neighbor by ten to one. Like their counterparts, the men wore a variation on the old British khaki, hobnail boots and berets.

And now, I was in India.

I ogled the narrow laneways of Amritsar, trying to take it all in. The fragrance of fried snacks from roadside *dhabas*[28] wafted alongside the stench of rotting vegetables, urine and excrement. Cyclists, scooters, pedestrians, cows, rickshaws and cars jostled; ringing, beeping, shouting, mooing, hailing and honking out their rights of passage. Frighteningly disfigured beggars whined routinely for alms. Urchins wandered through plentiful food markets, shooed uncaringly from one potbellied merchant to the next. Sacred cows roamed freely, eating at will. Fabric stores and sari shops displayed their dyed wares. Spice vendors sat behind pyramids of brightly colored powders. Voices and instruments screeched from tinny transistor radios on windowsills, barrows, bicycles and rooftops. The sky glared. The air quivered with frenetic life. My senses bulged.

I was surprised to learn that even foreigners were welcome to stay at the Sikhs' Golden Temple, not a guest house but the real thing, and that it was a popular stop for backpackers. A huge compound encircles the lake that in turn surrounds the famous temple itself. Rooms are provided for visitors in the outer compound. However, I was shunted from room to room until I landed amidst a group of Westerners, including Jacques and Annick, with whom I had a joyful reunion. They were delighted to see me on my feet and had just returned from Dharamsala, so I heard more enthusiastic stories of the Tibetans. It was late when we finally lay down side-by-side on bamboo mats, and fell asleep to the ceaseless hustle and bustle of pilgrims.

Next morning we bid adieu, and I set off for my appointment with Tibetan Buddhism.

15

DHARAMSALA

BRITISH INFLUENCE WAS NOWHERE more evident than in the stations and carriages of Indian Railways. Waiting rooms and the station master's office were all clearly labeled. Hand-painted signs in Hindi and English futilely requested travelers to refrain from spitting. Steam engines belched and hissed. Soot and smoke blackened the platform and its fixtures. The difference from England was that, on palettes and benches, in every nook and cranny, people cooked, ate and slept, oblivious to the hubbub.

In 1974 the million or so square miles that were India supported six hundred million souls,[29] mostly villagers. The country's rail network was available for all in first-, second- and third-class carriages. I entered the network for the first time at Amritsar, and purchased the cheapest possible ticket for Pathankot, third class, *unreserved*. The appended word seemed harmless enough, but I came to dread it.

Seats in this carriage weren't simply occupied, they were obliterated by a pile of humanity. Foot wells were filled with passengers and baggage. Families squeezed together in corridors. Above, people stretched out in wooden berths between luggage rack and roof. Three men were squashed in the WC cubicle—one on the crapper, one in the sink and the other propped between the two.

"Sixty-nine miles isn't all that far," I reminded myself.

Hours and a dozen stops later the Pathankot sign slid to a merciful halt outside the carriage window. My mind was set on the privacy of a hotel room, but as I left the station I was accosted by a cry of, "Dharamsala, Dharamsala!" Deciding to get it over with once and for all, I climbed on to the idling bus. Five hours later, four thousand feet into the Himalayan foothills and weary beyond words, there I finally was. The other passengers dispersed, the driver bedded down inside and I found myself standing in a sleepy little town. Where were the Tibetans? Too tired to care, I found a room and fell instantly asleep.

Next morning, I asked the lady who kept the hotel, "So where are the Tibetans?"

"McLeod Ganj!" She was surly.

"McLeod Ganj?" I repeated. "Sounds Scottish."

"David McLeod was lieutenant governor of the Punjab," she said with pursed lips.

"So where's that?" I asked.

"Up the hill," she indicated vaguely with the back of her hand. She looked me in the eye. "Why is everybody so interested in the Tibetans? This is India, you know."

I smiled, to show that I liked Indians too.

As the bus groaned uphill at walking pace I gripped the overhead handle. Tibetans filled the seats and aisles, giving off a buttery odor. When the bus finally disgorged me I walked into an unmistakably Tibetan village, its Indo-Scottish name notwithstanding.

The main street was dominated by a narrow-roofed structure, a series of rotating drums with Tibetan syllables carved in relief. An old man with shining eyes circled them, one hand fingering a rosary and the other setting one drum after another spinning. His lips moved continuously. An old woman followed, also muttering. She gave me a toothless smile. Half the people in the bazaar were fidgeting with beads and mumbling.

The buildings were various combinations of straw matting, brick and concrete, and swathed in colorful cloth awnings, rugs and paint. Florid

PRAYER WHEELS: under a narrow roof, rotating drums with Tibetan syllables carved in relief

strings of flags criss-crossed the sky. Roadside rocks were ornately painted with strings of syllables. Images were ubiquitous—faded grey photos of lamas from another century, pictures of the Dalai Lama at every age, paintings of beatific buddhas and ferocious demons framed in rich brocade.

Two monks walked confidently down the road, talking quietly with heads inclined towards one another. With rosaries tucked into sashes and hands behind their backs, they were sharp-eyed and neatly turned out. There were tall, burly Tibetans and small birdlike men and women, fat ones and thin ones with clear-skinned or pox-scarred complexions. Some were as white as me, some as tanned as leather. Young children played in the streets. Older ones worked alongside their parents, and were sometimes in charge.

Mangy dogs scavenged through piles of rubbish and decomposing foodstuff. They moved gingerly, ears down, tails tucked in, eyes flickering nervously. A bitch growled protectively over a meaty prize, surrounded by males.

Meat? I thought Buddhists were vegetarian.

The bustle was less frenetic, and the streets of McLeod Ganj hummed at a more tranquil pace than I'd grown used to. People smiled tremendously, the corners of their mouths and eyes deeply creased. Did they see something I didn't? There were serious and sullen faces too, but even they seemed at uncanny ease.

A monk walked down the road, arms behind, eyes cast firmly at his feet, a model of single-pointed concentration. He wore the yellow shirt and red robes of a monk, but his shaven head was pasty white and he had an unmistakably pointy, Caucasian nose. I grew excited.

"Excuse me."

He spoke with an English accent. "Hello."

"I, er . . . I was wondering, um . . . ?"

Why had I stopped him?

He smiled. "Have you just arrived in Dharamsala?"

"This morning. Well, last night but this morning really."

I'd gone stupid.

"You might be looking for the library."

"The library?"

"Of Tibetan Works and Archives."

"Yes, actually yes, I am. That's where, um—"

"The dharma classes are held? It's halfway down the hill to Lower Dharamsala. You must have passed it on your way up."

"Oh, I couldn't see out of the bus window. Too crowded."

"Not that way. Take the other road," he pointed to the far end of town. "You can't miss it. Gangchen Kyishong."

I repeated it.

"You've heard of it?"

"No, actually. But thanks. I'll have a bite to eat and make my way down."

Tibetan food was refreshingly bland, unlike the relentless spiciness of cheap Indian restaurants. With a full stomach and a hope that my journey might be entering a new phase, I walked to the end of the main street where the temple complex stood graciously against a hillside. It was maroon and saffron, trimmed with gold and blue. Underneath a Tibetan sign, a second line announced, "School of Buddhist Dialectics," and in its courtyard a young monk stood over a seated adversary, shouting and brandishing his rosary like a weapon. The seated monk responded briskly and I heard the din of other, unseen pairs and groups. Some were gabbling at extraordinary speed, shouting and mocking one other. They seemed to be at play.

DHARAMSALA: the baking plains stretched into distant haze

If Buddhism was about emptying the mind, I wondered how it was done, and especially what dialectics had to do with it. I'd read that Buddhism wasn't a religion at all, but a pragmatic way of freeing the mind, the point being something called Awakening. Could that wean me from the turmoil of my mind?

16

LEARNING

AN OPEN ROAD LED DOWN from the bustle. Perched on the very edge of the Himalayas, McLeod Ganj was backed by snowcapped peaks, while before it the baking plains stretched into distant haze. Early monsoon clouds drifted in, condensing in the cooler air.

Bent-backed men and women porters plodded uphill bearing packs two or three times their own size, held in place by a band of cloth running under the load and over the forehead. All proclaimed a cheerful "namaste" or "tashi deleg."[30] By the time I'd reached the grounds of Gangchen Kyishong, a mile or two down, I was quite cheerful myself.

The library was in Tibetan style, with rhombic walls that inclined inwardly as they rose. Freshly whitewashed, with primary red, blue, green and yellow highlights, it had a picture-book air. Inside, the entrance hall exhibited artefacts in a central display, while books stood open in mounted cabinets and scrolls hung on the walls. Beside each exhibit was a trilingual label, in Tibetan, Hindi and English. A distracted Tibetan man hurried from door to door, one hand in the deep folds of his finely tailored loose jacket, his air officious.

"Excuse me," I called out.

"Hm?"

"Can you tell me about the classes?"

"With Geshe[31] Ngawang Dhargyey?"

"Um, I suppose so."

"Every morning." He was already hurrying away. "Public teachings."

"What time? Where do I register? Is there a fee?"

"Ask one of the Injis, outside." he called out over his shoulder. "Try the canteen." His shoes clicked in the empty hallway.

Wondering what an Inji was, I stared at the waxed floor and noticed for the first time how disreputable my sandals looked, dusty feet and all. I made a note to do something about them, and turned to the hanging images—mineral colors on canvas, generously bordered with silk brocade. They featured all sorts of figures, from the beatific to the monstrous, all darkened by age. The books were loose-leaved, their pages two feet or more wide but just six or eight lines high. Built into the back wall was a floor-to-ceiling glass cabinet with dozens more books wrapped lavishly in cloth and trimmed with more brocade.

Out in the glaring sun I found myself squinting at a breathless girl. She was about my age.

"Have you seen Alex?"

"Alex?" As my eyes adjusted, I found myself gazing into a beautiful Anglo-Indian face.

"Alex Berzin. So, *have* you?"

"Don't know him, I'm afraid. I'm new around here."

"Oh, *everybody* knows Alex," she contradicted me. "He's translating the Compendium with Sherpa and Geshe and I wanted to ask him about the sunyata of bodhicitta. I mean if it's empty ... well, it's confusing, isn't it?"

"Sounds it," I agreed.

"Yes," she said. "What do you think?"

I shook my head. "I'm afraid ... ."

She interrupted me again, talking nonstop and sprinkling her sentences with unknown words. I managed a question of my own, "Can you tell me about the classes."

"With Geshe?"

"At the library."

"Yes, with Geshe," she said, and her eyes opened as if she now saw me for the first time. "Beginners at ten, advanced at eleven."

"I suppose I should come at ten."

"Oh, everyone goes to both. You always learn something." She looked around distractedly but asked, "So, where are you staying?"

I shrugged. "Just arrived."

"They rent rooms here, you know," she said. "Sure you haven't seen Alex?"

I was still shaking my head when she said, "Bye."

"Oh, by the way," I called after her.

She turned.

"What's an Inji?"

"English. You're an Inji. Actually," she laughed, "we're all Injis."

Like a gust of wind she was gone. Later I learned her name was Vivian.

By a quarter to ten next morning a couple of dozen Westerners had congregated outside the library doors. Vivian was questioning a young Tibetan monk with such vehemence that he seemed at a loss for words. No one paid much attention as I went in.

Against one wall in an upstairs room an ornamented seat rose some two feet above floor level. The room was laid with wall-to-wall mats. A few girls dusted and arranged flowers. Others, mostly young men, sat in meditation. I tucked myself away at the back and watched the room fill.

There was a rustle of robes and everyone stood with bowed heads. A corpulent Tibetan monk came in carrying the folds of his cape over his left arm. Everyone put their hands together, went down on their knees, and then rose again, repeating the sequence three times. I followed suit.

We sat and the teacher mumbled a recitation, his voice droning faster and faster as he unwrapped a cloth bundle. On an upturned silver base he built a pile of dried rice and jewels into a three-tiered pile, like a wedding cake. Some students had their own piles, other entwined their fingers. There were a few moments of silence. Then everything was bundled up.

The teacher spoke and the interpreter said, "Geshe reminds you that your prostrations are not for himself, but to prepare your own mind to hear these teachings of Lord Buddha."

GESHE NGAWANG DHARGYEY: built a pile of dried rice and jewels into a three-tiered pile, like a wedding cake

"Yesterday Geshe taught refuge in the three jewels—the teacher, the teaching and the community. Today he will describe the preciousness of human life."

The geshe described consciousness as a beginningless stream that moves after death into another body, not necessarily human. Lifetimes, he said, were counted as the grains of sand in the ocean, in billions of possible life forms. There were also hells of almost endless torment and the long, but not immortal, lives of gods. Humans, located between these extremes of pleasure and pain, were uniquely endowed with the potential to change the course of life, hence the preciousness of human life and the importance of putting it to good use.

As he spoke, I realized that I was already there. Ever since walking out on my education and the mundane goals of procreation, money and success, I'd been either desperately searching to make life purposeful or wallowing in self-pity because it wasn't. This was a good start.

Mention of Heaven and Hell didn't deter me. I was used to that. Having arrived at the doorway of Buddhism of my own free will, I had no problem taking such "places" as metaphorical. I'd read that Buddhism was unsuperstitious, and I meant to interpret it in that spirit.

The class came to an end and the first young monk was replaced by the one whom Vivian had been pestering. "Today," he began decisively, "Geshe will talk about relative truth and ultimate truth."[32]

I sat up.

"Relative truths are conventional; anything you can name, like a vase or a person." He pointed around the room. "These things seem to exist inherently," he paused, "but that's an illusion, caused by confusing a thing with its name."

A dark-haired man in the front row leaned head-to-head with the translator, who corrected himself.

"Sorry, not an *illusion*. A *delusion*. Nothing exists inherently because everything arises interdependently. This is the ultimate truth."

Geshe looked around with a grin. "Is that clear?"

There was a knowing chuckle from the front row.

"This may be rather obscure. Don't be discouraged if it's unclear. Ultimate truth cannot be discussed, only experienced. All ideas or opinions are conventions."

This explained why I'd been so confused for so long. I was stuck in the assumption that truth had to be a product of reason. However, as the geshe went into detail I found my new clarity clouded, ironically, by an impregnable wall of rational explanation.

"We take conventionally existent things as existing in themselves, independent of causes and effects. This is a mistake. All things are impermanent, and all come from causes and conditions, and are all composed of parts, so how can they be independent? The essence of a vase isn't in its belly, or its neck or handle. It certainly isn't in its parts when it's dismantled or smashed. Like this, we should meditate on the ultimate truth of the self; by seeking its inherent existence we discover that it doesn't exist." Geshe grinned again and looked around the room expectantly.

Vivian now put up her hand. "But Geshe," she asked, "What's the point of looking for something that's not there?"

Geshe slapped his thigh happily. "You think it's not there because I told you, because Lord Buddha says so. This is just a convention. Believing is better than not believing, and understanding is better than belief, but only direct insight frees you from conditioned existence! It's only ultimate when you realize it yourself.

"But I do."

Geshe roared with laughter. "If you understand it, why are you confused?"

She was perplexed.

"You see," Geshe continued seriously, "I told you it was difficult."

Some students were scribbling furiously in their notebooks. I wondered how it would be to listen and talk to Geshe without an interlocutor.

The two hours came too quickly to an end. Never had I been so completely absorbed in anything. I bought the Dalai Lama's thirty-page *Key to Madhyamika*, and his brother's memoir, *Tibet is My Country*.

I rented a room in the library complex, and was standing on the common balcony gazing at the knot of people outside the library. Nearby, another lodger muttered disgustedly, "Ridiculous!"

"What is?" I asked.

"Talking about it," he said. "You're just supposed to *do* it."

"Do what?" I asked.

"Mindfulness," he answered. "Meditation's got nothing to do with thinking, this is just more conceptualizing. The point is to stop the mind."

I'd read that somewhere. "Yes," I mused. "That's true, isn't it?"

It was puzzling, but it wouldn't stop me going to these classes. I couldn't get the easy laughter of the geshe out of my mind, and I couldn't wait for tomorrow's classes.

"So why exactly are you here?" I asked.

I turned to my companion, but he was gone. In his place was a girl who smiled and introduced herself as Felicity. Like me, she was a newcomer, and had just attended her first class. She was as impressed as I, and we chatted easily.

17

REPENTANCE

SOMETHING HAD CHANGED. My self-destructive near misses were evidence that my apparent love of freedom was just a fear of discipline. I now found myself amenable to moral order, and with that came a new confidence. All the ideas that had collaborated to confuse me now cooperated to my advantage.

I credited Buddhism for this new perspective. It confirmed that my sense of isolation and entrapment were self-imposed. I was no longer the odd one out. Uncertainty was normal. Life was unpredictable. Denial is rooted in the pretense that we know what's going on, and only when things get desperate do we break down and admit otherwise.

I still felt lost, but no longer alone. Awakening grew from an understanding that both the world and our knowledge of it are transitory, and that the more we seek happiness in such uncertainty, the more we set ourselves up. All emotions lead back to pain, just as pain gives way to joy.

God-fearing Westerners raised on promises of consolation and certainty may find this depressing but I now saw, buried in that truth, the key to freedom. There was more to meditation than peace and quiet.

It was good to stay put. The urge to avoid other Westerners was gone.

I was eager to fit in, and settled into the loose routine of a professional student. This all came to me surprising easily.

Like the library regulars, I came to look upon the young translators and the Tibetan-speaking Westerners with a sense of awe. Hands were put together at the mention of Geshe's name and it was tacitly assumed that the Dalai Lama and his two tutors, even Geshe himself, were "fully enlightened beings." I felt instinctively that it would be bad manners to suggest otherwise.

The fulcrum of social status in Tibetan society is the *tulku*, or reincarnate lama. Once "recognized" as the new incarnation of past teachers, young boys are ranked according to an arcane hierarchy that also determines the relative height of the throne from which they teach. In return, much is expected of them, notably grace, wisdom, kindness and, once they're trained, instruction. The library's two translators were tulkus, and were very likable. Many students concluded that they were buddhas, but who knew? What was a buddha anyhow?

My neighbor Felicity and I encountered each other daily on the shared balcony of the library's rented rooms.

"So what do you think of all this?" she asked. "D'you reckon you were a frog or something in your last life?"

We laughed.

"I don't see why not," I replied. "You might have been a Tibetan nun."

"Or monk?" she mused.

"What brought us here? And why do we stay?"

According to Geshe, some connection from past lives had brought us back. My life had been a mess until this opportunity had enabled ancient propensities to flourish, and now I was back on track.

The funny thing was, everything I was hearing and thinking did feel intensely familiar. I understood Felicity's hesitations, but I threw myself easily into this new way of thinking. The two levels of truth, the role of willful ignorance, the certainty of death and the preciousness of life all seemed self-evident. On the strength of that, I went along with the less obvious stuff. That actions have consequences isn't much of a stretch for a Catholic boy. That the stream of consciousness has no beginning or end, that there are beings "out there" who care for us, that beyond appearances lay true happiness; these were things I was predisposed to and *wished* to accept. There was doubtful stuff too, like Buddhism's weird description of the physical universe, but they didn't really trouble me, despite Geshe's insistence that they were real.

The monsoon was in full swing. The upper and lower towns of Dharamsala, tucked as they were into a nook high on the edge of the Himalayas, were pounded by wave after wave of unspent clouds that piled into one another and unleashed torrential loads. Everything was saturated. Wood and leather acquired a white patina of mold that faded to the touch and returned like fog on a mirror. The odor of mildew was rife. My room at the library, built against a low hillside, developed a wet patch that gathered into a stream, trickling across the floor and out the door. Insect life multiplied exponentially and fist-size spiders perched disconcertingly indoors, awaiting passing prey.

With the fervor of a convert I quit smoking and drinking, found a new sense of right and wrong and devoured the handful of English publications the library had to offer. There were straightforward accounts of daily meditation and contemplation, like Geshe Rabten's *Preliminary Practices*.[33] There was the philosophical challenge of the Dalai Lama's *Key to Madhyamika*. Jeffrey Hopkins' translation of Chandrakirti's *Analysis of Coming and Going* was a real head-scratcher, with phrases like, "The area being stepped on by a foot of a presently going goer is the being-gone-over." I tried to make sense of it anyway.

In this state of renewal I picked up a letter awaiting me, *poste restante*, in Lower Dharamsala. Dad rarely wrote to me, but he'd finally put pen to paper because Mum had learned of my conviction for shoplifting—in the worst possible way. Some chattering lady friends had sympathized with her "embarrassment," made oblique allusions and shaken their heads in commiseration. She went to Dad insisting on no half-baked explanations.

He'd had to admit he had few facts, and that he'd demanded no account from me, something that always struck me as peculiar. Perhaps his reaction had been tempered by a hidden shame of his own. In any case, she was angry, he wrote, that Dad, Philip and I had thought her too weak to bear the truth, and especially because her friends gossiped about her dishonor while she languished in blissful ignorance. She had a point.

I wanted to assure her that I'd regained my integrity, and set out to prove it by confessing my former depravity in minute detail. I began, "I don't give a cuss what anybody else thinks," and in my newfound piety was quite careless of her feelings. With a tone that makes me cringe today I explained that she had no reason to feel humiliated, for although I'd been proud of my exceptional skills at shoplifting and the admiration of others, I'd actually been a Robin Hood and given away most of my booty. Yes, my behavior had been perverse, but my motivation was altruistic.

Bells clanged in my head as I wrote, and I watched this defensive epistle take shape as if it were written by the hand of another. It wound its way down the page into the margin, and soon ran out of space. I wrote, "continued," and filled a second aerogramme from margin to margin, describing exploit after exploit in minute and cavalier detail. As I walked to the post office I reassured myself that Mum would take comfort in my newfound openness. She'd understand; she was Mum. I dropped

Aerogramme: confessing my former depravity in minute detail

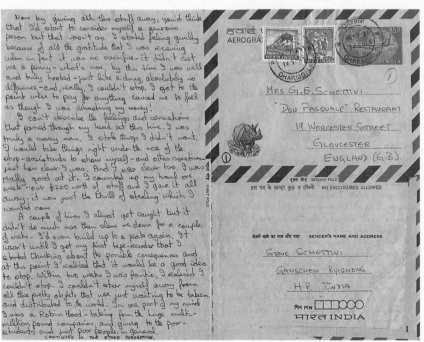

the twin time bombs in the post box and skipped merrily back into the protective shell of my new faith.

I sat to meditate each morning and evening, but never got very far. Hoping to fall into a state of complete absorption, I was more often carried away by distraction or boredom. After a few weeks it was clear that it would take more than a new belief system to dislodge the old mental patterns. I was still irritable, in particular when somebody walked noisily past my room or talked as I was trying to meditate. I was even irritated by my irritability, and although the joke wasn't lost on me the problem was real. The more I pushed myself, the more obstructions appeared. The more I hoped to cut through the underlying habits, the less possible it seemed. I needed patience, but I also wanted to experience Awakening! It made me want to scream.

I fell into increasingly vicious circles, sure I was getting it all wrong. The truth is, the quieter the outer circumstances, the louder the inner chatter; coming face to face with that reality for the first time is disturbing.

Geshe Dhargyey explained the difference between concentrative and contemplative meditation, the former for sheer mental strength, the latter to develop new mental pathways, but I needed hands-on instruction. I needed one of those courses that lead participants step-by-step through the meditative process.

Felicity said, "You should go to Kopan."

"Where's that?" I asked.

"In Nepal. Apparently it's very popular. I found out about it."

"Okay." I nodded.

She came back with an envelope of various colored pages, all covered in dense typewriting; one was an application form. "They call him the Hippy Lama," she said. "He speaks English. I was thinking of going myself. "Would you ... could I tag along? You know, a girl alone in India .... I mean, I *could*, but I'd rather not."

I would have preferred to travel alone, but agreed. I liked Felicity, but resisted my feelings. I'd had such bad luck with girls.

"So, The Hippy Lama it is."

We laughed.

We boarded the bus in Lower Dharamsala. It had been a couple of months since I'd met my first Tibetan and moved into the library compound. It seemed more like two years. I was quite sure of where I belonged and where I was going, and saw my life's mission ahead of me. My enthusiasm was unbounded. I hadn't told anyone yet, but monkhood was on my mind, and I even wondered if one day I might learn Tibetan. The voice of Mister Hayward still resounded in my ears, ten years after I'd been unceremoniously dropped from his French class—"Schettini, you'll *never* speak another language."

From Pathankot we traveled in a reserved second-class carriage—a luxury beyond compare. An express, it would still take two days and nights to cross the subcontinent at it widest point. Felicity chattered enthusiastically as the train heaved its great load of carriages out of the grimy station. We watched one village after another drift past at thirty miles an hour. The stifling heat, the clattering, rhythmic swaying of the train and the vistas of rural India cast a sleepy spell, as if we were stationary while the images of a time-locked world chugged past. Hundreds of millions of people plowed the land, led bullock carts, sat beneath trees, spat betel juice, offered their gods flowers and ghee, trudged down dusty roads, dodged honking vehicles, bartered food and goods, threshed harvested grain, married, loved, argued, gave birth, lived and died beyond the barred windows of our carriage.

It was the most foreign country of all, and yet India felt so like home. English was ubiquitous, often heard in upper-class, Victorian rhythms; rich, old-fashioned and more strangely authentic than my own tongue. It was also the lingua franca of commercial signs, many featuring dilapidated British logos. Post offices, banks and government bureaucracies had all been created under the Raj, and the arrangement of railway stations, the buying of stamps and tickets, the boarding of trains and storing of luggage were uncannily familiar. No matter what Indians had sacrificed to eject the British fewer than thirty years earlier, Anglophilia was rife.

Felicity was interesting, funny and attractive. I must have been in a narcissistic haze, however, because I remember feeling too irritable to fully enjoy her company. She'd traveled overland through Indonesia, Thailand, Burma and Bangladesh, and was no softie. I, on the other hand, was petulant and petty. I blamed the bilious aftereffects of hepatitis and distinctly recall hating myself even as I acted it out. Drugs had isolated me from this side of myself for years, but now there was no more hiding. In the hot, dreamy haze of the swaying rail carriage I imagined learning from the Hippy Lama how, once and for all, to take control of my life.

Dawn broke on the third day over Patna. Time lazily reasserted itself. Humidity hung like a lead blanket over the sprawling horizon of low roofs. A Sunday afternoon feeling pervaded the weekday morning.

"I don't fancy it here," I said, as we discussed finding a hotel.

"Well I'm not spending another night on a train." Felicity responded.

"Maybe we should fly." I wondered aloud.

Later that afternoon we lurched into the air at a hair-raising angle. "Perhaps," said Felicity nervously, "they think they're flying a rocket." The ascent was steep, and passengers standing in the aisle clung white-knuckled to the seats on both sides. Perhaps it was because we had to quickly climb above the Himalayan peaks, or it may have been, as travelers' lore had it, that steep, risky takeoffs use less fuel. In that time and place where even bus drivers turned off engines and coasted down-hill, anything was believable.

The stupendous view distracted us. Snowy peaks stretched from horizon to horizon, glowing deep gold as shafts of sunlight highlighted the mirror slopes against the dark cleavage of the valleys. Approaching Kathmandu, we banked steeply to starboard and the distant northern mountains came into view. I stared into the skies of Tibet. Shut up for centuries by steep passes and xenophobia, its borders were now secured by the Red Army, those within trapped in the madness of the Cultural Revolution. Trickles of refugees wound their way cautiously to the borders, and over the years a good quarter of all Tibetans had migrated into Bhutan, Sikkim, Nepal and above all, India, Buddhism's ancestral home,[34] unable to return. I wondered whether, in their place, I'd be as good humored as these refugees. The overwhelming cheerfulness of the Tibetans spoke eloquently of their spiritual resources.

The flight was as brief as it was spectacular, and the landing no less terrifying than the ascent. As we bounced along the Kathmandu tarmac

I vowed out loud that I'd take a train or bus, even walk, before I'd board another local plane.

Nepal was less populated and more relaxed than India. My first challenge was to duck through doorways, for Nepalese are particularly small. Then we went shopping against the cold. I bought an embroidered blanket and Felicity a thick jumper of coarse wool.

Backpackers stayed on Freak Street, where a hundred tiny hotels competed for their penny-pinching custom. Smoke from the world's best hashish wafted along alleyways and through windows. Nepalese temple balls and sticks crumbled easily, burned with gentle fragrance and brought a warm glow to the senses without clouding the mind, like a fine Bordeaux. Since leaving London I'd looked forward to sampling it in situ.

A boy approached. "Hashish! Mister, good hashish. Temple sticks."

My longings reached out, but I said as decisively as I could, "No thanks."

"You crazy? Far out hash, man. Far fucking out! Zero-zero, best shit."

I believed him, but I stuck to my guns. "I don't smoke."

He looked surprised, but not as much as I felt.

"Ah, fuck you!" he said halfheartedly, and turned away.

The regret I felt was eased by my new resolve.

Once we had a room, Felicity and I set out for dinner, I with the blanket folded on my shoulder, she in her new jumper. On the way back we encountered a beggar woman, a baby at her breast. I dropped some change into her outstretched hands but instead of thanking me she pointed to the blanket and asked, "For me?" She raised her arms to receive it.

I shook my head.

"Go on," said Felicity. "It's cold out there. Give it to her."

"I only just bought it," I said helplessly, and entered the hotel. Guilt forced me outside again several minutes later, but the woman was gone. All night long I listened to the bustle outside, staring at the ceiling and imagining her huddled against the cold.

18

MEDITATION

O N THE WAY TO KOPAN we passed through Bodhnath, where
giant painted eyes gazed down from the great stupa, an eerie,
hundred-and-twenty foot mound symbolizing the buddha
consciousness. Strings of prayer flags streamed in every direction from its
gilded spire. Monks, nuns and lay people by the dozen wandered over it,
turning prayer wheels and counting beads. Vendors sold religious wares.
It was the most cheerful religious monument I'd ever visited.

The walk to Kopan hill took us from the bustle, through terraced fields
and irrigated paddies into a wide valley. From a hillock in the middle, a
gilded roof rose like a ship at anchor, half concealed by a broad bodhi
tree. Prayer flags hung chaotically in every direction. Half way up the
hillside boy-monks laughed as they bathed in a gushing spring.

English signs directed us to the office, where books, incense, rosaries, bells and knick-knacks were on sale. A moon-faced American nun
retrieved our registration and asked for two-hundred rupees each, "for
food and lodging only; no charge for the teachings," she emphasized.

She handed us each a pile of booklets. "Here's some reading material.
You must attend all meditation sessions and maintain silence until lunch-

time. No leaving the grounds, no visitors, no non-dharma reading material, radio or music. Men and women sleep in separate quarters. Please
respect the vows of the monks and nuns. You must keep the five basic
precepts for the whole month and the eight Mahayana precepts for the
last fifteen days." She pointed to a wall chart where the precepts were
posted in large print.

"Total silence, right?" I asked.

"For the last two weeks," she confirmed.

Felicity stared, wide-eyed. "Total? Are you sure?"

I smiled. The nun nodded. As I opened the door she added, "Please go
easy on the water. Every last drop comes up on someone's back."

A marquee had been erected, and a bustle of western monks and nuns
was preparing the altar and throne for the beginning of the course that
evening. I wandered away, feeling free for the first time since leaving
Dharamsala, and decided to take a walk back to Bodhnath. I encountered
two women and a man on their way up.

"That's Ko-Pan up there?" the man had an American accent, Southern.

"Straight through the trees." I said. "It starts tonight."

"What starts?" asked the man.

"The meditation course. I presumed . . . ."

The older women laughed, too loudly. "Us? Good God no."

"We're just going to look," the other added, but the man regarded his
companions uncertainly. "Is that why you're here?"

I nodded.

"Are you a Boo-dist?" asked the man.

"Yes," I nodded again. I'd never said so before.

"Good gosh," said the woman. "Were you never baptized?"

"Oh yes," I said. "Catholic."

She looked horrified. "And now you believe in reincarnation . . . all
that stuff?"

"I think we're responsible for our own actions," I said.

"Christians believe that."

"Yes, but in Buddhism, there's no God to fix things up." I said. "Or devil
to blame the bad stuff on."

Both women looked at me as if I were mad.

*SWAYAMBHUNATH STUPA: a
120-foot mound symbolizing
the buddha consciousness*

"Buddhists believe in nothingness, don't they?" asked the man.

"This isn't nothing, is it?" I stomped on the ground.

"Yeah, but the point of meditation; it's nothingness?"

I shook my head. "It's not that nothing exists. We see something in things that isn't there. When we get past the preconceptions, we're free."

"Sounds like nothingness to me," said the man.

"*I'm* free!" stated the older woman.

"Not of your opinions," I retorted.

We stared down one other.

The younger woman was looking at me with suspicion. "So what's the point?"

"The point is," I struggled, "We're interdependent."

"Well I'm not interdependent with Buddhism," she said. "I'm a Christian."

"That's good," I said.

"Not good enough for you!"

"I like that Buddhism's open to other religions," I said.

"We'd better be getting along," the man interrupted. "Good luck to you," he stuck out his hand.

"All the best," I shook it and strode off.

My anointment at the age of thirteen as a Soldier of Christ had left me uninspired, but now here I was advocating a heathen faith in no uncertain terms. I understood that Buddhism was a practice, not a belief system, and yet here I'd been assailing unreceptive ears with mere words and ideas. I felt puffed up and silly, yet comfortable in my mission. Coleridge's notion of suspending disbelief ran through my head like a melody I couldn't shake. My heart was pumping. I felt fine.

The course began in earnest next morning with a young western monk sitting at the foot of the teacher's throne, gazing rather fearfully into his lap. He grinned sheepishly and said in a Dutch accent, "My name is Marcel. Lama asked me to come and talk to you. In fact," he added a nervous laugh, "he told me that I was to lead the meditation sessions." He paused. "Unfortunately, I'm completely unworthy."

A hushed laugh ran around the marquee.

"We'll start," he said, "with some simple breathing meditation to calm the mind and focus the attention. Watch your breath without trying to control it," he said. "Notice the air passing over the tip of your nostrils."

I did as he said, feeling my breath passing in and out and thinking how relaxing it was. I was meditating at last! Soon I'd have complete control over my mind. I was excited.

"Bring your mind back to your breath. Don't get excited."

Whoops! I wouldn't forget again. I focused back on the tip of my nose. Soon I'd learn deep meditation, and would become like this accomplished, modest monk. Perhaps I'd be a teacher one day . . . ."

"Don't allow thoughts or memories to distract you. Just watch your breath."

Damn! I started over.

His voice repeatedly lassoed my attention and dragged it gently back to the starting point. I felt I was making progress until he spoke again and I realized my attention had wandered once more.

"Don't be led astray by a sense of accomplishment or failure. Just watch the breath."

The urge to fidget was almost irresistible but I was determined to remain at least physically still, if not mentally. For fifteen minutes I managed. By the end of another quarter hour I wanted to scratch, to wriggle, to scream, jump up and shake every bone in my body. The effort to remain still was by turns exhausting, stiffening and finally deflating. I gave up any attempt at mental stillness and allowed my mind to wander freely. I wondered why I was there. I wanted to get back to it, but at that moment it was the last thing I felt like. If only I could take a break, I'd recompose myself and do it properly next time.

I cracked opened my eyes and saw Marcel in my peripheral field, awesomely still. I imagined him completely absorbed, blissful, perhaps even enlightened.

My knees hurt.

He spoke. "Bring your mind back. If you feel pain in your knees or anywhere else, use the pain as your object of meditation, instead."

Was he reading my mind, talking to me directly, and not the other hundred and forty-nine meditators? Or, perhaps we were all subject to the same mental wandering. If so, I was no better than anyone else! Pangs of self-importance thumped in my chest. I wasn't made for this.

"Come back to your breath. Don't compare yourself with others."

He *was* speaking to me. Or were we all in the same boat? I was there to develop a focused mind, and the bliss that comes with it, so they say. But I seemed so completely to lack the sheer mental power, and this was hard work. Had I failed before I'd even begun? Was it possible that I actually had no special gift for meditation? I'd actually started thinking I was a natural at Buddhism.

"Don't go anywhere. Don't think anything. Keep your mind fixed on the breath. Turn away from all distractions."

Yes, yes, easy for him to say. A still mind has no goal; so then what? Is there a difference between a point and a goal? I groaned inwardly. *Goal or point, what's the difference? Stop! Analysis is just another distraction. Back to the breath! My God!*

Was my mind *always* like this?

I peeked at my watch. Thirty minutes had passed, an hour remained. Marcel now introduced a new type of meditation. We were to imagine a Buddha in the space before us, light and goodness pouring from his heart into ours. Visualizing a hundred and fifty little buddhas, each attached to a meditator by his own luminous stream of spiritual nectar, made me want to giggle. As for negativity and frustration pouring from my bowels and joy and clarity filling my mind, I was too tired.

By the time we got to our feet only one thing was clear, that my mind had a will of its own. The controling "I" was supposedly just a figment, but it felt at once so real and so powerless!

I rubbed my eyes and headed gratefully to the steaming tea urns. Dense white clouds had crept down the far mountains and filled the valley floor. They lapped like waves at the foot of the hill, stranding Kopan like an island in the mist. I wrapped the blanket around my shoulders, cradled the hot mug in my hands and crouched at the edge of the plateau as the climbing sun peeled away the vapor in long wispy ribbons.

Breakfast consisted of gruel and fresh fruit. Afterwards we were to receive a teaching by Lama Zopa Rinpoche, the Hippy Lama's young ward. He looked embarrassed to be sitting on the high throne but put his hands together and began praying. The monks and nuns in the front row joined in, and there was a rustle as people flipped through their course notes. Sure enough, I found some transliterated syllables and did my best to keep up while tracing the English translation.

Lama Zopa opened his eyes and giggled, lowering his head so far that his chin almost touched his chest. Then making sure to avoid eye contact with anyone, he shifted his gaze from his lap to the empty space above our heads, and began. "Before, so far what we have done, that is, actually I will describe another time, it is however totally all this various things, these different things . . . all this purification . . . however purification is a method to pacify mental and physical suffering . . . each of these the different form of practices, have so much different explanation . . . so, I will describe another time."

You could have heard a pin drop.

His hands fluttered as he spoke and his voice had a birdlike quality. He stared often into space, expressing himself rapidly and repeating phrases over and over. He completely lacked the structure I'd grown used to with Geshe Dhargyey. His thoughts were interspersed with tall tales, Tibetan equivalents of the *Lives of the Saints* replete with miracles and magical happenings. The crowd hung on his every word and busily wrote them all down. I followed suit in the hope of gleaning something, and by doing so injected order into his ramblings. After the havoc of meditation it was good to deal with words and ideas, no matter how peculiar. Afterwards, I had another erratic meditation session before we broke for lunch to lounge in the temperate sunshine. We had a tasty combination of rice and vegetables, with sweetened bread for dessert.

That afternoon there was a murmur of conversation in the tent mingled with an air of expectation. I stretched my limbs in anticipation of forthcoming cramps and aches, keeping one eye on the entrance. Lama Yeshe, it was whispered, might pay us a visit. His appearances were unpredictable for his health was poor; two faulty valves had left him with an irreparably enlarged heart. The wait grew long. When his appearance seemed most unlikely, those nearest the entrance suddenly scrambled to their feet. By the time I was up and could see over everyone's heads, the Hippy Lama was sitting on the throne, smiling broadly. By now I'd learned that nobody called him that. He was Lama Yeshe, or just Lama.

We made three prostrations and settled down as Lama chanted a slow mantra. The monks and nuns joined in. I mumbled along. He closed his eyes and lapsed into expressionless silence. A few minutes later he looked around curiously, rocking from side to side and grinning. The silence was so prolonged, and he seemed so content to look at us, that all expectation faded. Then he began talking, picking his words like building blocks.

"Meditation that clarifies who we are," he began, "is worthwhile. But, if it makes you more confused, then it's not." He stared at us with curiosity. "If you come looking for academic explanations of Buddhism you will be disappointed. The purpose of this course," he stated firmly, "is to see our own minds for what they are. This is simple, not complicated." He smiled mischievously. The crowd rustled.

He fingered his rosary and scrutinized us. The audience fidgeted. He leaned forward intently, using words, gesticulations and facial expressions as a theatrical arsenal. He went over each thought thoroughly, like a writer working a paragraph, sometimes discarding whole metaphors and starting over. He smiled and laughed often, fully engaged in his task.

"All goodness and badness, highness and lowness, samsara and nirvana come from mind." He added civilization, houses, philosophy and doctrines to the list. "*Everything* comes from mind," he said. "All causation is mind—your self, your senses, your sense organs, your physical and mental energy."

His smile suggested it was a joke, but we were all ears. "You know," he said, "They say the East is more superstitious than the West, but in my opinion . . . ," he paused dramatically, "the West is far more superstitious. For example," he grinned triumphantly, "Supermarkets!"

There were a few hesitant chuckles.

In shaky English but with faultless command of his audience he elaborated a hilarious metaphor, parodying consumerism and the cycle of branding, advertising, desire and money. He reminded us not to take his ideas at face value but to draw on our own experience and figure things out for ourselves. "You check up," he admonished repeatedly.

He pointed out that we'd left the comforts of home to sit cross-legged for hours at a time in the hope of finding something to believe in. "People in the West," he commented, "are led to desiring objects that increase their need for more. But these things aren't satisfactory," he said. "Otherwise once you get one, you wouldn't want more; you'd be satisfied. But the more you've got, the more you want. Right?" he demanded emphatically. "Dissatisfaction is on the increase, not satisfaction!" He laughed sadly.

"Superstition makes you act, leaving an imprint in the mind that produces its own fruit, another action. Superstition is like the air moving over the ocean, causing waves, altering the shape of the planet, casting up landmasses. Just like that, superstition shakes the mind and creates shapes, colors and all kinds of different things. This is karma."

Making a motion of stirring liquid in a pot, he described the superstitious mind as deluded. "Your minds are like this, you know? The unclear mind perceives an unclear vision, which has nothing whatever to do with reality, yet the superstitious mind *still* believes in its object."

He made it clear that our sense of an unchanging self is illusory. We think something inside us is in control, but all we find is the mind's

LAMA YESHE: "You think you can choose your life? What an ego trip!"

rushing stream of conscious moments, nudging each other like billiard balls. Habitual reactions provoke overwhelming streams of karmic fruit, making us act in spite of ourselves. That's why meditation's so tough.

He continued, "The uncontroled energy produced by the deluded mind activates other karmic imprints, because karma is governed by the mind. Each time you act, you make karma. You have a billion, billion karmic seeds," he threw his hands in the air, "because every movement of mind is an action, a karmic movement. You understand? In one hour you make a hundred karmas. It doesn't matter if your body is sitting this way," he moved into an exaggerated meditation posture. "Your mind is still moving, shaken by superstition."

"You're driven by karmic seeds, by the force of your own accumulated actions, and still you think you have freedom of choice! But how do you know what kind of life you'll have tomorrow? You think you can choose your life? What an ego trip!"

Now he had us. "Why do you even want this kind of life? No one really knows what they want! Most decisions in your life are made by the uncontroled, superstitious mind."

He leaned forward eagerly, snapping his fingers in the air and saying, "Buddha's teaching is simple. You understand? Simple!" He looked around.

"Especially in the West, you think the mind is something permanent. This is the worst superstition. You don't remember how short and imperma-nent life is. You *never* remember! You can become a kind of social outcast by questioning life's permanence, by mentioning the unmentionable. And from your sense of permanence you make life plans that are *impos-sible*. They can never succeed."

He frowned, watched our response and pieced together his next words. "Maybe you don't understand what I mean by impermanence. Some people say it's the process of birth, then life, then death. But Lord Buddha explained impermanence as momentary change." He gestured to the tent and the surrounding buildings. "We see last year's Kopan like this year's; it's still here, so we treat Kopan as permanent, but it's not. You hold this misconception because you don't see the subtle, momentary changes."

He grabbed a roll of tissue, tearing off pieces and saying, "Perma-nence . . . I want this stuff. I want to use it, but I want to keep it." He grasped his head comically, "I'm losing it!" He paused. "Understand? I want more, more, more, more! It leaves me with an unpleasant feeling, here," he tapped his breastbone. "Grasping at permanence makes me want to have this thing *always*. Understand? Desire produces uncontroled action in the mind." His eyes were wide as saucers. "How could you think anything else?"

"You know, everything you learned in school made you more compli-cated. The teachers meant well. They tried to give you a profession, so you'd make money and be happy." He paused and looked around, "but this is just more superstition." A nervous shuffle ran through the audi-ence. "Superstition colors everything. If Buddhism makes you happy you might pursue those happy feelings through meditation, but this is just another form of grasping, just another ego trip. Now, checking up in your own mind to see what's really true, *that's* meditation."

He showed how we responded to Buddhism as consumers, with exag-gerated desire. "When you hear about Kopan and the fantastic medita-tion, you say, 'It's too much! It's incredible! Far out!'" Here was the hippy mimicry for which he was renowned. "Ya, Western culture's incredible. That's why you come, isn't it? But the Dharma won't help if your contact

MEDITATION: "Lord Buddha's teaching is so simple. You understand? Simple!"

with it just increases superstition. Even when we talk about reality, you like to hear fancy Buddhist words like 'sunyata,' but you don't want to see that your vision, all your vision, comes from mind! If you don't realize that, it's impossible for you to realize sunyata!"

"That's why Lord Buddha's teaching is so simple. Simple! You understand? Simple!" He snapped his fingers again and gazed at us. "You don't need to believe anything, just go into your own mind and check up, right now. Right now you can experience meditation. Awakening is realization that comes from the mind. That's all."

He fell silent and signaled to a nearby monk, who called for questions. He'd looked penetratingly into his audience from the moment he arrived, but now his intense curiosity came plainly to the fore. He wanted to hear from us. Somebody asked, "Could you please explain the reasons against the use of so-called mind-expanding drugs such as hashish and LSD, as well as their effect on the mind?"

"Well," he smiled wryly, "taking drugs is sometimes useful for Westerners. Because your way of life is so material and the mind is so completely ignored, those who take an acid trip sometimes go beyond the physical body and notice wider possibilities of the mind; they might even glimpse reality. That's if you take it once. But taking it all the time, hoping to experience sunyata, is just another superstition. It's impossible. The realization of sunyata never fades. You wouldn't come down." He laughed.

"Now," he became serious, "this is just *my* opinion. I'm *not* saying that Lord Buddha suggests taking hashish! I don't want you going and saying, 'That Kopan Lama, Thubten Yeshe, told me that Lord Buddha says it's good to take hashish.' This is *my* opinion, not Lord Buddha's. Okay?"

Another question came from the floor—"What is devotion?"

He rubbed his face. "I think there's dull-witted devotion and intelligent devotion. Intelligent devotion comes from understanding, from a clear mind. I saw a good example of dull-witted devotion when I was in Rome, with all the big churches. Some primitive people were looking around and saying, 'Ah, ooh, fantastic!' Well, they're devoted to a church, an expensive building. That's devotion," he assented, "but it's dull witted. It doesn't clear the mind; it makes it cloudy."

"You should avoid extreme devotion. A kind of dreamy mind manifests and sees holiness in objects that have nothing holy about them. Interesting, isn't it? It's very dangerous, you understand? Logical, reasonable devotion, with understanding, is good."

"Actually, the twentieth century needs skepticism. Why? Because it's too much! Everything in the West is too much! Understand?" His voice was quiet and yet he seemed to be yelling. "Too Much!"

We stared.

"You can't even begin to say what's right, what's wrong. Skepticism though, checking up, may help us find out. You know, when I was in America, someone offered me ice cream, and so I said, 'Yes please.' But that's not enough. Now I had to choose from twenty flavors." His tone rose incredulously. "I think I was confused. You know? It's too much!"

A monk leaned towards Lama and the microphone picked up his words, "Time's up."

"So," he recapitulated, "That's how it is in the West, too much. Without skepticism, I'm not sure . . . . Okay? That's all. I'm joking too much. Thank you . . . so much." He left the tent with his back stooped and his neck tucked in, but his eyes looked up, twinkling. He chuckled and reached for outstretched hands as he went, giving each one a firm clasp. And then he was gone. The marquee felt empty. We stood staring, a bedraggled, bleary-eyed bunch.

I walked out into the sun, smiling to think I had a whole month ahead of me. Over the edge of the hill, the clouds had completely evaporated and the green fields shimmered verdantly, still touched with dew.

19

KOPAN HILL

THE ROUTINE WAS FIXED, but my mental landscape churned unpredictably. Concentration came and went of its own accord. Sometimes the ninety-minute meditation sessions sped by. More often they dragged on endlessly. When I was low the urge to blame others was irresistible, and out came my righteous indignation. How could these people, fidgeting, rasping and coughing, impede my path to Awakening? How dare they? I learned to sit straight-backed and cross-legged, still as a tree trunk, and to ignore the searing pain in my knees. I figured I looked good, and took some comfort in the knowledge that no one knew what was going on inside. In my finer moments, I was embarrassed by myself.

I failed to get the powerful concentration and bliss of the meditative absorptions, but gained unexpected insights that, uncomfortable and unflattering as they were, I didn't really appreciate. Acknowledging my inner chaos effectively undermined my sense of certainty. Chinks appeared in my tempered armor of defence and denial. In the bigger picture, I saw that the mental patterns that had confounded me for so long weren't really so complicated after all. They alternated between dullness and nervousness, boredom and anxiety, comfort and pain,

hope and despair. The more I saw the mind at war with itself, the more
I commanded it to stop, and the more I realized that commands were
irrelevant.

The people that gathered on Kopan hill every morning that autumn
were largely of my generation. All were from North America, Europe
or Australasia and many sported the prizes of the hippy trail—sturdy
Afghan jumpers and Pakistani sandals, colorful Nepalese bags and blankets, Indonesian batik. Most were long-haired, scruffy and sallow-skinned
and from what I could tell, had used drugs, suffered intestinal diseases
and lost weight more or less like me. The few that had flown in recently
stood out with their shiny pink skin and machine-laundered clothes.

Although we were asked to keep to a strict discipline, some were
stricter with themselves than others. Asian veterans had an easier time
of it than newcomers, particularly with the low-calorie food, but only a
handful quit. Some slipped away for a few hours and returned surrepti-
tiously. Most stuck to the rule of silence pretty well and there weren't
many signs of real distress. It was good to recall that we were the self-
indulgent offspring of the world's wealthiest countries. We'd discovered
that such baseless freedom led into the mire; we wanted real help, not just
words. Lama took each of us seriously and with overwhelming affection.

Feeling the ground shift beneath our feet, however, we were also
reaching out to steady ourselves. Tibetan Buddhism was ancient and
anchored, colorful and exotic.[35] Lama never stopped reminding us, "You
check up."

Lama himself was a complex man. Perfectly traditional, he'd put his
hands together reverentially at the mention of any of his own teachers,
but many of them, including his peers, considered him a maverick. As
a child he'd been recognized as the reincarnation of a female meditator
and taken to a monastery for traditional instruction, but without being
given the title of Tulku. Apparently, his former gender didn't count.[36]

Due to his heart condition he hadn't completed the traditional geshe
study program, and so had had the time and freedom to meet the hippies
from whom he'd learned English, and whom he found so fascinating.
He grilled them for words and phrases that would help him express

the meaning of Buddhism in plain language, and when he later visited the West he turned the symbols of material society into metaphors of cyclic existence. So, while the Tibetan Library of Works and Archives was engaging Western scholars to develop an erudite lexicon and transpose the immortal words of Buddha Shakyamuni into English, Lama was learning all about supermarkets, ice-cream and chocolate cake. His affectionate enthusiasm left us feeling very good about ourselves and profoundly empowered by our potential as meditators.

However, we only saw him every other day or so. Lama Zopa's strange discourses left us by turns completely baffled or profoundly concentrated as we tried to follow. In meditation we sat for painful hours, focused when we could be, but more often drifting on clouds of mental wanderings. We reflected on what we'd learned, tried to accept uncomfortable truths about ourselves and became stoic in the face of daily sensory deprivation. Those who'd had a normal sex life suffered more than I, but one and all craved food. It wasn't that there wasn't any; the simple vegetarian fare was good, but there were rarely seconds and never thirds.

On the positive side, the setting of Kopan Hill in and of itself brought life into focus, and the vast Himalayas beyond were profoundly calming. More cerebrally, Lama's talks satisfied our burning existential questions just as well as they entertained us; the more serious his point, the lighter his touch. Also, there was a sense of progress as the month-long course unfolded. I certainly felt I was growing in knowledge and clarity, though I was horribly disappointed in my poor concentration.

As the mid-point approached Lama announced that we'd be taking Mahayana Precepts[37] each morning. This meant, among other things, reverting to one meal a day. He spoke at length about the significance of these temporary vows and built up considerable anticipation. It would be a tough fortnight, and we all wondered how we'd do. In the meantime, we'd all need Tibetan names for the daily ceremony.

I fixated on my forthcoming name change. I was ready for something momentous. With each new day my old life had become less real. In the perfect world of my own imagination I anticipated transplanting myself once and for all to become a new person in a new life. The day of the naming finally came and we filed past Lama to learn our new identities. I drew close and saw that Lama was holding a hat rather carelessly, from which each person pulled out a scrap of paper. I unfolded mine and looked up, hoping for a significant explanation.

He shrugged. "It's just a name."

As I stumbled back to my place over meditators and their cushions I told myself he was right, of course. He was right and that was that. Once again I'd been grasping at thin air.

The one-meal-a-day rule was the only precept that added to the rules we were already following. We ate just before midday. The vegetarian food passed quickly through me and within an hour my belly was protesting, and so was my mind. I didn't mind being empty in the morning and could have more easily skipped lunch in anticipation of dinner, but that wasn't the way it worked. And for Buddhist monks, the afternoon fast was a lifelong rule!

I managed better than some of the others. One afternoon I found a pale American sucking on his toothpaste tube. With a frantic look in his eyes he said defensively, "It's okay! It's not really food, is it?"

I couldn't help smiling.

"What I'd give for a steak," he continued torturing himself.

For me, the easy part was the silence. The urge to speak arose, of course, but I wasn't unhappy to watch the trapped thoughts circulate briefly and sputter to a halt. For some meditators, this was the biggest challenge of all, and they couldn't help breaking out into conversation, occasionally chattering in small groups. I walked away, but in that rarefied context every snippet of ordinary talk, concocted for the simple pleasure of exchanging words, sounded particularly bizarre. I thought it a wonder that anyone bothered to speak at all—ever.

Since arriving at Kopan I'd paid up front and never gave money a second thought. But when the course ended I was forced to open my money pouch again and face reality. I had just a few weeks to decide whether to find a source of income here in the East, or to go home. I sent a telegram to Dad and he sent me a ticket immediately.

I also heard from Mum. This was her first letter since I'd sent off my shameless confession and I opened it apprehensively. She declared that she couldn't believe what she'd read, nor recognize the writer. She was

ཐུབ་སྟེན་སང་རྒྱས

consumed by her shame and had pushed the offending pages to the very
back of her drawer in the hope they'd go away. In short, far from reaching
out to embrace her contrite son she'd cowered from my assault. This
wasn't what I intended, and I paid in guilt for my superciliousness. It was,
however, one of very few occasions when Mum spoke frankly about her
deepest feelings.

I returned to Kopan to wait. Most of the course attendees had left. I joined
a small group each day for meditation and arranged a private meeting
with Lama Yeshe.

When I entered his room his eyes lit up as if he were welcoming an
old friend. He leaned forward to welcome me. "Hello dear. Hello, hello.
How are you?"

"Very well thank you," I said politely. I couldn't help breaking into a
broad grin. Between outstretched arms I offered him a ceremonial white
scarf I'd bought at the monastery office.

Lama grinned back, took the scarf from my hands, draped it over my
bowed neck and pulled me up. "Are you comfortable? Food is good?
Accommodation is good? Some tea?" He called to his attendant in the
adjoining room.

"No, no," I said. "I'm perfectly fine thank you. We just finished breakfast."

"Oh yes, yes. Okay. Did you enjoy it?"

"Yes, actually. Thank you. The food is very good."

"Oh," he said smiling. "I'm very happy." He really seemed so.

"Unfortunately," I continued, "I've run out of money and can't stay any
longer." I waited for him to say it didn't matter.

"Oh dear, money," he said sympathetically. "Very important, isn't it?
Unfortunate but true. Can't live without it, can we?" He laughed as if the
truth was absurd.

To me, it was. "Lama?" I said vitally.

He leaned forward and his ears prickled to attention. "Yes dear?"

"I would like to devote my life to the Dharma."

"That's very good," he said. "You meditate every day, learn about your mind. Very worthwhile. You're returning to the West?"

"England," I said.

"England," he said, then asked, "I have some English students. Did you meet any of them?"

I shook my head, "No, I haven't been talking."

"Oh yes," he laughed. "No talking; too busy practicing meditation! You ask at the office. Someone will give you an address and phone number in London. You visit, meditate with them. Avoid bad friends, bad situation, drugs, alcohol, all that. Good friends encourage meditation. Bad friends encourage distraction." He laughed. "That's all."

I blurted out, "I want to come back."

"You want to come back here? To Kopan?" He was delighted, as if the good fortune were his.

I nodded.

"Oh, that's very good if you can, but it's not so important where you meditate. What's important is to continue with the Dharma."

I'd grown to look upon the Western monks and nuns with envy, but ordination seemed unlikely. All I said was, "Yes, I want to continue."

He put his hands together and said, "Geshe Rabten, my teacher, will teach in England, soon; in two or three months."

"Geshe Rabten?" I asked.

"A great Geshe," he said, dispelling doubts with a shake of his head and recommending him with wide eyes. "Fantastic meditation master. You study with him," he nodded. Finally, he gave me some pointers on keeping up a daily practice.

With nothing else to say I rose hesitantly on my haunches. Lama opened his hands invitingly, and when I leaned forward he held my head against his forehead and muttered a blessing. Then he tapped me playfully on the cheek and signaled me to go. I left according to Tibetan custom without turning my back to him. He kept his smile on me. As the door was closing I saw him slump. Then I was in the hands of his attendant, out the door and on my way home.

Leaving Kopan troubled me less than I expected. I was sure I'd soon return, and in the meantime anticipated the comforts of home and the West. More than anything else, I looked forward to drinking glasses of cool, clear water. On December 24 I flew to Delhi and transferred to a Trans World Airlines jumbo jet to London, en route to New York, taking my place with mixed feelings. After my bargain basement travels, the soft seats and carpeted floor of the economy cabin might as well have been first-class. The uncrowded space was pure luxury. I recalled Lama Yeshe's admonition that renunciation was the abandonment of craving, not of comfort. I tried to relax.

I'd had months to acclimatize myself to the unfamiliar East as I traveled overland mile by mile, but my return would take mere hours, and I suddenly realized that I was in the throes of reverse culture shock. I found myself encased by the cabin's tan-colored, molded polypropylene storage lockers, walls and ceiling, its smooth touch unreal. I felt a hole in the pit of my stomach as I saw through eyes I'd forgotten. The skin on the back of my hand was stretched taut over the knuckles, the deep pores and embedded grime standing out starkly under the cabin's metallic lights. In the clean, well-lit mirror of the in-flight bathroom I gazed for the first time on my hollow eye sockets, sunken cheeks and the sallow texture of a surprised, frightened face. In every nook and cranny, bones pressed outward like prisoners clawing the walls.

The plane took off, the warning signs went out and cigarette smoke began to drift through the cabin. A hostess placed a tray in front of me with plastic containers of food, drink and disposable cutlery. The vegetarian meal I'd ordered was as lifeless as a carcass. She returned later to dump valuable leftovers and sturdy containers alike into a rubbish bag, and I cringed for those who subsist at the grimy edges of Indian bazaars by selling jars, bottles, tins and plastic odds and ends. A poor Indian family could prosper from this rubbish, even the black plastic bag itself would fetch a useful penny. I squirmed.

As the plane droned over the Punjab, Iran, Turkey and Southern Europe however, I became philosophical. Such gestures were short-lived. Whatever one did in the material world would sooner or later come undone. The way to fulfill this life and the next, if there were one, was to unravel my own mind. Even as I returned to the comforts of home I knew with finality that I had to turn my attention inwards. If I valued one thing from my past it was the impression of the fearless, passionate Jesus. Like him, Lama Yeshe was no dry ascetic but a living, feeling man—the sort of man I wanted to be.

I arrived at Heathrow airport late on the night of Christmas Eve 1975. The crowds bustled bad-temperedly, and as my Indian fellow passengers dispersed and the crowd became increasingly European, I was given a noticeable berth. I collected my shabby rucksack and a rug-and-clothes roll and turned away from the carousel just in time to see my brother walking towards me.

20

WITH NEW EYES

PHILIP GREETED ME as if I'd just returned from a long weekend, making no comment on my appearance or asking after my health. We scooted out of Heathrow airport in Mum's Austin Mini and picked up the Westbound M40. The urban landscape was harshly lit, and so orderly it seemed surreal. He answered my questions in monosyllables. Only when I brought up the subject of the Don Pasquale did he finally began to speak, venting his frustration with Dad.

I waited for him to ask about me, but he avoided the subject judiciously. It occurred to me that he might have been more concerned with why I hadn't been *there*, than where I had been. Here he was working for Dad in provincial Gloucestershire when he should have been acquiring new skills in London, Paris or Rome. Dad had once wanted us all to follow him into the business, but Yolanda left, then I. The mantle of Dad's guilt fell squarely on Phil, who did what he thought had to be done. Meanwhile, I'd lived the high life on a government grant for four years, only to abort my degree and then gallivant around the world, returning to the security and comforts of home when money ran out. Whether Phil's silence was meant to shut me up or to prick my guilt I was too dazed to tell. I did however sense the clear imprint of Dad's sadness in him.

An hour later we passed through Cirencester and plunged into the dark old roads of the West Country. My childhood greeted me silently.

It was late when we pulled up in Worcester Street; number nineteen was still brightly lit and the door opened to a riot of color, conversation and good cheer. The gilt mirrors and sconces were adorned with holly and mistletoe. The air was alcoholic. Customers looked around curiously as I entered and raised their eyebrows when Mum crossed the room and wrapped her arms around me, laughing and crying and saying my name.

I carried my stuff upstairs, put it on the landing and wandered through this place I knew best. The frosted glass door of the living room opened on the deep-pile comforts of a blue woolen Axminster carpet. I gazed on the thick-cushioned settee and chairs, all pointing to the television, all soft and enveloping. In the kitchen, a turkey carcass lay half-dressed on the open oven door and the fridge and counters overflowed with holiday excess. I opened the back door and gazed over the streetlit roofs of old Gloucester to the illuminated tower of the cathedral, recognizing every old brick and stone and marveling that nothing had changed. The sound of the cathedral bells ringing the hour was as familiar as my own breath.

Mum came up.

"Restaurant closed already?" I asked.

"Daddy'll close up," she said. "I wanted to see you." She held my shoulders and sized me up. "You're so thin! Aren't you hungry?"

I shook my head.

"How about a nice cup of tea?"

I smiled. "That'd be great."

"Go and make yourself comfy then."

I went back to the room of cushioned chairs and perched on the low windowsill that overlooked Worcester Street. The streetlamps and shop lights traced my favorite childhood journey, up past the greengrocer to Mister Meadow's sweetshop. To the right I could see Archie Smith's television and radio appliances, and Lloyd's Bank. On my left the railway bridge crossed the road, advertising "England's Glory" matches in red and blue, yard-high letters.

Mum brought the tea and made sure I saw her eyeing my bag and bedroll. "Um . . . ," she began cautiously.

I followed her gaze. "Oh, d'you like my Nepalese blanket? It's been a long way with me, you know."

"D'you think it could make it's way outside?"

"What? You don't like it?"

"I love it darling," she said soothingly. "I just don't know where it's been."

I remembered the wide berth I'd received at the airport.

"Thank you," she smiled as I put it on the balcony. "Just in case there's something in it, you know, alive."

"You don't know where I've been either," I joked. "D'you want me outside too?"

"I want you here." Tears formed in her eyes. "Aren't you hungry?" she asked. "You're so thin! You must be hungry."

"I will be," I said. "Right now I'm just jet-lagged. I'm fine."

"Really?" she pleaded. "How are you feeling?"

"I feel fine, Mum. Don't worry."

Her eyes fixed on me indignantly.

"Sorry."

She told me that as soon as they knew I was in the Madyan hospital, Dad had moved heaven and earth to place a telephone call.

"Really?" I was surprised. "I'm sorry you didn't get through."

"Oh, but we did," she said. "It took hours, but an English voice answered. At first we thought it was you, but then he said it wasn't but he knew you and you'd just left that morning and you were well."

"That was the morning I left for Kalam." I remembered the grim days of Swat, thinking I'd never discuss them with Mum.

"We were quite worried," she said carefully.

"I expect you were," I said. "Sorry, Mum."

"Well, all's well that ends well," she said. "It's so nice to have you home."

Dad came in wearily and sat down. He smiled cheerfully and asked, "So how are you son?"

"I'm fine," I said. "How's business?"

"Oh, you know. Up and down."

"Busy night?" I said.

"Christmas," he said. "You know ...."

"Yes, I know. You're closed tomorrow?"

"Oh yes," said Mum. "Your cousin Robert's coming up, with Auntie Joan."

"Lovely," I forced a smile.

"Good to have you home, son," said Dad.

"Thanks, Dad, it's good to be here. By the way, thanks for the ticket."

"No problem, son," he smiled. "You're welcome."

I wanted to yell, to collapse in blood and tears and scream that I'd been to Hell and back, to be carried to the rooftops and hear him declare, "My son has returned!" and to be held with all his might.

Perhaps if I stepped onto the bridge he'd make a reciprocal move. But as I opened my mouth to speak, the gentle, suffocating cloud of home fell on me. I took a second breath, but Dad had stretched out in his deep wingback chair and clicked the remote control. The images of James Herriot's *All Creatures Great and Small* emerged from the dark. He impatiently tried the other two channels. The flickering TV set gripped the room, and I thought of the stillness on Kopan hill, that I should be there. Mum's settee gradually swallowed me and, finally overtaken by fatigue, I went upstairs, wrapped myself in a blanket and slept on the floor.

"Happy Christmas, Steve," my cousin Robert said.

"Happy Christmas, Rob." We shook hands. He was four or five years older, had an easy smile and London accent and was everyone's favorite cousin. He was over with his Mum, my Auntie Joan, Mum's older sister.

The four of us were sitting in the front room having a Christmas drink. They had sherry. I was on my forth glass of cold water. Dad, Phil and Maria were at church. Mum had gone to mass early because she was cooking.

Rob smiled genially. "So, how was India, Steve?" He was the first to ask.

I raised my eyebrows at the scope of the question and said, "It's a fantastic place."

"I heard it was pretty tough."

"Oh yes, it's hard too." A mosaic of grim images came to mind. "It's like Heaven and Hell all rolled up into one."

As he gazed at me, I wondered what he saw.

"So ... what was it exactly that you did over there?"

I told him I'd traveled until meeting the Tibetans.

"Oh," he was relieved to have something to grasp. "Buddhists, right?"

"That's right."

"So what do they believe? Who's their god?"

"They don't have one."

"Oh! So, um ... what *do* they believe?"

"That everything originates in the mind, that it's all interdependent and nothing exists inherently."

"Oh," he said politely. "I see."

Auntie Joan broke the ensuing silence. "I was in India, you know."

"Oh yes," said Mum. "During the war, wasn't it?"

Her story consisted of dates, times and names as she related the facts of her young life. "It was jolly exciting," she added without explaining how. She'd been a nurse, traveled exclusively in British enclaves and referred to Indians as "natives." Her experience of travel was at the other end of the spectrum from mine, and infinitely easier to chat about. She and Mum argued happily about dates and places until her peregrinations were all chronologically pinpointed. Once Mum was sure that the conversation was on a sufficiently vague footing, she bustled bravely, "Well, I must get back to my roast."

Dad, Phil and Maria returned, and once everyone had had a drink we sat in a circle to exchange presents. I was empty-handed, except for a tiny phial of duty-free Chanel No 5 perfume for Mum that I'd picked up on the plane.

"Oh," she exclaimed, "But this is terribly expensive."

I shrugged. "You like it though, don't you ...?"

"I love it darling, but did you spend all you had?"

I had no answer for such a melodramatic question, and shrugged. What was the big deal? I'd left India and didn't need the money any more. It was also a peace offering. Didn't she understand?

Everyone stared with pathetic, sad eyes. I realized I was as much a mystery to them as they were to me. It was nothing new, but now it stuck with strange finality.

Lunch was served, and I devoured the crispy French bread hot from the oven with relish. Ignoring the turkey, gravy and wine I added a few vegetables, followed it with a little pudding and declared myself stuffed. We were all polite and no one asked me anything more complicated than to pass the salt.

In the ensuing days, there was likewise no mention between Mum and me of our exchange of letters. As if it had never happened, she was all smiles and pleasantry.

Back insecurely in the bosom of my family my fastidious new ways didn't last long, and I realized with dismay that the benefits of my limited meditative experience were entirely reversible. My cravings had apparently been disabled, but only temporarily and circumstantially. As they reasserted themselves my appetite galloped along and I was soon sneaking down to the restaurant between lunch and dinner to tuck into the dessert trolley. I burst out of the size twenty-eight jeans I'd bought just days after my arrival and never wore them again. This wasn't an ideal diet but nor was it an altogether bad thing, because I had indeed become far too thin for my large frame. However, my body absorbed the increasingly

DAD IN HIS COMFORT ZONE: *I wanted to scream that I'd been to hell and back*

rich foods like a balloon even as my digestive system went into reverse culture shock. Philip prosaically described my flatulence as "rotten and stinking to high heaven," and asked me, for God's sake, to be more careful around the house. He had a point. I wondered if the hepatitis had left any residual damage, but Doctor Tom gave me a clean bill of health and everything eventually returned to normal.

Shortly after Christmas I approached Dad in his office as he sipped his morning coffee. He snapped a low-tar cigarette in two, pushed one half into his Aqua-filter, struck the flame of his Dunhill lighter and inhaled. He hoped these half-measures would lead him to quit, but his fingers and mouth worked habitually against his better judgment, and would eventually trump it with a fatal case of lung cancer.

"Dad," I said, "I want to pay you back for the ticket."

"That's up to you son. It doesn't matter."

"It does to me," I said. "I just have to get a job."

I was ready for any work, but I didn't particularly want to return to building or motorway construction sites. Now more than ever I'd stand apart from the other laborers.

"So what do you want to do?"

"Anything," I said. "Washing up?" I was hinting at Dad's frequent staff shortage at the kitchen sink.

He stared for a moment and ventured, "Philip could use some help in the dining room."

"Really? You'd let me in the dining room?"

He smiled. "If you were dressed properly ... of course! Your mother and I were hoping to go to Teresa's baptism, but we couldn't leave Philip alone."

Yolanda was now living in Rome and had just delivered their first grandchild.

"I could do that," I said.

Besides, I was enjoying the comforts. After a few nights on the bedroom floor I'd progressed to the soft bed. You'd think a few pounds of fat would make the floor less uncomfortable, but the reverse seemed to be true. It may have been a matter of perception, but my meditative percipience was dimming by the day.

Philip instructed me on the rules of grating fine Parmesan cheese, polishing silver cutlery, grilling Melba toast and laying impeccable tables, but he soon stopped looking over my shoulder. Best of all, I learned to work with customers. "A waiter's invisible except when he's needed," my brother explained, "And then he's in exactly the right place at the right time." Within this strict context, we put on a playful show of brotherly competitiveness that maintained the family feel of the restaurant and seemingly delighted the customers. I found the work conducive to mindfulness, and took pride in my newfound skills.

Nevertheless, I couldn't forget where I'd been and what I'd seen. The desire to sink myself into esoteric studies grew more compelling by the day, and the life I was living grew less and less so. Mum and Dad were happy to see me in the restaurant and, I imagined, would have loved me to remain. How would they take my departure?

Three months after my return I placed a wad of cash on Dad's desk and said, "Thanks for the ticket home." He counted it.

"This is too much," he said, removing the excess.

"It's interest," I said.

He shook his head firmly, "I don't need that, but thanks for this. I appreciate it more than you know."

"You're welcome Dad. Thank *you*." Never had things gone so smoothly at home.

"It's been great having you around," he said, "I suppose you're off now?"

"How d'you ...?"

He laughed. "I know you find it hard to believe son, but I understand you."

"You'll be okay in the restaurant without me?"

"I've managed for thirty years."

I felt sheepish.

"So where to?" he asked.

"A meditation course near Reading."

"With a Tibetan?" he asked.

"Geshe Rabten." I added grandly, "He's a debating tutor[38] to the Dalai Lama."

"You've got your whole life ahead of you. Just remember—"

"I know," I said, "You can't change human nature."

We each knew the other wouldn't budge an inch. He believed we were all sinners, should do what good we could and must pray to God that death would find us in a state of grace. To pretend we could emulate Christ was to commit the double sin of pride and blasphemy. To me, human consciousness and potential were limitless, and if Christ wasn't a role model what was the point? Dad took comfort in the thought that I'd sooner or later miss the security of the church and return to the fold. I could think of nothing less likely.

Dad now listened without arguing. He kept his opinions to himself and was no longer infuriated by mine. I thought I'd earned a little respect. While Philip was expected by Mum, Dad and of course Phil himself to remain faithfully at the Don Pasquale, I'd been given carte blanche to follow my nose. It didn't seem fair, but I didn't complain. Besides, the path I'd chosen wasn't exactly easy.

"Dad told me when you left the first time," Mum confided years later, "that you'd be all right, and that if we didn't give you our blessing you'd go without it. He said we shouldn't alienate you. Oh dear," she concluded as always, "I was so worried about you."

"Dad had faith in me?" I raised my eyebrows.

21

THE STARS LINE UP

I FOUND MYSELF AMONG a very different crowd this time. Gone were the multinational hippies, replaced now by a respectable, British middle-aged audience. The least orthodox was the translator, a lanky, pale-skinned American in threadbare robes.

Geshe Rabten sat straight-backed and alert, delivering his teaching in a measured, businesslike way. After Lama Yeshe's meandering and colorful talks, this was a return to the style of Geshe Ngawang Dhargyey at the Tibetan Library, with the refreshing difference that this was translated into a fluent stream of articulate English. Geshe's presentation too was thorough, methodical and systematic. He first outlined what he was going to say, then followed the outline like a table of contents, reviewing it as he moved from topic to topic. What his explanations lacked in spontaneity was made up for in clarity and in authority. He sat like a rock and spoke with the absolute assurance of Buddhism's twenty-five centuries.

Geshe Rabten was an instant receptacle for my projections. As he led us in meditation, he seemed the very embodiment of single-pointed concentration. I found that my miniscule experience, simply because it had taken place in India and Nepal, now lent me a certain authority, and I took the lead in assuring others that here was at least a great bodhisattva,[39] if not a fully enlightened being. Most people took easily to such assurances, although we had nothing more to go on than Geshe's scholarship, his Tibetan complexion and his monkish dignity.

The American translator too became a model for me. Tibetan syllables left his tongue like velvet and his translation into both languages was unhesitating. What excited me most was his free access to Geshe and, I presumed, his trust. If he could learn Tibetan, so could I. If he was close to Geshe, if he were a monk, so could I be. His name was Jampa Kelsang, also known as Alan Wallace.

After class, while watching Alan lope away to what I imagined were hours of profound conversation with Geshe, I felt a tap on my shoulder and turned to see a familiar face.

I couldn't put a name to it, for we'd spent a month together at Kopan without speaking. Now we belatedly introduced ourselves. His name was Rob and he asked if I'd be interested in helping set up a permanent dharma center.

"I'm not sure," I replied. "I'd like to study more."

Rob examined me. "What, are you going to become a monk?"

"I dunno," I gazed in the direction where Alan had disappeared.

"Well, you look the type," he said.

"Really?" I was distracted. I excused myself, followed the corridor and called out to Alan.

He turned.

"I wonder if I might speak to Geshe in private?"

"Geshe has reserved time for private interviews after lunch," Alan said. "He's free at one."

"One o'clock? Today?"

He nodded.

"Well, thank you," I stammered. "I'll . . . um."

But he'd already turned and was gone.

Instead of lunch I wandered in the grounds, and heading back just before the appointed hour, I saw a white-haired lady staring at me with a twinkle in her eye. I'd noticed her before and nodded politely. I timed my approach nervously and on the stroke of one knocked on Geshe's door. It was opened by Alan.

Geshe sat cross-legged on a Tibetan rug on the bed. He greeted me with a businesslike smile and looked a bit uncomfortable as I prostrated. Alan smiled and gestured me to sit at his side on the floor.

Geshe spoke and Alan said, "Geshe is very happy that you're attending this course."

"I'm very happy to be here," I said. "I was at the Kopan meditation course last year."

He nodded.

"When I was leaving, Lama Yeshe suggested I study with Geshe Rabten."

"Lama Yeshe and Lama Zopa are accomplished teachers," he said. "Have you been practicing since then?"

"I've been staying with my family, doing my best. But it's not ideal. I came here to improve my meditation."

"That's very commendable."

They were now looking at me expectantly. It was time to get to the point.

"I understand that Geshe has a monastery in Switzerland, and wondered if I could study there with him." I stopped breathing in the silence that followed.

"It's true that Geshe has students in Switzerland."

"And some of them, some of *you*," I turned to Alan, "are monks."

"Like Lama Yeshe's students," Geshe continued, "some wish to take the robes, to focus entirely on study and meditation."

"And is it possible to join them?" I asked. "I'd like to become a monk." I took a shallow breath.

"A worthy thought," he answered, waiting.

I forced myself to say, "So, could I become a monk? I'd like to study with you, Geshe. In Switzerland. As a monk, I mean. Is that possible?"

His expression didn't change, "You wish to come to Rikon?"

"Rikon?" I looked at Alan.

"Geshe's monastery."

"Yes, I want to come to Rikon." How clear did I have to be?

Geshe fingered his rosary and looked out the window.

He asked, "Have you got any money?"

"Money?" I laughed.

"Yes, for food, clothes and other necessities. Geshe can find you accommodation, and of course the teachings are free, but how will you live?"

"I, uh . . . ?"

"Perhaps you can work for a while and save up."

The prospect of going back to ordinary life scared me. The drudgery would drain my enthusiasm, and sooner or later I'd return to old ways. I'd taken it for granted that Geshe would be eager to recruit new Western monks and had expected to be welcomed with open arms. The last thing I'd expected him to worry about was money.

"Then," Alan continued, "Geshe will be happy to ordain you." These were the words I'd longed to hear but they seemed to come from a great distance.

Geshe smiled politely, friendly. He fingered the beads of his rosary and looked expectantly at me.

"Um, okay. Thanks then. I'll do . . . what I can." I shrugged, stood up and nodded impotently as Geshe reached forward and draped a ceremonial white scarf around my neck.

Alan left the room with me and as he closed the door on Geshe I asked, "How does everyone in Switzerland support themselves?"

"Some of us have a little money of our own and others do as Geshe says, working for a while. Another teacher there, Geshe Jampa Lhodro, actually works in a factory."

I was aghast. "How can you keep up a real practice if you're always running off to make money?"

"I'm sure it's difficult."

I was turning to leave when he added, "Of course, you could always find a *jindak*."

"A what?" I asked.

"A sponsor. Someone who'll support you."

"In exchange for . . . ?"

"Merit. Tibetan lay people traditionally support monasteries and monks, especially those who'd like to enter a monastery but can't, for one reason or another."

"How do I find one?"

"You'll have to ask."

"Ask?"

He nodded sympathetically.

Crestfallen, I headed back to the refectory.

Everyone was still at table, talking and drinking tea. I almost made it to the tea urn when I was intercepted by the white-haired lady. Her face was scarred on one side, and the left and right sides of her body seemed out of synch, as if each was receiving different signals. I thought she winked at me.

With no preliminaries she said in a triumphant voice, "I have heard you would like to be a monk?" Her accent was German.

"You did?" I recalled my conversation with Rob.

She giggled.

"How would you know that?"

She ignored my question. "Did you see Geshe?"

"Yes, actually I just did."

"And?"

I found her imperious, not to say intrusive.

"And . . . we spoke about my practice, and things."

"Did you ask to become a monk?" she demanded.

"Yes," I was irritated now. "Actually I did."

"And?"

"He said it was possible." That should get rid of her.

"But that is wonderful, no?" Her crooked face shone.

Her goodwill dampened my negativity, and I felt inclined to share my burden. "Well, it appears I'm not ready."

"*Why?*" She was amazed. "What did the geshe say?"

"He said," I stalled, discomforted, "He said, um . . . ."

"He said he would not ordain you?" She was incredulous.

"No, that he would. But there are certain conditions."

"Ah, so?" She looked expectant.

I sighed, "I have to get a job." That would shut her up.

"A tchob?" She was puzzled.

"Money. I need money."

"Ah," she grinned impishly. How much?"

I don't know." I looked up incredulously. What was the word Alan used—*jindak*? I shook my head. "If only I were Tibetan."

"Oh!" she said emphatically, "There is no need to be Tibetan."

I stared.

"Is there something you would like to ask me?" she prompted. "Something you need?"

She'd become coy, a little old girl with a secret.

"Well . . . ," I began.

Her eyes were as wide as saucers.

"I might . . . if there's an alternative to working."

She nodded.

"A sponsor."

"Ah, yes?"

It was my turn to nod.

"So?" she demanded.

"I don't know," I said.

"Oh, but you do. You must ask the question."

"If I were looking for a sponsor," I ventured, "could I ask you?"

"You would have to ask, to find out." She laughed.

"Would you be my sponsor?"

"Yes, oh yes," she exploded happily.

My God, I thought. *I'm going to be a monk.*

My benefactor's name was Sigrid Kremzow. "You must call me Sigrid," she said, "And I shall call you Thubten Sangye."

I was "her" monk, with all the perks that entailed. This included an open invitation to her home in Lugano on the warm side of the Alps and a stipend of two hundred Swiss Francs a month, a sum that Alan said would pay my food and supplies and leave me with a little pocket money. I wouldn't go hungry.

Sigrid had come to England partly in the hope of making such a match, and considered herself lucky to find me. I was tickled by my good fortune. Out of the blue, my future had arrived. I was free to study and meditate, and now I even had a worthy worldly ambition—to be a translator and teacher; to play a role in Buddhism's historic expansion to the West. My future was guaranteed. All doubts were dispelled.

Well actually, I wasn't entirely without doubts; my very sense of security was mitigated by an instinctive discomfort. Lama Yeshe had said, "If Buddhism makes you happy you might pursue those happy feelings through meditation, but this is just another form of grasping, just another ego trip."

He was right. I'd have to watch out.

However, my hesitations were no match for the way I'd decided to see things. I was determined that monastic discipline would help me overcome my drug dependence and kleptomania once and for all, and even silence my treacherous libido. I was on track so far, but the straight and narrow was precarious. I'd have to be careful until I reached the effortless state of Awakening, when everything would fall perfectly into place. As for exactly what form my practice would take, I'd ask Geshe. Of course! I should give him the good news.

In his room once more, I talked and talked, pouring out a detailed account of my years of confusion, stealing and drugs. I felt it necessary that he know what sort of person he was taking in. As I painted the garish self-portrait Alan looked a little doubtful, but Geshe laughed and pointed his thumb vaguely over his shoulder. "You wouldn't have lasted much longer out there. You're lucky you got to me when you did."

"You mean . . . I'd be dead?" I asked.

Geshe now roared with laughter. Seeing this side of him both refreshed me and relieved me of a burden. Alan smiled.

We got down to details and it was arranged that I'd return to Gloucester to tell my parents, then attend Geshe's next meditation course in Rome before heading to Switzerland, where I'd be prepared for ordination.

As I left the room I realized he hadn't questioned my mental or emotional capacities—my suitability for monastic life. Perhaps, I thought, he could *see* monkhood in me. I was comforted to think of my new teacher's telepathic powers and the secure cocoon in which I'd be bound.

Back in Gloucester my joy wasn't reflected in Dad's face. He went a little pale, although his features remained steady. He let Mum do the talking.

"A monk?" asked Mum. "Oh dear, is that what makes you happy? You want our blessing?"

"Well, I thought you'd be happy," I said. It had never occurred to me that the advantages of being a Buddhist monk weren't self-evident. "I've got direction now, something to work for. A life of contemplation and teaching is good, isn't it? You know, being a Buddhist doesn't mean I can't be a Christian too."

"Oh?" she said faintly.

"It's all about compassion and insight."

"Compassion?" She stopped fidgeting.

"Christ and Buddha both taught love and compassion."

"Oh," Mum tried, "that's good. That's very good, isn't it?" She turned to Dad.

I smiled hopefully. Dad's expression didn't change.

"Well darling, I'm happy if you're happy. But what will you *do*?"

"Do?"

"Every day; what will you *do*?"

I shrugged. "I'll be living the life of a monk, studying, meditating. Eventually I'll be a teacher."

Dad broke his silence. "What about money?"

"That's the great thing," I said excitedly. "I don't need it."

"Everybody needs . . . " he began, but turned away.

I thanked him silently for biting his tongue. "Well the accommodation's free and so's the teaching. I just have to pay for food and supplies."

"How much is that?" Dad asked.

"About a hundred and fifty francs a month."

"Swiss francs?"

I nodded. "It's not much really."

"Oh, really? And you expect us to give it to you?"

"Well, no," I said. "All my expenses are covered."

"What d'you mean covered? By whom?"

"By someone else." I was reluctant to say.

His eyes narrowed. "What are you talking about?"

"I've found a sponsor. A lady."

"A lady?" Mum looked up.

"Yes, a student of Geshe who wants to support a monk."

"A stranger?" asked Mum, incredulous.

"Yes," I said. "A German lady."

Her voice rose. "German? She's *German*?"

Like the bombs that once rained down on her.

Dad asked, "Just how will this woman support you?"

"She's going to send me money each month."

"And if she changes her mind?"

"Then I'll find another sponsor."

Dad picked up the newspaper from the side of his chair, opened it, stared, folded it twice and slapped it on the table. Then he stretched back in his chair looking into space.

"She must be quite a woman," said Mum.

"She's just a Buddhist," I said.

"And she's German," said Mum, trying to sound indifferent.

The news was delivered. I set off early next morning and arrived three days later at the convent of Grottaferrata, just outside Rome.

Set among the woods and vineyards of Frascati, the abbey of Grottaferrata was a great setting for a meditation course. The rose gardens were exquisite and so was the food. I was pleasantly surprised, even after Pope John's recent reforms, to find this community of Catholic nuns willing to play host to a group of Tibetan Buddhists. Some of them even sat in on the teachings.

Classes were conducted very much as at Pangbourne, although Alan had been replaced by a hesitant young Tibetan, Gonsar Rinpoche. An additional translation from English to Italian slowed the pace still further, but I didn't mind. If anything, it gave me more time to mull over each of Geshe's statements before he moved on to the next. I followed patiently.

During a morning break I took a French door from the teaching room and found myself on a lichen-spattered path. I clasped my hands behind my back, as I'd seen monks do, and walked meditatively through the spring air into a garden of flowering roses, watching my weight shift from one foot to the other, taking each step like a breath. My eyes sank into a narrow field of view extending like a cone before me.

As I turned a corner, a foot and then a leg intruded into the cone, dissolving it and leaving my gaze resting on an attractive girl.

She sat on the verge sunning herself, and remarked, "Isn't it beautiful here?"

"Lovely," I shifted my smile from her face to the general beauty around.

Moving unnecessarily to one side she patted the grass and said, "Here." My legs obeyed.

"You looked very serious coming around the corner. Were you meditating?"

"Not really," I answered. "I wouldn't call that meditation."

"Oh, I *am* disturbing you."

"Not at all! There's plenty of time to meditate and as you say, it's a beautiful spot." My voice was unfamiliar to me.

"Yes." She leaned back on her hands, exposing her neck to the sky. "It's so nice to be in the sun again."

I asked. "Where are you from?"

"I've been living in Zurich, with Frau Kalff."

"Oh?" I asked.

"Yes," she giggled. "The big lady," and nodded her head back in the direction of the meditation room. "I'm from France, but I live in Maine, although I've just left." Her French accent had a New England edge.

"And now you're in Zurich?"

"For the time being." She looked around the garden.

I followed her eyes. "You'll be returning to Maine then?"

"I don't know. My husband is there."

"Oh," I said.

"He arranged for me to stay with Frau Kalff."

"A friend?" I asked.

"A therapist."

My brow furrowed.

"She's a psychologist." She looked up in surprise. "You haven't heard of her?"

"I'm afraid not."

"Oh, she's quite famous."

"Really?"

"Yes," she cocked her head to one side. "What about you? You sit very straight, you know. I was watching during the teaching. Where did you learn to meditate so well?"

"That's not meditation," I exclaimed. "It's just sitting. My mind's a mess."

"Really? Mine too," she said, "I couldn't believe it! But you seemed so serious in there, and when you came around that corner just now."

"Well, I was *trying* to meditate."

"You've done this before."

I nodded.

"But you're not one of Geshe's students."

"A new one. I'm going to join him after this course."

"You're going to be a monk?" Her eyes were wide.

I shrugged.

"Celibate?"

"Yes," I was abashed.

"What will you do in Rikon? Tell me about it."

I stretched out. "Well, I'll be studying Tibetan, and debate."

"And you'll meditate?"

"Of course."

"Frau Kalff wants to study you," she said.

"Me?"

"All of you. Geshe's monks."

"Is she a student of Geshe?"

"Sort of," she said, "She wants to make this East-West bridge—you know, the psychology of Buddhism, the collective unconscious and all that. I'm not sure Geshe approves."

"Oh?" I said. "So she wants to see what makes us tick."

The girl stuck her hand out. "By the way, I'm Lucille," she said.

"I'm Steve." We shook.

"Frau Kalff was a personal student of Carl Jung. You've heard of him, haven't you?"

I nodded.

"She uses Sandplay; you play with a box of sand, make shapes and add figures. Actually, it's fun but it's supposed to be therapeutic."

"Isn't it?" I asked.

"It helped me put a story together," she reflected. "But I don't know . . . ."

"When I read Jung," I ventured "I wanted to be a psychologist."

"Now you're going to be a monk instead."

"Yes."

A bell chimed. She looked at me. I looked back. "What?" She demanded.

"I don't know," I said. You're just very . . . ."

"What?" She laughed insistently.

"Nice."

She grinned.

"I usually shy away from people," I went on. "Especially girls. But you're easy to talk to."

"You're very sweet," she said.

Over the ten brief days of the Grottaferrata I stepped indulgently into an idyllic world that I didn't believe in for an instant. I liked Lucille very much, and especially the feeling of being liked in return, but my intentions were unchanged. There was barely time for the blossoming romance to clash with the meditative life when it came to an end.

The course was over. It was time to leave.

"It was so pure," she smiled sadly.

"You know," I responded, "Sometimes a monastery's just a temporary environment, to strengthen your practice. Who knows, one day I might give you a call."

"Don't say that," she shook her head. "Let's just enjoy this for what it is."

"But I want . . . " I hesitated.

"You're going to be a monk. I'm married. What's complicated?" Then she grabbed my hand and said, "But you're so sweet!"

It was time to head for Switzerland, to join Geshe and my fate.

22

CLOSE QUARTERS

I LOOKED ACROSS THE MANICURED RIVER Töss åt pale green fields and deep green forest. The village of Rikon Im Tösstal consisted of a couple of roadside shops and a few houses. Downstream, a bridge crossed the river and the road split in two, one branch heading up a forested slope and the other past sprouting crops towards an encircling arm of the same forest.

I followed the road up to a tall concrete building half-concealed in the trees, its door and windows recessed. An engraved brass plate on the wall stated rather starkly, "Institut Rikon." I initially walked right past it until the farmland broke free, but soon turned around, came back and pressed the bell hesitantly. There was no sound. I knocked, but the heavy door bruised my knuckles. I took a step back and pressed again. Still nothing.

Taking a deep breath I turned the handle. A narrow corridor gave way to a sunlit landing; a square stairwell led down into the bowels of the building. Dust motes floated in tall shafts of incoming sunlight. From where I stood the living meadows outside the windows looked surreal.

To my left was a Tibetan scroll painting. With a sigh of relief I put down my bag.

Doors were spaced regularly along the parallel walls to left and right. With a metallic click a doorknob turned, a pool of light opened from a small room and Geshe Rabten stepped out, backlit by light pouring from his own room. He wore a sleeveless shirt and ankle-length robe. I'd never seen him without his upper robe before.

"Oh!" he grinned. "You come. *Tashi Deleg*."

I returned the greeting.

Geshe put his hands on his hips, pursed his lower lip and thrust it towards the stairwell. He said, "Gonsar."

Gonsar what? I wondered.

Geshe stared curiously at me before furrowing his brow, sticking out his lower lip once more and repeating, "Gonsar!"

"Gonsar . . . ?" I repeated stupidly.

At that moment the neighboring door opened and a very large monk emerged. When he saw me he placed one hand formally over the other and said interrogatively, "*Guten Tag?*"

"Hello?"

"Hello," he said in a resonant voice. "My name is Lhodro." Looming deferentially on one side he exchanged some words with Geshe.

"Geshe says you will find Gonsar downstairs. He will translate"

"Oh," I said. "Yes. Should I go and get him?"

"I will go." Despite his large frame he stepped silently down the stairs. Geshe cocked his head to one side. "Now Gonsar come," he pronounced. Shifting his weight from one foot to the other with a waddling gait he returned to his room.

A slapping of slipper heels on the stairs announced Gonsar's arrival. "Hello, hello!" he said breezily. "So you have come!"

In his room, Geshe took the scarf from my outstretched hands, placed it round my neck and tapped my head.

Gonsar translated, "Geshe is glad that you have come. Are you now free to settle down here and study?"

"Yes, I am." I nodded.

"Geshe is pleased that you have overcome so many obstacles to be here. It shows that you are resolved. Now you can live in Schwendi with the other Westerners."

"Schwendi?" I asked.

"Oh, it is a nearby village. I will show you."

Geshe spoke again.

"You should begin by learning Tibetan and memorizing the basic texts. You know Jampa Kelsang, don't you? Alan?"

"Yes," I said.

"He will show you where to begin."

"And my ordination?" I asked.

"There is no hurry. First, begin your studies."

Gonsar gave me directions, and I headed off down the hill.

I turned left, headed for the furthest corner of the valley and was soon damp with perspiration. The road turned into a gravel path flanked by two dairy sheds and ended at an L-shaped block building, where a group of red-robed Westerners sat around the doorway debating. With their pasty, shaven heads they looked like children playing dress up. I found the image inappropriate and pushed it out of my mind.

The seated monk sprang to his feet. "Looking for us?" he asked in an English accent.

Alan said, "Welcome, Thubten Sangye."

The Englishman said, "So you're the new bloke. Hi, I'm Steve. Good to have an ally against these Yanks."

"Geshe said I should stay here. If there's room, of course"

"That makes a dozen," said another American."

"A biblical number," I smiled.

"Oh, are you Jewish?" He stuck out his hand. "I'm Arnie Possick."

"Nice to meet you, Arnie. No, I'm not. I'm . . . um, an ex-Catholic."

"Gee, I wonder if I could become an ex-Jew," he laughed gently.

"You'll have to leave your privacy at the door," said Alan. "But we've got a spare mattress and plenty of muesli."

Another monk leaned in the doorway, his feet wedged in one corner, his shoulder against the opposite doorpost and his head cocked to one side. I recognized him from the Grottaferrata course. Tall and thin as a stick, a bald patch shone clearly though his cropped head. He raised a leisurely hand and put it on my shoulder and shook his head. "Muesli!

These guys are crazy. I'm Piero. You can eat with Claudio, Massimo and me." He drew himself up to his full height, glared at Steve and said, "We eat well on the path to Awakening. We renounce attachment, not good food and health."

"Don't listen to that lot," said Steve. "They're degenerate."

Piero's grin sagged a little.

"Actually . . . ," I began.

"But I heard that you are Italian," Piero frowned. "Is true?"

"Sort of. Half and half."

"Half Italian?" exclaimed Steve.

"Porco Dio!" said Piero. "Half English?"

Alan interrupted, "Let's get back to what we were doing."

A third American sauntered over, tall and loose-limbed. "I'm Brian," he said. "Glad to know you."

I shook his hand. "I suppose you all met in India?"

"Arnie and I studied with Geshe in McLeod Ganj," he nodded. "When His Holiness[40] asked him to come to Switzerland, we came too. Then Alan and the others. So Steve," he asked, "You want to be a monk?"

"Of course," I said. "Don't you?"

"Well, Steve," he said thoughtfully, "I don't know. I'm not sure I want to," he said.

"So why would you?"

"For Geshe," he said.

"Surely Geshe wouldn't ordain you against your will."

"Of course not," he said, "He'd like me to be willing."

"So you'd do it for him?"

"Could be," he said. "I sure do love him." He looked up. "How 'bout you?"

"I don't know Geshe that well. It was Lama Yeshe who suggested I study with him. I definitely want to learn debate."

He stared as if I might be a little crazy. "Well, Geshe's an amazing teacher."

"So why the hesitation?"

"Ah, Steve," he said doubtfully, "It's the chastity thing."

"You have a girlfriend?"

"Not right now."

I shook my head. "I've had enough of all that. It's never brought me anything but misery."

"Well, I can't argue with that," he said without conviction. "Come on, let's eat."

Alan was putting things out in the tiny kitchen—yogurt, rolled oats and some dried fruit and nuts. Five of us squeezed around the table and Steve mumbled a Tibetan blessing over the table. Everyone tucked in.

"What about the others?" I asked.

Steve scoffed, "The Italians won't eat this."

I looked at the uncooked oats.

"See," he said. "A perfectly balanced diet, no cooking necessary."

"But doesn't it give you gas?" I asked.

They stopped chewing and looked up. "Gas?"

"Uncooked cereal's a bit hard on the digestion, isn't it?"

They looked at one other.

"Do you think that's it?" Alan asked Steve.

"I dunno," he replied. "The Tibetans eat flour all the time. They just mix *tsampa*[41] with their tea. Live on it for months, sometimes."

"The barley's dry-roasted before it's ground," I said. "It's cooked."

Arnie said reflectively, "You know, I thought we should cook it."

"Yuck," said Brian. "Porridge."

"Not if you dry-roast it," I said.

All eyes were on me, so I said, "I'll show you." I took a large skillet from under the counter and put it on low heat, stirring in the oats. A toasty aroma gradually filled the room and the mixture grew dark and crisp. I added nuts, threw in a pinch of salt and dumped it, hot and steaming, into the bowl with dried fruit. The yogurt sizzled as Alan, Steve, Arnie and Brian spooned it into to the mixture.

Happy as a child, Brian burped, scraped his chair and scuffed his heels. "Come on Steve," he invited. "I'll show you around."

The main room held three mattresses, three upturned boxes and an altar laid with seven brass bowls of water, burning tea candles and incense. It was colorful with the mustard-yellow and maroon fabric that covered monks, books, seats[42] and a dozen other things. The room was shared by

Arnie, Steve and Alan, whose head leaned over a Tibetan book, his faded robe stretched taut over his shoulders, his fingertips tracing a line of text, the air around his body bristling like a Van de Graaff Generator.

The next room was Piero's, which he shared with his roommate Claudio. There were two more rooms upstairs, plus a crawl space in the windowless attic, all occupied.

A flurry of activity and the booming sound of Geshe's voice announced his arrival. He clumped heavily up the stairs. Brian greeted him delightedly and Geshe nodded to everyone in a businesslike way. He looked into rooms and put questions to Alan, even climbing the lower steps of the attic ladder and interrupting the meditation of a French monk, Bruno.

"Geshe says you should move into Brian's room," Alan translated. It was the obvious place. It was a large room. I couldn't ask for better, but somehow I'd always equated my ordination with a situation of perfect tranquillity.

There must have been a look of dismay on my face, because as Geshe left Alan said consolingly, "One day we'll each have our own room. A permanent center's on its way." This wasn't the first time I'd project my expectations onto Tibetan Buddhism, nor were they the most far-fetched.

Between the monks' house at Schwendi-22 and the apartment rented by a group of lay people there were three Americans, one Frenchman, a Swiss, four Italians, one Canadian and one Englishman, plus me. Five were monks and three of the Italians spent long periods in Italy, where they were founding a center for Lama Yeshe. There were also two women and a child.

The common Tibetan word for woman, *kye-men*,[43] means "low-born" or "lesser-born," and while socially enlightened lamas might suggest that they're not *really* lesser, Tibetan women were subject to the disadvantages typical of most feudal societies. However, the Western women around Geshe, as well as those in Dharamsala and Nepal, expected equal access to all forms of instruction, and most lamas seemed happy to oblige.

On the other hand, Tibetans are especially fond of the tantric female Buddha Tara, whose wrathful form is widely esteemed. This is an aspect of what's known as "highest yoga-tantra" (the extraordinary path), which supposedly supercharges your practice by transforming negative energy into pathways to Awakening. Many Lamas proclaim that this transforms women's usual disadvantage into natural advantage. Still, every Tantric text begins with the caveat that the extraordinary practices are ineffective or even dangerous for those not thoroughly grounded in the *ordinary* training. The absurdity is that many Tibetans, and now Westerners too, practice tantric ritual to the exclusion of all else, as if it were magic.

Despite the crowded conditions and cultural differences, I liked the microcommunity and settled in quickly.

Weeks passed, and then months. There was nothing to do but study. Recreation consisted of walking in the nearby woods or further afield. It was a pretty spot, though far from the spectacular mountains for which Switzerland is famous. The silence of the coniferous forest just minutes away was the backdrop of many a conversation. I picked Steve's brains about everything we learned, listened to Brian's stories about the great lamas of Dharamsala or heard in detail from Arnie about Vipassana meditation, the other Buddhism, and the popular teacher S.N. Goenka.[44]

I wanted very much to believe that the Buddha was onto something, and that's quite simply what I did. Geshe's mission was to teach us as he'd been taught, and he tried to build into our minds the same grid of Gelug scholarship that framed his own. I did my best to be receptive.

We were not starting out as Geshe had done, however, with a clean slate. I may have chosen to reject my Catholic background, my subliminal training as a Western consumer, and the mishmash of academic theory I'd picked up at college, but that didn't make them go away. Questions arose that, when I tried to ask Geshe, couldn't be formulated in Tibetan—not by Steve, not by Alan and not by Gonsar. Steve made me think when he said, "I learned Tibetan in order to speak to my teachers about absolutely anything, but not everything translates."

My wish was to become a translator and teacher, but I understood that this would require greater subtlety and interpretation than I'd anticipated. We'd have to absorb the essence of the teachings first, put them into practice and only then expect to find ways to express them in our own language. That would take years; if not a lifetime.

The date of my ordination was fixed, but I still had unfinished business with Lucille. We arranged to meet secretly and I stood on the platform of Kollbrunn railway station, feeling like Humphrey Bogart on the tarmac in *Casablanca*.

I'd hiked through the woods to get to Kollbrunn, one stop distant from Rikon. Clutching a paper bag of fruit and chocolate I watched the station clock tick and stared at the tracks. The train arrived, Lucille jumped off and we embraced. I inhaled her hair.

"You look well," she said as we walked away.

"You too."

"It's nice to see you."

I smiled.

"So, today we stop time," she said.

"Briefly, yes."

"I think Frau Kalff might be suspicious."

"What did you tell her?"

"Nothing."

"She doesn't know you're here?"

"She knows I'm somewhere she wouldn't approve. Otherwise, I'd have told her."

"Why shouldn't we be here?"

She raised an eyebrow. "You're going to be a monk."

"I'm not yet."

"You know what I mean. Maybe you have doubts."

"You'd think so, wouldn't you?"

We walked for a while in silence until she said, "And eventually, I'll be going home."

"To Maine?"

"There or somewhere else. The point is, I can't stay here forever."

I stopped. "Should I be confused? I'm happy to be here with you, *and* I'm looking forward to being a monk."

She shrugged, and took my hand.

We'd reached the edge of the forest and followed a path to a small clearing. Sitting on a fallen tree, our ears gradually opened to the scurrying of birds and tiny feet. Insects murmured. The distant buzz of a chain saw cut the air. We spoke of the blue of the sky, the warmth of the air and the absence of other people. She opened a bag of sandwiches and we ate. We lay back in the warm air and grew drowsy in each other's arms. Time passed.

"So!" she roused herself, "This time next week you'll be a monk."

"Yes."

"And we'll never see each other again."

"Not like this." I pulled her to me.

She pushed back. "No. That would spoil everything."

"Why?"

"It would."

I felt a moment of resentment, but nodded. "You're right."

At last the sun dipped over the trees, the air cooled and Lucille looked at her watch. We rose without a word and retraced our steps slowly.

She stood in the doorway of the departing train with tears in her eyes, and her fingers slid out of mine. The train passed down the track and around a bend. I continued to stare, long after the metallic ringing of the rails had ceased.

23

A Day in the Life

A FEW DAYS LATER, Brian and I were summoned to the monastery, where the monks of the Rikon Institut awaited us with a couple of upright chairs on the landing outside Geshe's room. A large cut-throat razor was produced, though no water or shaving soap, and the party began. Brian went first, and the bland patina of his head was quickly exposed, leaving only a slender tuft of hair. Geshe leaned back with folded arms and cracked jokes that kept his monks howling with laughter.

I sat quietly, understanding very little and wondering how I'd feel after all the excitement died down. By the time all my hair had been swept up and disposed of I felt just fine, sure of my decision and looking forward to the irrevocable transformation of my life. What did I have to lose?

Brian too was in a great mood, but then he was always happy around Geshe.

"We look like Hare Krishna devotees," I told him.

"Now," said Geshe, "You'll need some offerings. The shops shut soon."

"We can't go out like this!" I said. Hair cuttings covered our clothes and shoulders and our scalps were pasty white with bloody nicks.

Brian said, "Come on Steve, we might as well get used to it." He clapped me on the shoulder.

"I suppose so," I said doubtfully.

Half way down the hill we passed a Swiss couple heading upwards and said the obligatory "Greutzi." They nodded to us and returned the greeting courteously without batting an eyelid. Down in the grocery shop, however, the staid Swiss shopkeeper eyed us suspiciously. Brian and I couldn't look at each other and keep a straight face; as we left the shop we burst into laughter. Our arms were full with bags of biscuits, fruit and tea for the ceremony next day.

In the morning, Arnie and Steve helped us fold the twelve-foot loop of the lower garment and bind it with a sash. The slippery folds threatened to slide through the binding as we walked and I fretted, "I'll never get it back in once it comes out."

Brian's mood from the night before, in which he bathed in Geshe's presence, had disappeared. "I don't know about this Steve," he said.

"Well you're all dressed up and on your way, aren't you?" I said stoutly.

"Yes," he said hesitantly. "On my way." His pace didn't falter. "You know," he reflected, "Geshe told me back in India that I should become a monk."

"Did you want to?"

"Not really."

"So what did you say?"

"I said, 'Sure Geshe-la. I'll become a monk when you move to Switzerland."

I laughed. "You were bluffing?"

"Well heck, Steve. How was I supposed to know he'd end up here?"

In retrospect, Brian's reaction was far more understandable than mine. Today I find it amazing that I didn't give even a second thought to what I was doing. At age twenty-three, with a strong libido, even though it had been persistently frustrated, I turned my back on everything I'd known to commit myself to a life of celibacy.

The Rikon monks were wrapped in ceremonial yellow robes. Gonsar indicated our places and Geshe welcomed us from a low throne. We went down on our hands and knees three times.

Gonsar placed a white scarf around our necks and translated as Geshe explained his role as our ordaining abbot. The scarf represented the white clothing of the householder, a lifestyle we would now renounce. Geshe held his right hand above and left hand below in a gesture of handing over, and we ceremonially received a begging bowl, our robes, which we were already wearing, and the other implements of a monk.[45] Geshe joked about handing us robes we were already wearing, but warned us that the ceremony was serious nonetheless.

"The text says," Gonsar translated, "that the robes distinguish you from lay people and protect you from insects and weather," and continued with an explanation of each item's purpose. Geshe now approached and cut the final tufts of hair on our heads with scissors.

We went on our knees and it was explained how the monk's life is superior to the householder's because there are fewer fetters and distractions, and more opportunities to accumulate merit.

"While listening to this advice," said Gonsar, "You should look upon your abbot as a wise father and yourselves as sons in need of guidance." The white scarf was now removed and Geshe addressed us by our Tibetan names. We took refuge,[46] pledged to respect the abbot and wear only the robes—especially avoiding white or black clothes, fringes, sleeves, ornaments, or jewels, and hair longer than a finger's width.

The preliminaries over, we recited the vow after Geshe, a few words at a time. I understood the gist, but not the words, and knew my accent was atrocious. The monks smiled.

"You should think," said Gonsar, "that you have received the vow not only in words but in your mind, and rejoice."

Lhodro Rinpoche stood and announced the exact time of ordination to the congregation, to establish our seniority. We should henceforth respect and defer to our elders.

Finally, the assembly offered prayers of auspiciousness and threw rice in the air. The white scarves were handed back to us, this time as the more commonplace token of a symbolic welcome.

Geshe told Brian and me that we were now dharma brothers. "Usually," Gonsar translated, "monks are ordained in large groups. When there are few, the bond is closer. You are just two."

We looked at each other. I thought I should feel extraordinary. I was a monk! We shared lunch with the Rikon monks, were congratulated by the others as they arrived for debate class, and continued with our studies.

We were heading back when Brian said again, "I don't know about this Steve."

He didn't look exactly troubled, but neither was he joking.

"It's a little late now, isn't it?" I said.

"Well, I don't know if I'm going to be a monk for life."

"That vow we just took . . . ," I reminded him.

"Oh, I've already spoken to Geshe about that," he said. "If and when the time comes to move on I won't feel bad."

I'd met few people quite as frank as Brian; he was guileless, you might say honest to a fault. I wondered for a moment if I too might return one day to lay life, but this hardly seemed the time to dwell on it. However, I noticed that the mere thought scared me.

The routine of Schwendi-22 was far from settled. Classes were interrupted due to Geshe's responsibilities as Abbot of the Rikon Institut, which had a fairly large Tibetan community,[47] and he also traveled to give teachings elsewhere in Europe. This gave us time to reflect on how we were doing, and to adjust to our situation.

Fully ordained Buddhist monks have 253 rules, not all of which seemed entirely practical in twentieth-century Switzerland, and for a while our interpretations were split down cultural lines. On the whole, the Anglos and lone Gaul (Bruno) among us were punctilious, the Italians laid-back. Much to my surprise, Geshe regularly ate an evening meal and appeared to be quite flexible about the fine print. His only demand of us was that we go slowly and take the long view. Most Tibetan Lamas found Westerners of our generation addicted to instant gratification, an approach inimical to Awakening. By contrast, they approached their spiritual goal as a multi-lifetime endeavour.

Alan, Steve, Arnie and Bruno were all in favor of the afternoon fast. I thought it a great idea, though my stomach didn't agree, and Brian went along with it too. The idea is that once the noon meal is over and done, the remainder of the day can be spent entirely in meditation. While we

GESHE RABTEN AT RIKON WITH LAY STUDENTS AND WESTERN MONKS
(AUTHOR FAR LEFT): *celibate young men in our sexual prime*

were enthusiastic about what we were doing, this caused sufficient difficulty that we sought out Geshe's advice.

"These rules were laid down by Lord Buddha and there's a great virtue
in following them," he said. "On the other hand, you're all studying hard
and," Geshe chuckled, "may be susceptible to *lüng* disorders. So watch
your health, and if necessary, eat."

Lüng[48] is a subtle "air" that supports consciousness in the body. What
are known in Tibetan medicine as lüng disorders often take the form
of nervousness and sleeplessness; these were in fact the order of the day.
From dawn to dusk we studied, meditated and even walked with uncom-
promising seriousness. This made for snappy moods, and the petty irrita-
tions of close quarters were at times all too evident. Medicine was ordered
from Dharamsala, consisting of bitter black balls to be chewed and swallowed with hot water. All we really had to do was relax, but that was easier
said than done. We were driven and impatient for progress. Relaxation

seemed like a waste of our precious, short span. In any case, all forms of entertainment, including shows, books and music, were proscribed.

The fact that we were all celibate young men in our sexual prime didn't help. I'd assumed that with ordination my libido would atrophy from disuse, but once again my body saw things differently. Quite apart from that, I missed the emotional friendship of women.

There was also the stress of being perceived by our Swiss-German neighbors as crackpots in drag, a situation that wasn't helped by living in an insular farming community. They were used to us, but strangers stared, sometimes laughed. It was nice that Tibetan grandmothers smiled, put their hands together and bowed, but we didn't see that much of them.

We did our best to take all this in our stride. If anything, the fact that it was a struggle fortified our sense of mission and self-worth. Awakening was a dream of freedom, and I clung to the idea that there would one day be a breakthrough in which all this would become effortless.

The resolution was both less dramatic and more satisfying than I would ever have anticipated. Returning one Sunday morning from a long walk, I was surprised to hear music coming from our house, even more so to trace it to the large room. Through the open window I saw Alan and Steve standing, staring into space, rapt by the echoing tones of Vivaldi's Spring concerto. I raised my eyebrows; Steve turned to me with barely suppressed glee and said, "Geshe *ordered* Alan to relax!"

"Alan?" I raised my eyebrows and glanced at him. His expression didn't change.

"Well," Steve laughed. "All of us. Where's the harm?"

The sun streamed through the window. The sky was brilliant blue. The late spring crops rustled in the breeze. The world outside was like a stage set, and we the players in a great Technicolor epiphany. In a moment our earlier sacrifices became irrelevant.

"God," I murmured, "it's wonderful."

It came to an end and we played it through a second time.

From that point forward we took a more measured approach, much to the relief of Massimo, Claudio and Piero. The music had come from a borrowed cassette recorder belonging to Helmut, a prospective monk, and we soon each acquired our own players and headphones.[49] A small collection of tapes made the rounds—Vivaldi concertos and Beethoven, Mozart and Sibelius symphonies. We relaxed other rules, making dietary exceptions when it seemed practical, and eating an evening snack from time to time. The frequency of lüng disorders declined.

The music opened a door not, as stricter abbots might fear, to rampant hedonism but to something far more seditious. Beethoven in particular struck a chord in my own cultural core; here was something distinct from the Asian values I'd been trying to pursue to the exclusion of all else. I saw that to understand myself, it might help to understand it.

Frau Kalff now came into the picture, offering us an opportunity to delve into ourselves and our cultural icons. Having renounced Western culture and gone to Buddhism for psychological succor, this was an about-face for us. Who better to guide us than a Jungian psychologist, a personal student and neighbor of the master himself.

Whether she intended to bring her eclectic life's work under the Buddhist canopy or, more likely, the opposite, Frau Kalff was fascinated by the vast Tibetan repertoire of symbols, and by Geshe's learning. I doubt that her feelings were reciprocated. While visiting her house, Geshe had seen the Buddhist images he revered side by side with statues of Shiva, stone carvings from Africa and other objets d'art, and he dealt warily with her. However, he also had a job to do, and Frau Kalff was an important hostess of public teachings with the right connections and her own public venue. On the basis of that pragmatic relationship she asked for Geshe's consent to bring us, his Western monks, into her sand-room. I imagine that he was inclined to refuse. Diplomatically, he didn't.

Frau Kalff's medieval house in Zollikon had survived the centuries well. Its cellar walls were several feet thick and its floorboards as stout as tree trunks. The place creaked with unexpected life. She lived here with her son Martin, and Lucille, who still hadn't gone back to her husband. She stood at a distance and caught my eye as I turned. I nodded to her and almost smiled. It took me a moment to realize I shouldn't approach. Instead, I joined the monks in the sitting room, and awaited my turn.

When it came, Frau Kalff explained the process. On a table in the center of the room was a box with several inches of sand. "Most people begin by just putting their hands in it," she said. "You may add water if you wish, to shape it." She pointed to a jug and moved to a stool on one side, indicating the walls. The shelves, from floor to ceiling, were crammed with figures of thousands of animate and inanimate objects.

"Use anything you like. There's no need to think of anything in particular; just play."

I stared at it stupidly, embarrassed.

"Please don't be shy," she soothed professionally. "This is all confidential. Our conversation stays within these four walls."

As I moved my hands through the sand they took on a life of their own, and a pile formed. I pushed one corner into a high ridge, tamped down a firm plateau and moulded the top into a protected hollow. Then, trying to think serene thoughts, I turned my attention to the plain below. I put a farmhouse, trees, farm animals and a few figures, placing them among the undulations of the sand until the pastoral mood was right. I stood back.

Frau Kalff's leg shifted from the stool to the floor and her breathing changed perceptibly.

I stared a little longer. "Okay, I'm finished."

"Really?"

I turned to her. "Don't you think so?"

"I don't know," she said. "Just . . . you spent so much time on that hill in the corner."

"Yes?"

"Hm," she barely assented.

I looked again. The peaceful scene was a concoction, what I *thought* I should create. Some plastic toy soldiers on the shelves caught my eye, like ones I'd had as a boy, but they seemed inappropriate for a young monk. I scanned all the shelves, returned to the soldiers, and with a sense of time running out I grabbed a handful. The plateau was perfectly prepared for them. In a few moments I added tanks and field guns, and the farm was ready for bombardment.

"There," I was breathless. "That's it."

She got off her stool and made a show of examining it. "It's menacing."

"Do you think so?"

She looked up. "Soldiers attacking a farm?"

I shrugged. "I suppose so."

"Are you afraid of being destroyed?"

"Not at all." I spoke with all the confidence I could muster.

"Then perhaps you wish to destroy," she said gently.

"Well," I shuffled my feet, "I haven't mastered the Perfection of Patience yet . . . ."

"Tell me," she smiled. "Would you like to live in this farm?"

"With those guns up there?" I snorted.

"But otherwise?"

"Otherwise?" I looked at it abstractedly. "I . . . I suppose so. But . . . ."

She waited.

"But how would you know they weren't there?"

"The soldiers?"

"They're hidden. You wouldn't know."

During one of Geshe's longer absences I attended one of Lama Yeshe's courses at Coniston Priory, an old manor house in north England's Lake District. The huge Victorian folly was infested with dry rot and Lama's students had picked it up for a song, on condition they restore it.

This was my first trip as a monk and I decided to wear my robes en route, pointed fingers and sniggered comments notwithstanding. Crossing the English Channel, freezing winds tugged forcefully at the folds of my lower robe and almost exposed me even more than I'd anticipated.

Arriving in Coniston, however, I was received with open arms. A small group of students was fighting against time to tear out thousands of rotted beams and replace them with new wood, and the place was a dusty building site. It was backbreaking volunteer work that no afford-able wage could have justified. It took them weeks to make a handful of rooms habitable.

As usual, Lama Yeshe's young ward Zopa Rinpoche took some of the burden off his guardian by teaching most of the classes. He was rambling and difficult to follow. However, one discourse, clear as a bell, was seared in our memory. While talking about the brevity of human life and the uncertainty of its end, he told a story about one of Lama's students, years earlier in Dharamsala, who lived in a rickety old A-frame hut. She'd just heard a discourse on the very same subject and he was wondering out loud just how deeply she'd contemplated the teaching when an explosive laugh erupted from his chest. "And then, and then . . . ," he slapped his side, "the ridge pole broke. Snapped in two. And the roof fell." He wheezed, describing how the house had collapsed, crushed her skull and killed her instantly. He repeated the punch line, slapping his thigh each time, laughing at our trust in the sacredness and security of life.

. A hush had fallen. The audience chewed lips and fidgeted. The fact that no one joined in his laughter seemed to tickle Rinpoche even more.

The climax of the ten-day course was the ceremony of the Great Wish,[50] conducted by Lama himself. He called for the room to be filled with light and we brought there every candle we could find. Some were in candlesticks, some stood on saucers or were fixed in cups or on bits of broken tile.

CONISTON PRIORY (AUTHOR FAR-RIGHT, FOREGROUND): with Lamas Yeshe and Zopa, and author's white-haired benefactor, Sigrid Kremzow (standing, rear)

Imagine a cavernous Victorian ballroom, furnished only by its crumbling plaster mouldings, huge sash windows and heavy oaken doors. A teaching throne and altar stood against one wall. Long-haired young men and women stood, heads down, blankets draped over shoulders, thumbing rosaries and mumbling mantras. A thousand candles created a mosaic of softly flickering shadows as the temperature rose. Candles melted together into formless clumps, one or two filaments wicking wax to the flame, some sputtering, others burning black smoke. The sound of the room was that of crackling, fizzling, dripping candles.

Lama Yeshe arrived with his finger to his lips, and spoke in whispers of the vow we were about to take. "This is more important than any moral precept. Compassion for other sentient beings means feeling for them, putting yourself in their place, like Christ. Loving others is to give up attachment to your own little ego, to embrace the big universe of sentient beings. This Great Vow destroys the dualistic mind and makes you blissful. Bliss makes you tireless and free. Nothing is more important. Sunyata is difficult, very subtle; but love is not complicated. Anyone can practice it. You are taking the vow, 'I will not rest until every Sentient Being is Buddha.' You think about it first."

We remained in silence for some minutes before he spoke again, leading us through a simple recitation. The mood was solemn, the heat tremendous and the quality of light and shadow like the painting of a Dutch master. When we got up I felt the precept seared into my consciousness with a brilliance I'd never experienced at my ordination.

On my way back to Switzerland I stopped in on Mum and Dad in Gloucester, and they saw my cropped head for the first time. They were welcoming but skeptical, clearly waiting for me to outgrow my latest phase.

24

OF THINGS UNSPOKEN

DEBATE TRAINING ISN'T THE ONLY approach to Buddhism, by any means. Different traditions emphasize other forms of study, and all four Tibetan schools teach the three yanas—Hinayana, Mahayana and Tantrayana—the narrow, broad and hidden vehicles, respectively. Practice of the broad path is said to require all the skills of the narrow, and tantra depends on a thorough grounding in both. This isn't always evident from the way tantric rituals are made available. The Dalai Lama, for instance, often performs the Kalachakra initiation ceremony at large public gatherings, knowing that many have little or no training at all. Merely attending the ceremony without understanding is considered a blessing or karmic imprint that will ripen in future lifetimes, and not a transmission of the truly secret elements, so no harm is done. However, the whole notion of tantrayana and of imprints can strain the average Westerner's credulity, especially since Buddhism is widely appreciated in the West for its 'scientific' approach.

Nevertheless, the attractions of Tibetan Buddhism are many, and not everyone is in search of scientific dispassion. Those interested in ritual and esoterica find much to be excited about. Piero and Claudio were very much in this mold, and didn't really have their hearts in the debate training. However, they put great energy into tantric ceremonies. Every so often they'd prepare an elaborate ritual, and after hours and sometimes days of secrecy would emerge from their darkened, incensed room in a state of exhausted elation.

Piero and I had bad chemistry; or, as we'd say in those days, bad karma. Although he was an elder monk he didn't pull rank and instead worked hard to make me like him, but my distrust only grew. The more he worked on my defences the stronger they became. He'd put his arm around my shoulder, incline his head towards me and say, "You know Thubten Sangye, I like you. You are a nice guy. We're both disciples of Lama Yeshe. Really, we're dharma brothers. You think so too—no?"

I'd look at him.

He'd squeeze me. "Can't we get along?"

"I don't see why not." I really couldn't explain my antipathy.

One day he announced, "I have just the thing for you."

I waited.

"You should make tsok. You need *guru yoga*."

Tsok is an offering ceremony—a tantric ritual—and guru yoga is the essence of tantra, in which one visualizes the guru as Buddha, absorbs him or her, and regenerates oneself in the same physical/mental image.

Piero put his hands together reverentially. "I've asked Geshe Rabten-la in his loving compassion to give the Vajra Bhairava initiation. Do you know this manifestation of Buddha?"

I shook my head.

"The Great Destroyer. He belongs to the highest and most secret class of tantra. It's a great opportunity. A great privilege to develop fantastic deep meditation and reach[51] full Awakening in one lifetime."

"Uh-huh," I nodded.

In fact, Piero's reminder of Lama Yeshe had indeed touched a nerve. I was pleased to be studying with Geshe Rabten. He was kind and a gifted teacher, but his methodical, scholarly style touched me very differently from Lama Yeshe's ebullient, free spirit. The truth was, I felt rather guilty about my tepid feelings for Geshe. After all, he was my ordaining abbot and de facto teacher. I decided to talk to Brian.

"I love Geshe," he said simply.

"And he loves you?" Why couldn't it be that simple for me?

"I don't judge him by ordinary standards of love and friendship. I choose to see him as an enlightened person who loves all sentient beings. I don't expect any favoritism."

I asked, "You've received secret initiations, haven't you?"

He looked out the window. "Well," he said at length. "I don't know how to answer that. Is there something you want to know?"

"I mean, from Geshe?"

Brian straightened up. "As far as I know, Geshe doesn't give highest yoga tantra initiations. I know people who've asked, and he always refused. Says debate's more important. Perhaps to his Tibetan disciples back in India . . . I really don't know." He laughed, "I'm sure I wouldn't ask!"

I said, "Piero and Claudio have asked Geshe for this big initiation, and they want me to go."

"Really?" he looked intrigued. "Well, we'll see."

Sure enough, Geshe passed the ball on the initiation, asking a colleague, Geshe Jampa Lhodro, to conduct the ceremony instead. I asked Brian whether I should go.

"Far be it from me to influence you one way or another, but you should think carefully about the relationship you're entering into. During the ceremony and from that day forth, you're expected to see Geshe Lhodro as Vajra Bhairava—the wrathful embodiment of the wisdom of all the buddhas. You're bound to the initiating lama for life, so you'd better be comfortable with him."

I thought about that for a minute and asked "Will you come?"

He picked his words carefully. "I already have my guru-yoga practices and don't want to compound them with another Lama."

Brian spoke often and warmly about the Dalai Lama's tutors and other lamas in Dharamsala. I imagined he must have received all sorts of initiations from the highest sources, and was envious. I knew my motivation couldn't have been worse, but I wanted *in*, to the inner sanctum. Still, my doubts remained.

"I don't know," I told Piero.

"Oh, Thubten Sangye," he was exasperated. "This is a precious opportunity." He put his hands together at his heart and fluttered his eyelashes.
"Geshe Jampa Lhodro is a kind, compassionate lama, and by the power of
your mind you can transform him into the deity." He shook his head. He
pleaded, "I would hate for you to miss your chance."

It was Claudio who tipped the balance. He was loud, intense and
pushy, but I liked him. "Come Thubten Sangye," he boomed. "How can
you turn your back on this great initiation? Imagine if in three years[52]
you are fully enlightened, how many sentient beings you'll help." He
roared with laughter.

And so one morning I walked with Piero and Claudio to the house of
Geshe Jampa Lhodro. As we waited for the door to open, Piero counseled,
"Instead of a small Swiss apartment, we're entering the divine mansion.
Everything is made of light. All is bliss, especially your mind. You too are
Bhairava."

On the wall hung a large painting of Vajra Bhairava in all his azure
glory—a buffalo-headed figure grinning hideously, nine faces dripping
blood, thirty-four arms clasping weapons and sixteen legs trampling
enemies. He wore a necklace of fifty moist human heads, his hair was
made of fire and his penis was erect.

Geshe Lhodro was a shy, gentle man. He recited from a thick book,
periodically taking an article from a small arsenal of implements beside
him, including a bell and *dorje*, a finger drum[53] and a ritual vase. He
used them with hand movements as he chanted. The scene was at once
strangely evocative and utterly incongruous.

The ceremony was long and tedious. By the time the moment of initiation arrived I was fidgety. Piero signaled me to lower my head. Geshe
bonked my head with the vase and I imagined myself pure and full of
bliss. It wasn't unlike my first communion.

As we walked home Claudio explained the commitment and described
the special hells reserved for those who transgressed the tantric vows, of
which secrecy was just one. "From now on," he pointed out, "you must see
yourself as Bhairava in every thought, word and deed."

My head swam with the immensity of the task, especially when I read
next day a translation of the daily meditation. It was a visualization of

VAJRA BHAIRAVA: *nine faces dripping blood,*
thirty-four arms clasping weapons and sixteen legs trampling enemies;
he wears a necklace of fifty moist human heads, has hair of fire and an erect penis

vast proportions and immense detail, making Catholic ritual look like village theatrics.

"What makes it different from rote?" I asked Steve.

"Well . . . if you're not actually absorbed in incredible concentration, nothing at all I should think."

"What about the karmic imprints?"

He laughed dryly.

"Don't you believe in them?"

"Well of course, when you do something it leaves an imprint—that's how we develop habits. But I wonder what sort of imprint I'm leaving when I recite something I barely understand. I've been to those ceremonies and to be perfectly honest, I don't see that I *received* those initiations. I'm quite sure my mind wasn't a suitable receptacle."

"But you do believe they're the Buddha's teachings?"

"You mean all that stuff about Buddha teaching them in the heavenly realms? And about being kept secret by the Nagas for five hundred years? And about Nagarjuna fetching them back from the underworld?"

"Well, when you put it like that—"

"I mean . . . really!"

"Well, don't you have an opinion?"

"Ye-es," he prevaricated.

"And you don't believe it."

"I don't see any compelling reason to. I mean, it's pretty convenient, isn't it? After all, what was Gotama all about? Awareness, mindfulness, looking objectively into your own mind. Even if he did teach the tantras, which I doubt, they're obviously not for ordinary people, and certainly not for a bunch of Westerners who've only been studying Buddhism for a few years, sometimes not even that. And then there's bodhicitta—having absolutely no self-interest whatsoever?" He raised his eyebrows.

Now I was shocked. "You don't believe in that either."

"Don't misunderstand me. It's an amazing idea—very appealing—but I don't *experience* it, at least, not with any great continuity. And every tantric text makes the point that unless you've developed bodhicitta you're really not going to *get* the initiation."

"So belief's got nothing to do with it?"

Steve frowned. "Belief's always got something to do with it."

Steve's skepticism resonated for me, and yet I looked forward to the day when tantra would become a real experience. I trusted that it could be transformative. Its subtext was, "taking the goal as the path," and its power lay in the "pride of being the deity"—seeing oneself unwaveringly as a fully enlightened, wrathful buddha, able to extinguish conventional pretensions without a moment's hesitation.

As Steve pointed out, the immediate challenge was practical. It demanded meditative and concentrative powers that I simply didn't have. One day I'd do a Vajra Bhairava retreat and make it a part of me once and for all. I promised that my daily recitation wouldn't descend into rote, but it wasn't long before I was racing through it at breakneck speed, like everyone else.

Brian made no show of rapture as he recited his daily commitment. Neither did he question its value. Steve kept his commitment, but made no pretense of accepting it at face value. These two had become my friends, each like one of the two sides of my brain. Analytically, skepticism was my yardstick. Emotionally, I kept the faith. The two formed a dialectic that spurred me with sufficient focus to stay on track and enough doubt to remain alert. The fact that it left me vaguely uncomfortable was actually reassuring. To this day, the deadening weight of comfort, security and certainty makes me nervous.

25

HALCYON DAYS

G ESHE RABTEN'S FOLLOWING IN EUROPE grew steadily as several regional groups took shape. They consisted of philanthropists, businessmen and people of all walks of life who wanted to be a part of the growth of Buddhism in Europe. What became known as the Geneva Group seized the initiative to establish a permanent center for Geshe and his Western monks. Just after a year in Rikon, we learned that a property had been purchased near Lausanne.

It seemed that not only the occupants but the very bricks and mortar of Schwendi-22 exhaled a sigh of relief. After living like sardines in a can, we'd soon have room to swing a cat. We'd also have direct access to Geshe, more classes, additional teachers and an extended lay community. Classes would expand. We'd all begin to teach.

Rumbling like an empty box, the wooden funicular rose a thousand meters through the vineyards overlooking Vevey and deposited us eleven minutes later at the terminal. Mont-Pèlerin was a resort village above Lake Geneva, facing a dazzling array of snowcapped peaks. Dozens of little flags fluttered in the crystalline air and the village center was dominated by the pretty terrace of the Café du Relais. Apart from several restaurants and hotels, the entire commerce consisted of a grocer, a bakery and a post office. The round-topped cap of Mont-Pèlerin lay behind, forested in clumps, scattered with alpine pastures and chalets. It was uniquely, Swissly picturesque.

Our new home was on a knoll a couple of hundred meters up the route de Beaumaroche. French doors opened at ground level onto a sloping apron of grass. Damson trees flowered in front. A large horse chestnut tree partly obscured a burned-out house on the far side, run-down and ready for rebirth.

The chemin de Dérochoz turned sharply behind a third, low building and led to the rear entrance. Our voices echoed excitedly through the ground-floor refectory and kitchen. Upstairs, dormitories and bedrooms faced south, a glass door opening onto a common balcony and unobstructed vista. Rolling vineyards fell away towards Vevey and the lake. From the far shore the land climbed again into snowcapped mountainsides. Behind them, the alpine horizon rose to the jagged Dents du Midi[54]—a landmark of my trip to Italy with Dad, my passage to India, and now my daily life.

The Geneva group had formed under the eagle eye of Anne Ansermet. Her father Ernest was the celebrated director of Les Ballets Russes, and she grew up with the likes of Igor Stravinsky and Pablo Picasso dropping in for dinner. Decades later, as the privileged daughter of a Swiss national icon, she was familiar with the drawing rooms of power and could get things done. Drawn to Buddhism at the age of seventy, she'd traveled to India and been ordained by the Dalai Lama himself, whom she described proudly as her guru. Other members of the fund-raising group ranged from business people and industrialists to friends and all sorts of ordinary Buddhists. It can't have been a simple matter to set up a Tibetan Buddhist monastery in the staid canton of Vaud for foreign ex-hippies with no income, but she had the pull to get it done. In time, our neighbors realized we weren't dangerous fanatics. We were referred to as "*le culte*," but generally tolerated.

Known around the center as *Anila*[55] Ansermet, she was an energetic and imperious force to whom we owed the privilege of our unfettered lifestyle. The Geneva Group put a roof over our heads and visas in our passports. Our individual sponsors provided funds for food and books, and we gave ourselves up to a life of study and contemplation without the slightest material worry. Visitors to the center often brought gifts for the community or sought out monks with such unexpected needs as a dental bill or traveling expense. They were eager to help.

In time a new sign appeared in the doorway—Tharpa Chöeling, *Centre d'hautes études tibetaines*.[56] Our sponsors looked on approvingly, confident their money and time were well spent. The nucleus of married and working lay students from Rikon rented a large house and became a satellite of the monastic center. Geshe's growing reputation brought people from far and wide, even from Dharamsala. Some studied, some helped in the administration or financing and some worked in the kitchen or garden. Most respected of all were the studious, and the core group from Schwendi were the stars. Our days of splendid isolation were over.

With this also came more specific goals. We may have looked to our neighbors like just another religious cult but we never doubted the historic moment of our mission. We'd been sure of ourselves back in Schwendi, but now with the backing of respectable citizens we had new credibility in our own eyes. We were to become translators and teachers, lynchpins in the transmission of the sacred Buddhadharma to the West. For now, we'd study. Later, we'd be sent to train others.

Geshe's commitments as abbot of Rikon Monastery prevented him from joining us for the time being. The largest room on the top floor was set aside for him, and a carpet had been laid from wall to wall. Brian said, "Helmut put this in for Geshe. What a lovely gift."

"Helmut?" I queried.

"The Austrian boy. Tall. The one who lent us the tape recorder. Vivaldi?"

"I never actually met him."

"Well, he'll be joining us."

"Another monk?"

"Eventually," Brian said. "Not right away though. Seems he's a computer whiz and Geshe wants him to finish school first."

"Really?"

"Seems so." Brian was as surprised as I.

Geshe soon came down for his first week with us and it was a delight. We had only to walk down the hallway for classes and it was exciting to find him wandering though the building and stopping to chat. Brian had taken the small room beside him—one with neither a balcony nor a view—and fell happily into the role of personal attendant, tidying his room, bringing him tea and helping out in any way he could. He also interpreted for him from time to time, but from day one most of the important-looking people from Geneva were ushered in and out by Alan, who was first choice as translator.

We drew up a schedule of daily language classes, with Alan and Steve as teachers. We also set aside time each afternoon for debate.

The moment Geshe returned to Rikon and we were left to our own devices, things went quiet. We studied and meditated as usual but also went beyond the traditional curriculum. Just as classical music had become a source of relaxation and surprising productivity, Western books became a source of inspiration and vocabulary. Even Alan, the most conservative among us, was exploring particle physics and seeking parallels with Buddhist epistemology. A new biography of Alfred Einstein made the rounds. Steve developed an interest in Protestant theology and buried his nose for months in Paul Tillich's monumental Systematic Theology.[57] Carl Jung's writings on subjectivity, myth and synchronicity stirred my imagination. Even novels like Dostoyevsky's *Crime and Punishment* were popular—nothing lightweight for us, but otherwise we were omnivorous.

One morning in the new center I encountered a tall young layman in the monk's corridor. Was he lost?

"Hello?" I asked questioningly.

"Hello," his voice chimed with an Austrian accent and he lowered his head deferentially. "How are you?"

"Fine, thank you." I replied, "Um . . . who *are* you?"

"Oh!" he seemed surprised. "I'm Helmut." He thrust his hand out.

"And you're here to see . . . ?"

"No one," he laughed. "I'm going to my room." He pointed to the door.

"You're going to be ordained?"

"At last, yes! Geshe gave me this room."

"Oh!" I smiled with a discomfort I couldn't account for. "Well, welcome to Tharpa Chöeling."

"Thank you," he nodded formally.

I nodded too, and headed for the stairwell. "Breakfast," I explained.

"Ah yes, breakfast," he laughed, a little too loud.

As I went down it clicked. This was the owner of the portable tape recorder that had filled Schwendi with Vivaldi's *Stagioni*. How long ago it seemed. I reran our conversation in my head.

We converted the small building on the corner of the property into a temple. Insulating boards were laid on the concrete floor and covered with industrial carpet. The walls were painted in traditional Tibetan style, a horizontal stripe separating the upper and lower walls. Helmut put together small wooden boxes, turned on their sides to provide a cubbyhole for prayer books, bells and other paraphernalia for each monk. At the apex of the T-shaped room, the altar was tiered like a wedding cake, spread with brocade and jammed with statues, pictures and coconut oil lamps. The teaching throne was in front. On one side stood the Dalai Lama's inordinately raised seat, a feature of every Tibetan temple; his photo rested on the cushions.

Each morning we took our places face-to-face down the length of the temple, spread our mats[58] and followed Brian's lead. The Tibetan language is rife with onomatopoeia, but no word sang quite so appropriately as *oomze*, the person who leads the chant. Brian had a deep voice and among us was the best able to approximate the unique Tibetan resonance between belly and chest. The rest of us weren't even close. Listening each morning to our assorted warbles and mutterings I sometimes didn't know whether to laugh or cry.

There we were, a bunch of Westerners who'd given up on God, praying together daily. As Buddhists we didn't believe in a creator, nor even that any buddha could enlighten us. Instead, we called on the buddhas and bodhisattvas of the past present and future to witness our determination to follow in their footsteps.

Our sleepy drone never rose to a truly tantric roar, and it was usually a relief to emerge into the early morning light. One morning, after days of overcast skies, we came out to thick shafts of sunlight pouring though breaking clouds onto Mont-Pèlerin. Brian grabbed a chair and sat in the warmth, waiting for the breakfast gong.

Crockery, cutlery and butter passed through the hatch from kitchen to dining room. Piping-hot tea gushed from large Thermos flasks. Pots of jam, giant tubs of peanut butter and Marmite were littered with fragments of oven-fresh bread crust. Thick slices were slathered in butter. Biscuits and fruit—the remnants of recent *tsok* offerings—were quickly depleted. The Schwendi müesli bowl stood on one side like a relic.

The gong sounded, doors opened and feet pattered, slipped, slid and slapped as everyone headed for the refectory. Even Alan became talkative.

"Thubten Sangye," he asked, "How is the memorization of your *lo-rig*[59] definitions coming along?" He sat in perfect monkish posture, one hand on his lap beneath the table, the other tidily lifting bite-size pieces of buttered bread into his mouth.

I almost choked on my bread. "Oh," I answered. "I'm, er, still working on it."

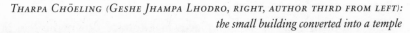

THARPA CHÖELING (GESHE JHAMPA LHODRO, RIGHT, AUTHOR THIRD FROM LEFT): *the small building converted into a temple*

Several pairs of eyes shifted in my direction, then back towards Alan.

"Well, keep at it," he said encouragingly. "Before you know it you'll have *ta-rig*[60] under your belt and you'll be on to *prajna paramita*."[61]

I smiled in reply and stuffed some bread in my mouth before I could be called on again to speak.

"Yeah, prajna paramita," said Steve laconically. "Let's all memorize the Perfection of Wisdom."

Alan's gaze fixed on him inscrutably. "Well Jampa Thubkay," he used Steve's Tibetan name, "Can you think of something more important?"

"Well, developing wisdom for one. That's more useful than memorizing stuff, isn't it?"

Alan gazed at him for a moment. "Quite. Point well taken."

Steve grunted disinterestedly. Alan cleared his plate and slipped away to his room.

"Jampa Thubkay?" The incredulous voice belonged to an English monk in his twenties. This was Lawrence, strangely young for his years. "Don't you think we should memorize texts? Geshe said we should, you know."

"Don't get me wrong," Steve said. "I think it's great that Geshe's got all the textbooks memorized. If it were as easy for me as it was for him I'd have done the same thing long ago. But you've got to keep it in perspective, haven't you? I'm not going to do it to the exclusion of studying and meditating. I mean, that's the actual *point*, isn't it? It's why we're *here*."

Lawrence laughed a little hysterically. "Okay, okay. Just asking." He looked around the room helplessly, as if expecting some moral support.

Eckart, a German monk who'd joined us at about the same time as Lawrence, squinted antagonistically.

Lawrence continued, "Look, I was only asking, wasn't I? I mean, we're s'posed to do what Geshe says, aren't we? What about you Thubten Sangye?" he turned towards me. "You think Geshe knows what he's doing, don't you? Of course he does—doesn't he?"

I shook my head, nonplussed. Lawrence was scatterbrained, some said unhinged.

"Shut up now, Lawrence," said Eckart threateningly.

Helmut now stood up with deliberation. All heads turned to the tall, awkward Austrian. "Well," he announced," I'm going to go to my room to memorize *some* texts and meditate on *others*." He laughed alone and carried his dishes to the kitchen sink. I stared. How were we to take this newcomer who, with every sign of humility, presumed to conciliate us?

Since spoken and written Tibetan are so different, we studied them in separate classes. Alan taught Colloquial Tibetan while Steve led the scriptural form.

Learning the spoken language requires an understanding of Tibetan social hierarchy. It includes formal and informal distinctions similar to those in Romance languages, like the familiar *tu* and formal *vous* in French;[62] but it goes much further, shifting whole lists of nouns, verbs and adjectives into higher or lower gear depending on whether you're addressing a superior, a peer or a subordinate. The formal language is obligatory when addressing lamas and teachers, but there's a more rarefied court language too, a super-honorific reserved for the 'highest' lamas. We muddled along as best we could and most Tibetans tolerated our lack of finesse. We were, after all, Injis[63] and not too much was expected of us, for the time being.

Another peculiarity of the spoken language is its forms of greeting. There's no real equivalent of "hello," or "how d'you do?" Instead, when Tibetans bump into each other they ask, "Where are you going?"

"That's a bit nosey, isn't it?" I reacted.

Alan laughed. "Tibetans have their own ways of being discrete."

"But it's like that in India too, isn't it?" I said. "Privacy's hard to find."

"It's an Anglo-Saxon thing," laughed Claudio. "You guys are so uptight."

Alan gave him a withering look.

"You see?" Claudio's grin just grew wider.

I couldn't help smiling.

Arnie worked with Alan to put together a rudimentary phrase book, for we had no textbooks or learning programs to turn to. This provided vocabulary and grammar, but we had few native speakers to practice on and conversational fluency didn't come naturally. Geshe suggested we speak Tibetan amongst ourselves instead of our own languages, and for a while Alan tried to initiate Tibetan conversations at mealtimes, but it never really took off; we simply lacked the skills to express our overflowing minds.

Steve's reading classes were another matter altogether. From the very beginning we plunged into philosophical texts from the very heart of Buddhist theory. The slow going was perfectly suited to the subject matter, and small efforts were quickly rewarded. Some texts—especially those meant to be memorized—are arranged in cryptic verse that chop and combine words to fit the meter. To understand some of the most brutally compressed abbreviations, Steve went to Geshe and passed on his inter- pretations to us, so these classes were about more than just language.

The first difficulty was the sheer foreignness of its sounds. Tibetan grammar, structure and etymology are pretty simple. Until the eighth century Tibet was a disunited borderland, rife with bandits and having little in the way of cultural baggage. Early translators had a free hand to give the written language its present form, just as modern English was shaped by medieval translators of the bible. The difference was that in the intervening centuries Tibetan didn't have to stretch, adapt and twist itself to accommodate an unending progression of world views and scientific disciplines. Apart from the problem of translating terms without exact equivalents, putting clear old Tibetan into modern English often adds a spectrum of meanings that simply doesn't exist in the original.

ARNIE IN THE OFFICE: *helped put together this rudimentary phrase book*

Steve took a democratic approach to translation, inviting everyone's opinion. Each term prompted a list of English candidates, many of them open to broad interpretation. He turned us into miners of the English language and I realized that to become a good translator I'd have to broaden my reading, a prospect that by this time was more appealing than I'd expected. I understood now how absurd it was to even think of rejecting the cultural roots of my Western thinking and self-awareness.

Sundays were a day off, sort of. There were no language or philosophy classes, but Geshe delivered a public teaching in the temple in the afternoon, and the dozens of visitors from Geneva, Milan, Paris, Hamburg and Munich gave the day a holiday feel. The temple mats and table-boxes were tightly piled into a corner to make space. Many arrived early, either to sit quietly in the temple or to socialize with the monks, drinking tea in the refectory or sunning themselves on the graveled terrace, all eager for some interesting conversation. Some of the monks showed up purely out of duty, others to enjoy some refreshing company.

Alan was generally busy upstairs, translating for Geshe's visitors. Steve's dry humor drew the intellectual types, mostly men. Brian was in his element, usually surrounded by laughter and at least as many women as men. Arnie was often found in subdued conference with board members of the Geneva group; he'd recently become Tharpa Chöeling's secretary.

I enjoyed the company of outsiders, though I was unsure whether I was really liked. I measured myself against Alan's brilliance, Steve's probity, Brian's warmth and Arnie's modesty, and always came out wanting. Our visitors' feelings were hard to gauge, for lay people generally deferred to those in robes. I hoped in time that my practice would make me worthy of genuine respect. In the meantime, I was as dignified as my insecurities allowed. We were the recipients of these people's hopes and projections— not to mention money—and it would have been ungracious to burst their bubbles. This left me feeling somewhat fraudulent.

The temple was always packed by the time Geshe entered. He settled onto the throne and everyone went down on their hands and knees— staid businessmen, scientific professionals, monks, Swiss matrons and hippy cowherds alike. The silence settled. Geshe sat shyly but spoke with confidence from the very first word. "All beings," he began, "seek happiness, and wish to avoid suffering."

I sat on one side, watching expressions of hushed awe, concentration and delight pass over the faces. Ripples of laughter followed Geshe's slightest hint of humor.

Geshe spoke about the futility of attachment, describing the human body as a "putrid, dirt-filled machine."[64] He quoted from the *Bodhicary-avatara*, a contemplation designed for monks to overcome sensual desire:

> *I have no wish for a small dirty maggot*
> *Which has come from a pile of filth,*
> *So why do I desire this body, which by nature is grossly unclean,*
> *For it too was produced by filth?*

> *Not only do I not disparage*
> *The uncleanliness of my own body,*
> *But because of an obsession with what is unclean*
> *I desire other bags of filth as well.*[65]

A man put up his hand, said he was a doctor and commented that the human was body something of great beauty—a miraculous machine. A couple of younger monks sniggered at the man's ignorance and Geshe patiently explained that he was quite mistaken. The doctor persisted, describing at length the fine balance of a healthy organism. The translator faltered. Geshe frowned and asked whether peeling the skin off a lover's body wouldn't change one's feelings from lust to disgust. The doctor commented that his concern was with objective, not subjective, truths and restated that the body's inner workings were subtle beyond human imagination. Politely, Geshe disagreed and moved on.

Afterwards, I was approached by Diane and Juliet Brooke, English twins who worked in Geneva.

"What did you think of that doctor, then?" Diane asked breathlessly.

"Think of him? Well, scientists study the workings of nature. I'm sure it's often awe inspiring."

"But you don't agree with him, do you?" asked her sister.

"Why not? Because Geshe has a different point of view?"

"You mean they're both right?"

"It's got nothing to do with right and wrong," I said. "They're talking at cross purposes, aren't they?"

They looked at one other and burst into giggles.

I slipped away.

Back in my room, I closed the door and breathed a sigh of relief. After having traveled so far and given up so much, it wasn't easy to admit that their schoolgirl giggles could so easily deflate me.

I sat in meditation posture and closed my eyes, but without even noticing myself get up I soon found myself pacing the room. The hum of conversation called to me, and yet I was afraid of it. I'd joined a monastery to get away from society—no, that wasn't quite true. I'd joined to escape my desire to be social. I didn't trust people. No, that wasn't it either. I didn't trust myself with people. Aha!

To go down again was to court disappointment once more, to risk my fragile self-esteem. But I was a Buddhist monk and this was part of the job. While I was preoccupied by this rational chatter, it was the combined desire for the company of others and aversion to my own that propelled me out the door and back downstairs to the crowd. There I sipped tea, smiled and spoke animatedly about the wisdom of Tibet, all the better to drown out the endless rubbish in my head. I was still confused by my own feelings and it would be a while before I realized that like all other human beings, I was guided more by emotions than by ideas.

Tharpa Chöeling was developing a reputation within the Western dharma community for elitism. The reason was simple—to study with us you had to learn Tibetan. Only the Sunday public teachings and occasional general courses were fully translated. The core debate classes were sometimes aided by Alan or Steve, but even in translation every phrase was peppered with Tibetan terminology.

The charge originated from the ranks of Lama Yeshe's students rather than from any authoritative source, but it wasn't just squabbling; the relative roles of study and meditation were a familiar bone of contention. If Awakening was *an end to views*—the nonconceptual experience of reality—then intellectual study was downright oblique. Only meditative practice could arrest the discursive mind. Lama Yeshe certainly encouraged a lot of meditation, but he also gave many discourses—powerful, effective, attitude-changing thoughts and ideas.

Geshe's priorities were unambiguous. Again and again he repeated, "Study first, meditation later." To him the path to Awakening should be traced like a map. Without it, you don't know where you're going.

My affection for Lama Yeshe was unlikely to change because of the judgmental attitude of some of his disciples. Besides, it had been Lama's suggestion that I seek out Geshe in the first place. At the same time I was finding myself more at ease with Geshe Rabten. In spite of his reputation as a scholar, and his severe opinions, he was warmhearted, especially when Brian was around. No one else was more relaxed with Geshe, or so able to bring out the simple Khampa[66] in him.

Lama Yeshe and Geshe Rabten were both alumni of Sera-Jey college, a student and teacher who praised one other on every occasion; not just politely but effusively. Western followers, however, were sometimes less diplomatic, unable to believe in their own path unless someone else's was wrong. Nothing was said against Geshe himself, that would have provoked outrage, but charges were leveled against his students. For a start, we were wasting our time learning Tibetan; after all, we could study with Lama without having to divert so much energy from the actual practice of the path to Awakening. And then there was all that effete, self-aggrandizing debate. We spent too much time on sterile intellectualization.

Those who thought it necessary rushed to defend Geshe Rabten's traditional methods and pointed out that Lama handed out bits of tantric practice without the mandatory initiation, spoke appalling, hippy English and took inexcusable liberties in his translation of key dharma terms. He tinkered with venerable, age-old traditions. He elaborated the intricacies of mental attachment using toilet rolls as props and expounded on the twelve links of interdependent origination using metaphors of supermarkets and chocolate cake. He skipped over the long-winded Sanskrit terminology. He insisted that ultimate truth was "simple." In the halls of Tibetan spiritual power, it was said, heads were shaking.

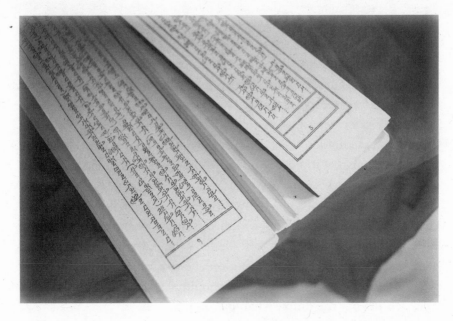

A TIBETAN BOOK: wasting our time learning Tibetan?

Something all Tibetan teachers had to deal with sooner or later was the urge of Westerners to seek instant gratification. We expected measurable meditative progress and quick results. Lama Yeshe and Geshe Rabten each approached this obstacle in their own way, and each attracted a different type of student. Lama used this desire as a hook to engage people, and whether their tantric bliss was imaginary or not, got them to sit down and face themselves. Geshe confronted our expectations head-on. He told us to slow down and explained repeatedly that the point of studying was to understand what we were meditating upon. *Slowly* was one of the few English words he knew; he used it all the time.

I loved studying with Geshe Rabten's students. I was inspired, if a little awed, by Alan's prowess and intellectual clarity. On the other hand, I wouldn't have traded my troubling conversations with Steve for all the tea in China; his implacable questioning was the very essence of Buddhism. Without even realizing that he was doing it, Brian constantly reminded me that emotional realities stood in sharp contrast to the convenient, compulsive rationales with which we defend ourselves. And of course, I never forgot Lama Yeshe. Like no other Tibetan teacher I ever met, he displayed an intense interest in his audience, and his teaching was an act of personal creativity. If I were to become the teacher I wanted to be, he'd be my model. Like him I'd use colloquial language and get to the point without pretense. Had he been more available, I would happily have stayed at his side, but he was surrounded by thousands of followers, and I'd never have the one-on-one access and personal attention I enjoyed with Geshe Rabten. Lama was constantly on the move from one country to another, and one dharma center after another sprouted in his footsteps.

It was through Lama's inspiration that I thought it possible to climb over the centuries of commentary and get to the Buddha himself. That meant identifying and separating the "Tibetan" from the "Buddhism," and what better place to start than with the whole traditional package?

Geshe Rabten had risen from impoverished ignominy to become one of the foremost debaters of his time, and his only wish was to give us the same opportunity. His teaching, his explanations and above all his person exuded the reliability his name implied.[67] After each class we aired our points of view, interpreting and juxtaposing the traditional teachings with Western ideas, exploring doubts and objections. His was a very different influence from Lama Yeshe's, but in no way contradictory. However, he never learned English.

Nothing would have made us happier than to include Geshe in these conversations, but all attempts to express them in Tibetan usually made him either laugh or frown. Steve was the first to suggest bluntly that there was no point in trying. What could bridge the precision of Tibetan terminology to the ambiguity of Western philosophy? Perhaps it was just a matter of semantics. What, I demanded, was an example of an important issue that wasn't adequately addressed in Tibetan Buddhism.

Steve didn't hesitate. "Guilt."

I was stumped. We were studying Buddhist "psychology" at the time, the fifty-one states of mind,[68] none of which could by any stretch of the imagination be translated as guilt—that gnawing, self-destructive undermining of one's own freedom to act. Nobody claimed the list was exhaustive, but this was a glaring omission.

"Perhaps," I said, "it's not an issue for Tibetans."

"Even if that were true, which I doubt, it's an issue for us."

I felt something like the tearing of cloth within me. So Buddhism wouldn't answer my every question. It couldn't even pose them all. I'd already seen that we should dig into our own culture for a vernacular to express the purpose of Buddhism. Now I realized that we'd have to explain our own truths, even if they were irrelevant to the Tibetans. We were climbing the distant mountain of Tibetan language only to gaze back, fascinated, at our own valley. It was surprisingly compelling.

26

THE JOURNEY WITHIN

NATURALLY ENOUGH, our hardworking patrons looked upon the lifestyle and freedom we had with some envy, but being a Tharpa Chöeling monk wasn't as easy as they, or even I, had assumed. To the casual observer my life probably looked restrained and focused. I went to the temple with the others, or meditated alone. I studied hard and participated actively in colloquial and scriptural classes. I read complex books and listened only to serious music. I walked on Mont-Pèlerin by myself or in deep discussion with others, my hands determinedly behind my back. My focus was the monk's lifestyle and my dream was Awakening, a state of mind described by the textbooks as "perfect" and "omniscient." That would be an added bonus; all I wanted was a quiet mind; mine was fragmented and willful.

At the same time, this newfound respectability was distracting me. I knew it was due to the robes I wore and not to any inner change, but my head swelled with self-importance. Visitors and younger monks saw in me imaginary qualities I didn't deny. Balanced precariously between life-long feelings of inadequacy and a newfound self-esteem, I didn't know how to walk away from this seesaw. I might have benefited from an old

Catholic confessional, but lacked the courage to share my mortal weaknesses with anyone, even Brian, whom I trusted more than anyone.

In search of guidance I turned to the *Bodhicaryavatara*,[69] the text over
which Geshe and the doctor had disagreed that Sunday afternoon. As
legend has it, its author, Shantideva, was despised by his fellow monks at
Nalanda University[70] for just "hanging around eating, sleeping and shit-
ting." His colleagues invited him to address the general assembly, fully
expecting he'd make a fool of himself. When the big day came, however,
he astonished his colleagues by describing the entire path to Awakening
in eloquent verse and, in a magnificent coup de grâce, expounding the
nature of ultimate reality whilst floating up and fading into thin air.

I found these verses, and hoped they'd help me put my problem in
perspective. Like Shantideva himself, the book doesn't pull any punches.

> *Stupid, ugly, feeble and everywhere disrespected.*
> *Tough people bloated by conceit*
> *Are also counted among the self-important;*
> *Tell me, what is more pathetic than this?*

> *Whoever seizes self-confidence in order to conquer the enemy of*
> *self-importance,*
> *He is the self-confident one, the victorious hero,*
> *And in addition, whoever definitely conquers the spread of this enemy,*
> *self-importance,*
> *Completely (wins) the fruit of a Conqueror, fulfilling the wishes of the*
> *world.*[71]

I went off to meditate with the assurance of one who'd found the answer,
pondering the difference between self-*importance* and self-*confidence*.

Distinguishing concepts from one another requires just a few words,
but separating these two variants of self-worth in the wavering reality of
your own psyche is another matter. Two years of meditation had brought
me a modicum of self-control, but it had also forced me into a corner. I
had to accept that my mind wasn't just a pile of ideas in need of organization but a torrent of intertwining currents that could, and usually did,

SHANTIDEVA: expounded the nature of ultimate reality, floated up and faded into thin air

sweep away my best intentions in a heartbeat. Clearly identifying even one mental event was hard enough, transforming its nature seemed beyond my powers. I had one of those realizations in which something absolutely obvious is invested with startling new clarity—what I wanted to do with my mind and what it actually did were simply two different things. Meditation wasn't putting me in charge, and I wasn't sure it could. Progress in meditation is almost a contradiction in terms. It's not about seizing the reins but letting go.

I'd been trying to control every moment of my life as if I knew exactly what was worthwhile and what wasn't. The result had been neurosis, lüng and failure. Even if some sort of self-control really was possible, it would have to be oblique. I'd always been drawn to the Zen practice of meditation through activity. I took up calligraphy and discovered that the simple act of guiding a flat nib into the angular shapes of the Tibetan alphabet could be just as meditative as sitting in the full lotus[72] position.

For hours at a time I kept my head bent over my desk and turned out handwritten books at a steady rate, trying to remain focused and mindful. A part of me still vaguely believed that you had to be cross-legged to meditate properly, but at the end of the day I actually felt better. Bit by bit I accepted that it didn't matter how I sat; it's the mind that counts. And even there, it's not about acquiring knowledge but dropping preconceptions. My transcriptions were nothing to be proud of—they were riddled with spelling mistakes, but the exercise was therapeutic.

I also prepared Geshe's food. I'd always liked cooking because I enjoyed eating, but now I learned that slowing down to watch the movements of my fingers, wrist and mind turned chopping onions and slicing peppers into a meditation. Wanting to serve Geshe the best, I paid extra attention to detail by, for example, stirring his yogurt from a gelatinous curd into a smooth cream.

I'd been doing this for months when one day he picked up the tub, looked into it pensively and asked, "How come you take the lid off?"

"To stir it," I said proudly. He'd noticed!

"Maybe you could leave it on in future."

"But stirring makes it creamy," I protested.

"That's right."

"You mean . . . ?"

"I don't really like it creamy." He looked sheepish.

"Oh."

"But thanks anyway."

It was strangely difficult to accept that he actually preferred something I considered inferior, but of course my opinion was arbitrary. In fact—I took a deep breath—it was unimportant. I'd put so much brow-furrowing effort into battling ego-clinging and generating universal love that I hadn't even noticed the rigidity of my everyday thoughts. It's innocuous enough to prefer one thing over another, but to *believe* in your preference adds a burden that we end up carting around. It's onerous, it's preposterous, and it's the foundation of a million disappointments.

While this little truth was sinking in, I was also training Eckart as an alternate cook. He paid careful attention to my instructions and, like me, wanted only the best for Geshe. But now I was confused. What if Geshe actually disliked the way I made his noodles or cooked his vegetables? Did he dislike me substituting basil for cilantro in his meat dumplings? What if I was teaching Eckart the wrong way?

Fortunately, Eckart developed his own style. Besides, Geshe wasn't really much of a critic. As a penniless young monk he'd foregone the ritual ceremonies, where itinerant monks could earn some free food and drink, to spend all his spare time in the debating courtyard. He just happened to prefer his yogurt unstirred.

I sometimes cooked for the community too, especially on holidays. My speciality was a giant chocolate cake filled with Gruyère cream and encased in melted Swiss chocolate. Such luxury reminded me that meditation didn't have to be the antithesis of material life. It had finally dawned on me that my path wasn't going to be handed to me on a platter just because I'd joined a twenty-five-hundred-year-old tradition. I had to figure things out for myself.

The new monks had come from England, France, Italy, Austria and Germany. Only a few now attempted to learn Tibetan, but Geshe accepted anyone with a sponsor or the means to support themselves. I'd hastily assumed that his willingness to ordain me was a personal vote of confidence but, in time, I came to see the mundane truth—he'd just been doing his job, building a group of monks.

Nevertheless, Tharpa Chöeling, although a very pleasant place to live, was a far cry from the intense and intimate learning environment of Schwendi. Of the original group, Claudio, Piero and Massimo had left for Lama Yeshe's institute in Italy, never to return, and Arnie was entirely preoccupied by his administrative duties. Alan and Steve, overwhelmed by demands on their time, became increasingly reclusive. Apart from the scatterbrained Lawrence, we were joined by a cripplingly shy middle-aged German, a terminal, desperately hopeful cancer victim and a host of starry-eyed youngsters.

However, they weren't all like that. Helmut proved perfectly capable of learning Tibetan and did so in record time. In the weeks following his arrival I hardly saw my new neighbor. He spent hours in his room and through our common wall I often heard the murmur of rote memorization. Within weeks, he was speaking to Geshe without a translator, and when I asked how he did it he said, "Oh, I'm rather stupid really," concluding with an explosive laugh, "I just memorized Chandra Das."

The Tibetan-English Dictionary by Sarat Chandra Das was a thick black tome. As ludicrous as his claim was, I believed it. His accent was unformed, his enunciation wooden and staccato, but he'd built up a considerable vocabulary. In no time he was speaking better than I.

Helmut's sheer mental horsepower led to talk of an innate bond between him and Alan, but it was soon apparent that Helmut didn't share Alan's intellectual curiosity. In fact, he exhibited no particular drive towards either study or meditation. His only apparent desire was to serve Geshe, and he placed his entire stock of time, energy and money at his guru's disposal. One day, he turned up with a beautifully polished maroon Volvo, his gift to Geshe, and we soon heard of a new retreat center in the Austrian Alps, also donated by Helmut.

Helmut's behavior towards the rest of us was impeccable. He was unfailingly self-deprecating, always deferred to older monks and shared his possessions unselfishly. He also had long, confidential discussions with Geshe.

Some of us felt left out. I didn't know what to do with my jealousy; I just knew it was a nasty emotion. I broached the subject with Brian as we rambled through the pastures above Tharpa Chöeling. Brian had translated some of Helmut's early meetings with Geshe and described him as an exemplary disciple who followed Geshe's instructions to the letter.

"But Geshe treats him differently from the rest of us, doesn't he?" I probed.

"Oh, I don't know about that," said Brian, looking uncomfortable.

With no training in administration, Geshe had been called out of solitary retreat by the Dalai Lama to help build Buddhism in the West. Unlike the funds provided to him by the Geneva Group, Helmut's contribution was not managed by a committee and presumably came without strings. No one else in Geshe's circle could be counted as both a benefactor and a close disciple.

Nevertheless, none of us was more familiar with Geshe than Brian. He was his personal servant, getting him up in the morning, preparing

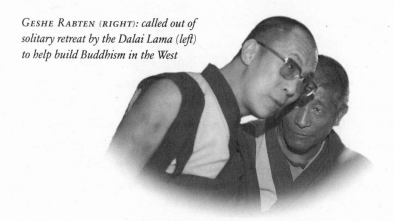

GESHE RABTEN (RIGHT): called out of solitary retreat by the Dalai Lama (left) to help build Buddhism in the West

his bed at night and accompanying him on walks. He knew how to joke around and get a belly laugh from Geshe without ever crossing the line. I suspected that Brian was as confounded by Helmut as I was.

It had taken me years to relax with Geshe but Helmut had walked straight into an intense relationship. He'd grown up without a father, and my own had been an indecipherable paradox. Were we seeking the same thing? Never mind Helmut. What, I wondered, did *I* want from Geshe?

Given the lifestyle, philosophy and culture that I'd chosen, the obvious answer was, "a guru." I'd struggled with the notion of guru devotion[73] since I'd first heard dharma practitioners speak of their lamas with awe as "fully enlightened beings." It never seemed very Buddhist to me to presume that one knew the mind of another, but I was just happy to be accepted, and followed their lead. It soon devolved into simple etiquette—the virtually autonomic habit of putting one's fingertips together when naming a lama, just as I'd once learned to nod my head whenever saying the name "Jesus." The need to respect one's teachers was mentioned frequently, but I never received clear instruction on relating to a teacher, or even imagined that it might need to be spelled out. Only years later did I understand the many shades of respect and the various relationships one might form with various teachers, preceptors and tantric masters. At the upper end of the spectrum, which is where in our eagerness we all wanted to be, one looks upon one's initiating lama as a living buddha, omniscient and knowing at all times what's best. In the wrong hands, of course, this is a shortcut to tragic misunderstanding or outright abuse, and accounts for the dire warnings in tantric texts about those who are not suitable vessels, referring to both gurus and disciples.

Geshe had wisely preempted the issue by refusing to give highest tantric initiations, but I never decided to what extent I could or should question his judgment. Now, my envy had me emotionally charged. I subliminally imagined that Helmut had won something that might have been mine. My actual relationship with Geshe had always been confused with inchoate longings for a guide, a father and a savior. Now they were coming to a head.

27

ADJUSTMENTS

GESHE'S RENOWN WAXED FAR AND WIDE, but he was no longer able to accept every teaching invitation he received. He usually traveled with Alan, Steve or Brian, who might also be sent out to teach whilst Geshe was busy elsewhere. Bruno and Elio were in growing demand as French and Italian translators, not just for Geshe Rabten but also for other Tibetan teachers touring the European dharma network. What were once brief interruptions to our studies were growing into periods of desertion, when half or more of the residents took leave.

Geshe had been postponing a teaching tour of America for several years, but could do so no longer. Alan and Brian were to accompany him. A friend of Geshe's, Geshe Ngawang Nyima, would move in while he was away, but otherwise Tharpa Chöeling would have a skeleton crew for the summer. Those of us who remained felt distinctly unsettled.

Before he left, Geshe made a long-awaited announcement—a permanent assistant for Geshe had been found and would be joining us as soon as the paperwork was complete. That would take several months. He was the very highly ranked ex-abbot of Ganden[74] monastery, Geshe Gendün Zangpo. I asked Geshe what he was like.

"He's my friend," Geshe said.

The thought flashed though my mind, *Was he being circumspect?*

Young Aldino, a wide-eyed Italian monk, spoke up. "He is a fully enlightened being, no?"

Geshe furrowed his brow and replied sternly. "He's a great lama of course. He was abbot of Jangtse college, one of the most important colleges of the Gelug tradition. I want you to listen to him as you would to me."

The good news provoked sighs of relief. We'd just have to get through the summer and then Tharpa Chöeling would finally be stabilized.

In the meantime, Mum and Dad were coming. Now I'd show them I wasn't a numbskull. Philip had been down for a week in the spring and confirmed that I wasn't in a cult. Then our family doctor Tom Durkin and his wife had dropped in for a public teaching. Tom was the one who'd recommended the child psychologist when I was a boy, and from him I now learned for the first time of Dad's reaction to being told how to raise his own son. In any case, their glowing report, combined with Philip's, gave my parents confidence, and they turned up with unexpectedly open minds.

Dad was a changed man, *threadbare* was the word that came to mind. Thin and preoccupied, his sadness and silence had deepened. Mum put on a brave face. He smiled wanly. They avoided my questions about his health. My cropped hair and funny clothes didn't seem to bother them. Geshe Ngawang Nyima met them in the common area, seated at the table like everyone else, not cross-legged and regal in usual Tibetan fashion. I translated as best I could. Mum was impressed by the incomprehensible sounds pouring from my mouth and amazed when the Mongolian teacher responded. Even Dad agreed I'd found my feet.

They seemed proud of my cleverness but uninterested in what I was doing with it. I wanted them to understand there was more to a spiritual path than feeling secure, but their protective walls were securely fastened. As we took pleasure trips around Lac Leman and chatted inconsequentially, I saw them face-to-face with mortality. Ideas, beliefs and differences melted and we accepted each other without question. The highlight of

our tourist week together was a cog-wheel train up the slopes of Les Pléiades where we ate a tourist lunch, stared out at Les Dents-du-Midi and lay down in the *alpage* under the late summer sun.

I was eager to resume my studies, but bid them goodbye in the shadow of Dad's frailty, saddened by the ravages of time.

Geshe Zangpo finally arrived, round-headed, soft-spoken and sweet-natured. We anticipated a new era in which constant interruptions and fractured community life would be a thing of the past, and crowded into the temple for his first class.

I could hardly make out the new geshe's broad Amdo accent. Alan was translating, and even he kept turning back to the teacher for clarification. When Steve began frowning, I listened more carefully, and noticed that he was reciting long chunks of memorized texts, apparently without explanation. When Alan pressed for more detail he responded with a sheepish look. Now even the younger monks were sitting up.

"Well," said Steve as Alan led Geshe away. "That was a dead loss."

My mind raced for explanations. I reminded myself that Geshe Rabten was, after all, the main teacher. Perhaps Geshe Zangpo had been foisted on us by the Tibetan authorities. Geshe Rabten mustn't have known that he wasn't much of a scholar, must he? But then, how could he have vouched for him in such glowing terms?

By contrast, the Sunday afternoon crowd welcomed the new geshe in no uncertain terms, and he charmed them immediately. There were questions from some more discerning listeners but for most, his warmth and presence more than made up for his pedantry. Besides, general teachings posed no obstacle, and he was a master of ritual.

I presumed the others would share my disappointment. Brian went out of his way to be diplomatic. Steve didn't, but neither was he weighed down by it. Alan's thoughts were anyone's guess. Helmut showed no particular interest in Geshe Zangpo and was as well disposed towards him as to anyone else, except Geshe Rabten, for whom he reserved special devotion.[75]

I probed Eckart as we left the temple one afternoon.

"I don't know," he said. "Maybe Geshe's manifesting skilful means."[76]

"What?" I expostulated. "You can't explain away everything as skilful means."

"Why not? What d'you mean?"

"Well, maybe sometimes Geshe makes a mistake?"

He turned away as if I'd struck him. "I don't think that," he said. "I choose not to think that."

"Why on earth not?" I called after him. But he was gone.

With one eye on the passing shadows of doubt in the faces of my fellow dharma practitioners, I watched them maintaining their beliefs at all costs, and recognized that I'd been doing the same for years. Was this what it meant to take refuge in buddha, dharma, sangha?[77] I didn't think so. There's a difference between faith and dogma, between suspending disbelief and hanging on for dear life to a belief system. I was willing to believe that the Buddha taught something that couldn't be immediately grasped, but he himself urged his followers to keep an open mind and to judge all practices by their consequences, not by consensus, not by the teacher's status—not even by mere reason.[78] If all I'd wanted was a sense of security, I could have remained Catholic.

I began to separate the subjects on which I had to take Geshe's word from those I could judge for myself. It was refreshingly straightforward. On the other hand, I was disturbed that some of my companions saw only what they wanted to see, and felt myself crawling out on a limb—

away from the community. I was also angry about having blinkered myself. Denial's a useful crutch in an emergency but a dangerous way to cope with inconvenient doubts.

Of course, this is all retrospection. At the time, my motives were muddled and my irritation, as usual, sprayed in all directions. One day, with guilt and angst, it all came tumbling out. "How come," I asked Geshe Rabten, "Geshe Zangpo is just reciting textbooks and doesn't explain them?" I expected a cataclysmic change in our relationship, but Geshe just scratched his head and said he'd think about it. He subsequently simplified his assistant's responsibilities, presumably because others raised questions too, though presumably with more diplomacy.

It got me thinking. Many of us had come to the Tibetans young and disillusioned by the hubris of our own culture. Our hosts were colorful, passionate and masterful promoters of their own, so it wasn't surprising that we'd grown starry-eyed. As we grew familiar with them, especially those of us who learned the language, I felt it important to see them less as repositories for our fantasies and more as human beings.

Some, however, just couldn't give up the thought that they were associated with otherworldly beings. They embraced the dharma like a security blanket and spoke of The Path as if it were etched in stone. I felt no such certainty, and these people triggered my distrust now more than ever. To me, the way to Awakening was shrouded and shifting, clear only in fleeting glimpses.

Becoming gradually less intimidated by my disappointments, I began to air them freely. Some older monks grew wary of me, some younger ones fearful. My relationships with Steve and Brian remained firm, counterbalancing what would otherwise have been increasing isolation.

Steve welcomed my doubts without a second thought; he'd never shied away from his own and remained studiously undogmatic, although his drive was detached and cerebral when compared to my existential angst. He'd translated several Tibetan classics, and now decided to write his own books. They were dryly intelligent, and shone a light on things taken too often for granted. If not one already, he was becoming an iconoclast.

Brian listened sympathetically to my issues, but they weren't issues for him. His path was quite simply the personal relationships he'd forged with Geshe and the other lamas he'd known in Dharamsala, something far too tangible to be swayed by my doubts and bad humor.

What we shared, however, was a dimming of our vision for Tharpa Chöeling. Geshe's fame was growing and he was in too much demand to teach us regularly. The assistant geshe, brought in expressly to compensate for the teaching shortfall, wasn't up to the job, and no replacement was in the books. Both Steve's and Brian's responsibilities had grown, to neither one's great satisfaction. When the Tibetische Zentrum in Hamburg got its own geshe, Steve was called upon frequently to translate, and would eventually be named their resident interpreter. The workload was light and left him free to pursue his explorations in writing.[79]

Meanwhile, Brian began to express his homesickness, and started to prepare Geshe for his eventual return to America.

Our third summer on Mont-Pèlerin had been deadly quiet, and it didn't look like things would be getting any livelier. I was even sought out by younger monks and lay people as the senior resident teacher-translator. I did my best, but wondered how long it would be before they realized that I simply wasn't ready.

Seizing upon the practical fact that fluency in Tibetan would require practice, and considering that good teachings were less available than ever at Tharpa Chöeling, I decided to return to India.

I planned my announcement carefully. One evening I knocked on Geshe's door, nudged it open and leaned inside. He was at his prayers and held a page in midair as he glanced up at me, not looking very amenable to interruption.

"Something important?" He sighed. I knew that frequent traveling was hard on him, and thought he must miss his ramshackle retreat hut on the slopes above Dharamsala.

I nodded.

He dropped the page, pulled a corner of the book cover over the pages and leaned back. I closed the door behind me and sat on the carpet at an angle from him. His reading table lay between us.

"I'm not happy with my Tibetan," I began.

I waited for him to remind me of my progress, of the fact that this interview was being conducted without a translator, but he just stared.

Groping for words I mumbled out my desire to return to India and my reasons. His brow furrowed. I finally came out with the words, "so it'd be good to go to India," and fell silent.

When he'd judged the silence sufficiently long, Geshe sat up and said, "Your Tibetan's doing fine. I don't think you need to go. In fact, if you want to know my opinion, I'd prefer you didn't go. However, it's your decision, not mine. If you really want to go, go."

My face lit up. "Thank you," I said.

He frowned at me. "Thanks for what? I just said I didn't want you to go."

"Oh," I replied.

"But I won't stand in your way. You decide."

"Oh. Okay."

He nodded towards the door. I stood up.

"You think about it," he commanded. "I'll think about it too." He kept his eye on me until I reached the door.

Next morning after breakfast Alan summoned me from my room and we walked together to Geshe's room.

"Geshe asked me to translate so there'd be no misunderstanding."

I nodded.

The door was already open.

"Are you quite sure you want to go to India?" Geshe began.

"Yes," I nodded firmly.

"And the purpose is to improve your Tibetan?"

"Yes, exactly."

"Then," translated Alan, "Geshe doesn't think it would be a good idea for you to be wandering around India aimlessly. He can arrange for you to stay at Sera."

"Geshe's monastery?" It had been reestablished in exile in South India, far from Dharamsala.

"Yes. You can stay in his house and teach English to the boys."

To a certain extent I'd still be under Geshe's watchful eye, but I'd also feel less guilty about ignoring his wishes. I'd also learn Tibetan, for sure.

"Are there any Westerners there?" I smiled.

"Not to my knowledge," Geshe said, unsmiling.

"Then it would be perfect." I didn't feel exactly excited about it, but his suggestion was more than reasonable.

He underlined his statement: "Like I said, I'd prefer that you stay here. You have all you need to study, learn and progress in your studies and your dharma practice."

I squirmed.

"Do you understand?"

"Yes," I said. "But my Tibetan really isn't getting any better here."

As Alan translated Geshe waved his hand dismissively. "I'll write to the abbot, Geshe Legden. He's my friend."

"Thank you."

He waved me out with the back of his hand. I'd been looking forward to meeting people I'd heard so much about in Dharamsala. On the other hand, if I went there I'd end up speaking English much more than Tibetan, and Geshe was right—drifting around, even from one Dharma community to another, wouldn't do me much good. A stint at Sera Monastic University would get my Tibetan up to speed in no time, and would help me clarify the Tibetan in Tibetan Buddhism.

It didn't take long for word to get around that I was leaving against Geshe's wishes. Most of the monks understood, but some of the lay people, on quite a different wavelength, were somewhat aghast. I'd be glad to get away from these starry-eyed people and see more closely how the Tibetans put their Buddhism into practice.

28

SERA MONASTIC UNIVERSITY

I WAS WEDGED AGAINST A WALL, trying to stay out of the flow of the madding crowd, looking at the departures list in Bombay Central railway station.[80] A middle-aged Indian man spied me, frowned, peeled off from the criss-cross crowd and made for me like an arrow for its target. What, he demanded to know, did I think I was doing?

I sized him up. He looked agitated, but rational. "Well, I'm checking out the trains to Bangalore."

"I mean," he stared intensely, "What are you doing with your life?"

"I beg your pardon?"

"Look at you," he said. "You're American, European?"

"English," I said.

"You're educated. Your family must be worried about you. You're wasting your life. Get a job. Look at you in that...that *getup. Do* something!"

I stammered, "I am doing something," realizing, and resenting, that he'd put me on the defensive. "I'm studying."

"Go home," he commanded with burning eyes. He turned and was swept into the river of people.

If he'd intended to sow doubts in me, his outburst had the opposite effect. I'd come all this way in search of spiritual refreshment, and
meeting a confirmed materialist just reminded me of the dreary middle-
class life that had left Dad so deflated. Still, I wondered what demons
had prompted this anonymous counselor to warn me against the ancient
values of his country. He was on my mind all day.

It was a two-day train ride to Bangalore, another three hours by bus
to Mysore, then two more to Bylakuppe. Finally, after a timeless, spine-
jarring scooter-rickshaw ride over unseen potholes to the looming silence
of Sera Monastic University, I pulled up in the pitch-black night to the
barking of dogs and shouting of unseen children.

"*Su ré?*" shouted a dozen excited voices. "Who's that?"

I announced my name and that of Thomtok Rinpoche, Geshe's
student. This made no impression and the question was repeated a dozen
more times. I tried another tactic. "I'm Geshe Rabten's student," Within
seconds a light was shone in my face and I at last heard the dignified
voices of adult monks. I was led into a small courtyard where a kerosene
lamp illuminated half-a-dozen anxious, deferential faces.

Dying embers were rekindled. Water was boiled. Soon, scalding hot
bowls of tea appeared along with a pile of sour bread rounds. Thomtok
Rinpoche's servant continued to feed the stove and only with the greatest
difficulty did I convince them that I'd gladly accept their hospitality next
day, but that for the time being I wished they'd sleep, so I could too.

I lay on my cot in Thomtok Rinpoche's room. Near my feet, through
an unglazed, barred window, a monk stood motionless, lean and sallow-
faced, for long, ominous seconds. Suddenly, his mouth gaped with blood-
red fangs and he lunged through the bars for my ankle. I screamed and
awoke in a sweat, looking around with no certainty that I'd woken up.

I was indeed lying in Thomtok Rinpoche's room facing that very
window, but all that lay beyond it was the silent night. I stared into it
until the eerie sound of blown conch shells called the monks to morning
prayer. I'd been in foreign places before, but always on my own. For the
first time, I was connected. Things would be expected of me.

Thomtok was up as I placed my feet on the ground. He told me to
stay in bed.

"It's okay," I said. "I should come."

He handed me a wooden bowl. "Here, you'll need this."

Outside, the shadows and silhouettes of human forms converged on the main temple. The first thing that hit me as I passed through the great doors was the cloying odor of butter, the second was the massed presence of the monks. The glow of hundreds of butter-lamps revealed the faces of those attending the altar, which stretched along the back wall. The monks took up positions in facing rows, those in authority front and center. These were the abbot and ex-abbots, *oomze*, *geshes*, senior administrative monks and tulkus,[81] young and old. They sat on thrones of varying height, each according to its occupant's rank, and wore ceremonial yellow robes with tall, crescent-shaped hats.

Thomtok, clean-shaven and well-dressed, took his place in these upper echelons and left me hovering uncomfortably. A middle-aged monk beckoned me and I sat down gratefully at his side, taking stock of my plebeian neighbors as the chanting began. Although it wasn't the least bit tuneful, the rhythmic rumble was deeply pleasing.

The vast majority, at least two-thirds, were children or teenage boys. All stared in my direction, nudging, giggling and whispering. They wore plain red robes, mostly faded, some threadbare. Each had his own wooden tea bowl. There were three or four hundred. It felt more like a boarding school than a monastery.

Latecomers were still scurrying to their places as a stern-faced, polished-headed prefect patrolled the rows, thumbing the beads of his heavy rosary. With an eagle-eye he stepped into a seated area and flicked it sharply at the back of a boy's chattering head. The victim yelped and clutched his skull as his companions muffled nervous giggles.

Still sleepy, I pulled my upper robe over my shoulder and closed my eyes, but too much was going on around me. They opened again involuntarily, revealing row upon row of boys, jostling and whispering, glancing constantly at the prefect's last-known position. He had a knack of appearing where he wasn't expected.

Would I one day belong here? I wondered, hope against hope. If not among my family, nor even in Switzerland, then why here? Why *not* here? I didn't tell myself this was a long shot, but I knew.

I turned my attention to the facing rows at the head of the assembly. The adults were relaxed in their authority but the eyes of the child-tulkus, drifting more cautiously than the other boys, were less so. Hopelessly conspicuous, they were as impeccably behaved as altar boys.

The chanting continued as a line of aproned monks appeared at the entrance, hauling great kettles. At a signal from the prefect, a dozen boys jumped up, wrapped their upper robes around their middles and carried steaming tea into the ranks, staggering under the sloshing weight, and filling one bowl after another with remarkably little spillage. By the time the last carrier straightened his back you could have heard a pin drop.

The *oomze* began the food blessing, the congregation growled the four stanzas and the final moment of silence was broken by a deafening communal slurp. The tea was salty, buttery and refreshing. The abbot made a few announcements and prayers resumed before the assembly finally arose. Boys ran pell-mell and the monks chatted loudly as they returned to their houses. Within minutes all that remained in the huge hall was the lingering smell of butter and a few attendants at the altar. I emerged feeling dazed and still sleepy. The middle-aged monk who'd made room for me was waiting outside. He asked my name.

"Thubten Sangye," I replied.

"Oho," he remarked. "Gen[82] Rabten didn't give you that name."[83]

"No," I replied. "It was Lama Yeshe,"

"Oh yes," he said thoughtfully. "Thubten Yeshe, right?"

I nodded. "Yes. D'you know him?"

"Of course. He's a Sera Jey monk, isn't he? We're from the same house. He's got lots of Inji[84] students."

I said, "Yes. He speaks English, too."

"Really?" he seemed perplexed. "Thubten Yeshe and I are brothers."

"And you are . . . ?"

"Kayang," he chuckled. "Gen Kayang."

"Geshe Kayang?" I asked.

He laughed with embarrassment, "Geshe, yes well . . . not a very good one. Just call me Gen."

"So you and Lama Yeshe are both students of Geshe Rabten. When you say brothers, you mean dharma brothers?"

He nodded, adding, "He's not really a Lama, you know".

I never quite figured out when and when not to use the title of Lama, it's generally, but not always, applied to a *tulku* once he begins teaching.

He went on, "He was a woman in his last life."

"Yes, I know."

"A woman lama indeed!" He laughed good-naturedly at the oxymoron. "But," he added respectfully, "She must've lived a good life, because she managed to get reborn as a man."

I stared. He didn't blink.

"Anyway," he said, his hand on my shoulder. "You seem like a good lad."

He took my hand warmly. I decided not to hold his archaic views against him.

"See you around," he said, and headed off.

I watched him waddle away, wondering why so many Tibetan monks ended up walking that way.

I returned to find Thomtok Rinpoche, his servant and half a dozen boys rummaging through my suitcase and passing anything of interest from hand to hand. They were unfazed by my entry and didn't even look up when I demanded to know what was going on. I was angry, but not quite sure how to express it, if at all.

Thomtok was disappointed, but not in my behavior. He asked reproachfully, "You don't even have a watch?"

I frowned at the bulky, shining timepiece on his wrist and shook my head superciliously.

Someone picked up my old battery-driven razor and found the switch. It vibrated gently.

The youngest, a boy of six or seven, passed it to me. "Show how it works," he demanded.

I passed it over my stubble. He laughed at the touch of my cheek, part rough and part smooth. The others came over to feel.

Now I pushed past to stuff my things back into the suitcase and close the lid. Thomtok looked rather shocked. I couldn't come up with a Tibetan word for "private," and wondered if there was one.

Thomtok promptly changed the subject, and I sat down.

"Geshe-la is well?" He had a very soft voice.

"He's well," I said. "Traveling a great deal."

"Working for the welfare of sentient beings," he stated.

"We don't see much of him any more."

"You have him more than we do." He gestured to the surrounding houses. "Many of us are his students. We miss him terribly."

"But you have many geshes here, don't you?" I asked.

Thomtok laughed. "Not like Geshe Rabten."

"Really?" I was surprised.

"He became serious. "No . . . no really! Geshe Rabten's not just another *gen*," he referred to the familiar abbreviation for "teacher" with which boys addressed their housemaster. "He's a great meditator. He's patient and kind," he looked away and wiped his eye. "So kind."

I'd never really thought of Geshe's Tibetan disciples as more than a vaguely remembered, distant family, but Thomtok's memories were anything but distant. His display of emotion gave context to Geshe's past and I saw something of their communal pang. I felt sorry for this young man who shared such a sense of longing for his lost country. This was the price, I reflected, of belonging.

My own inability to identify with family, religion and country began to look like an advantage, albeit an uncomfortable one. For a brief respite I thought I'd found my place at Tharpa Chöeling; Now, I was pushing away such feelings again, this time more deliberately than ever. The yearning to belong had led me astray. My path lay in the resolution of my own insecurities, not indulgence in those of a commiserating group. My loyalty should be to my own integrity, without regard for comfort.

Yet here I was, moving into one of the most homogeneous communities on the face of the planet, one whose allegiances had been collectivized to a razor's edge by its exile from Shangri-la.

Taking a deep breath, I resolved to keep my eyes open and mouth shut.

Without warning, the abbot showed up with a small retinue, all of whom proclaimed themselves brothers[85] or students of Geshe Rabten. I had no idea at the time, but it was an unusual honor to be visited by the abbot, as opposed to being summoned to his rooms. We exchanged white scarves and he accepted Thomtok's place while the others arranged themselves in positions of more or less formality.

Just when I thought the meeting was winding down, a procession of serving monks entered, carrying plates of food sculpted into cones and pyramids. The table before me was laid out and everyone leaned forward.

With some discomfort I realized that they intended to watch me eat. I invited them to join in, but they laughed preposterously and stared expectantly. I forced down a little from each dish, eating with what couldn't have been a very convincing smile. When I finally leaned back they didn't hide their disappointment. Only later, when I saw the daily fare, did I appreciate just how sumptuous this meal had been.

My welcomes continued for several days as the powers that be lined up in pecking order to greet the new English teacher. I grew impatient for things to settle down; I just wanted to take up my duties. However, this was less straightforward than I'd anticipated. The building of the schoolhouse was "behind schedule," and all my questions about its progress were greeted by a wall of polite smiles.

Sera Monastery, actually Sera Monastic University, is a uniquely Tibetan institution. Let go of any image of tranquillity and imagine a busy, male village of criss-cross laneways and little redbrick houses bursting with monks. Some are engaged in fieldwork, some in building, cooking or administration, but the dominant activity is memorization. Each morning, the boys and young novices add a few more lines of scripture and ritual verse to their stock of recall, usually within earshot of an attentive tutor. To help it sink in, this is done aloud. Because each boy sits with a dozen others and is surrounded by a dozen similar houses, it's done as loudly as possible. The result is a cacophony. They each begin by rapidly repeating the Sanskrit syllable *dhih*, like a machine-gun, to invoke the patron buddha of wisdom.[86] The acquisition of new material ends around lunchtime, and afternoons are devoted to reciting everything memorized to date. Once each monk is full grown he's etched thousands of pages permanently in memory. On countless occasions I'd watched Geshe Rabten retrieve any quote he wanted at a moment's notice.[87]

In the evenings, younger monks continue their recitations while the older boys, now receiving explanations of the memorized texts, assemble in the debate courtyard. If recitation is cacophonous, debate is bedlam.

SERA MONASTIC UNIVERSITY: let go of any image of tranquillity

A dozen or so monks gather around a cross-legged respondent while one stands to ask questions. The idea's not so much about right and wrong as getting the defendant to contradict himself.[88]

I watched a burly youngster in the hot seat twirl his rosary while the questioner respectfully posed some preliminary questions, and they settled on a thesis. Once satisfied, with upper robe wrapped around his waist, the standing monk stood back on one leg and brought his hands together with a resounding clap. The time for modest discussion was over.

The hands separated, respectively closing the doors on lower rebirth, and lifting sentient beings from samsara.[89] The first question was followed by a barrage of others until the respondent struggled for an answer. The questioner pounced mercilessly, circling his head with his hand and screaming. The defendant strained, shouting his answer, apparently trying to change his mind. One of the others jumped to his feet, but was promptly pushed from the circle. He staggered back, holding the questioner with one hand and insisting on an answer. Others joined in the shouting now while the two on their feet wrestled for their place. There were gleeful laughs, sympathetic smiles and sheepish looks.

The competition is fueled largely by testosterone. Around the court-yard arms, legs and loose flaps of monastic robes were pushed, tugged and dragged. There was taunting, sometimes sneering. There were inter-ruptions. Spittle flew and emotions ran high. I watched an older monk turn grey-faced with dismay, the slapping hands of his adversary crashing inches from his nose. Laughter echoed. The air was electric. It was pure sport. I was repelled and fascinated.

At Sera, personal status is won and lost on the debate courtyard, and with it, sometimes, self-importance. A public defeat, especially during the new-year[90] geshe examinations, can be a crushing experience. I even heard of monks occasionally coming to blows. The stakes are high for what's considered in other Buddhist circles to be of little significance—intellectual prowess and social standing. I wasn't inspired to take part.

However, I was pressured from every side to do so. Why would I not want to sharpen my mind, learn every detail of the stages of the path and even be led into a meditative state of nonconceptual perplexity? I tried to explain, but my claim to seek what the Buddha *really* meant fell on incredulous ears. Debate[91] was the manifest path of these Gelug monks, and that was that. In time, I learned to blame my poor memorization skills instead, but the harm was done; I was now an arrogant Inji. Still, I had no wish to devote my next twenty years to the study of arcane texts.

There were other objections. Although everything's theoretically up for question, novelty is closely monitored. In the final analysis, the path taught by the Buddha must be right because the Buddha is omniscient; if he isn't, the path is pointless. This tautology isn't as superficial as it seems, for the Buddha's *skillful means* meant that he taught people according to their capacity to understand,[92] and there was much to unravel in his words. Here lies fertile ground for debate.

Don't imagine, however, that the field of Buddhist theory is a relativist quagmire. I was chatting casually with some young monks one afternoon in 1981 when the subject of the American moon landing came up.

"You believe *that*?" they asked, almost simultaneously.

I had to think for a moment before I reluctantly admitted that as much as I'd always considered it a fact, it wasn't something within my direct experience. "Yes," I declared. "I *believe* it."

With adversarial gusto one of them rose to his feet and reminded me that the wind that destroys the universe at the end of the æon blows

continuously, just above the summit of Mount Meru, destroying everything in its path—including American spacecraft. I jumped at this diversion from scriptural rote and entered cheerfully into the spirit of things.

However, it soon became clear that this was no intellectual exercise.
When I suggested that the four-continents model wasn't an exclusive
Buddhist description of the universe,[93] he became perturbed. Worse still,
I responded to his scriptural citations by stating that not everything the
Buddha said was provable or even necessarily right.

The mood now changed. It wasn't simply that their faith rested on
the consistency of the Buddhist canon, but that they had nowhere else
to turn; their very frame of reference was under attack. Unlike physi-
cists who might one day treat matter as waves and the next as particles,
these boys had no alternative world view. The look in their eyes was pure
emotion; whether resentment or fear, it made little difference. I'd questioned their sense of security, and crossed the line.

My gaffes didn't put me entirely out of favor. Lama Lhundup, who was
in charge of external communications, invited me periodically for tea
and a chat in English. Prospective students also attached themselves to
me for the same reason, and most of the monks who saw me walking in
the monastery compound greeted me in a friendly fashion. I avoided my
native tongue as much as possible, and my fluency in Tibetan progressed.

Although I'd been feted on my arrival, I was now subsisting on daily
monastery fare—meager, broken, gravelly rice with a spoonful or two of
watery dal. Each of the two Sera colleges (Jey and Mey) had its own grimy
shop stocked with the occasional banana, rounds of sweet white bread,
boiled candies, soap, toothbrushes and other items. For a few paisa, you
could even buy an aspirin or a tetracycline[94] tablet, but fresh fruits and
vegetables were virtually unheard of. Just five miles away in Bylakuppe
they were available in abundance, but few monks seemed to care.

Thomtok's servant explained why. "Back in the old country we hardly
grew vegetables," he said dismissively. "We had yaks. You know yaks?"

I nodded.

"Maybe you think so, but you don't really. The best milk, fantastic
butter, plenty of meat . . . and delicious, hot blood." He stared. "Boy, that

A MASTER AT DEBATE: Geshe Ngawang Dhargyey, upper robe wrapped around his waist, stands back on one leg and brings his hands together with a resounding clap

blood was delicious." He threw his head back dramatically and convincingly mimicked the gesture of pouring the thick liquid down his gullet. "It was *so* good. Then we didn't care how cold it was outside, our bodies stayed toasty warm."

"Really?"

"It was the land of snows," he pointed to his knees. "This deep. We had no heating, none!" His hand rose to throat level, and he shivered. "We smeared butter on our bodies to keep out the cold. Otherwise, your skin would crack open." He leaned forward with bulging eyes, took out a large cube of raw pig fat, sliced off thick strips of lard and slid them down his throat. "Bet you can't do that!" he said, grimacing.

"Probably not," I agreed.

"Mmm! Delicious." He smacked his lips.

The sound of nervous laughter behind made me turn, and there was Thomtok smiling weakly. "He's just playing."

I nodded.

His eyes flickered uncertainly.

The market was an hour's walk or more, an opportunity to get away from the same old compound for a few hours, pick up some tropical fruits and sample the fare of local coffee and vegetarian meals.

The road from the monastery was an oxen track widened by the occasional scooter taxi and the passing of the monastery jeep on official business. Spindly trees with broad tops and no lower foliage, the remnants of forest canopy, dotted the landscape like orphan parasols. The eroded ground underfoot became fine dust in the heat and sticky mud in the rains. After my shoes had been sucked off my feet a few times I reverted to the all-season plastic sandals worn by everyone. Summer and winter, everyone carried an umbrella to stave off rain and sun alike.

Other refugee compounds nearby housed the lay communities that provided fresh blood for the burgeoning monastic population. In later years, there'd be a surge of new Tibetan refugees, and a prejudicial distinction between Tibetans born in India and those from Tibet, but to date there were few arrivals from the old country. The greater contrast was between the Tibetan settlements that were poor but prospering and the mud-and-straw huts of the rural Indians, whose poverty was inured.

It was along this road one day that I recognized Gen Kayang returning from the village. He stopped me with the usual, "Where are you going?"

I replied with the only other greeting I knew, "Tashi Deleg."[95]

He laughed at my untimely New Year wishes, clapped me on the back and gave me a friendly lecture on Tibetan usage. As water buffalo passed by he pulled me to one side, assuring me that I didn't want the boys laughing at me. He had no airs and called me "aro," roughly equivalent to the English "mate," and invited me for dinner that evening. I became a friend of the household and often sat with him and his boys around the fire, dropping thumb-size dollops of dough into the dumpling soup.

Gen wasn't a handsome man. His lips puckered in the corners and gave him a perpetually pensive look. Flared nostrils added a porcine

THE MONASTERY ROAD: little more than an oxen track

appearance. His thick-rimmed spectacles were of nineteen-forties vintage, fished out of a jumbled pile in some Indian bazaar. Unkempt brows sloped into a broad forehead and the heavy-lidded eyes beneath added a touch of sadness. A stubble of hair covered his scalp and cheeks, white with some remaining grey. On the other hand, he dignified himself with hands folded gently behind his back, an erect posture and a restrained though prodigious belly. Faded, tattered robes and lusterless, worn skin added to rather than diminished his presence. Like most of his fellow monks, a grin or belly laugh lay just beneath the surface.

Geshe Kayang had no rich, overseas students to send offerings. Rather, his was one of several Sera Jey houses that depended upon subsidies from Geshe Rabten who, like all émigrés, took it as a personal responsibility.

Every week or two, a Muslim butcher pushed into the monastery compound a bicycle laden with bloody cuts of fresh beef and swarming with flies. Geshe usually managed to dig up a few rupees for a piece. Together, he and the boys chopped and mixed it with chives or cilantro, wrapped small balls of the mixture in dumpling dough and arranged them in a bamboo steamer. These were *momo*, the Tibetan national dish. Leftover gristle and bones went into the next day's broth.

Gen loved to confuse me with his rough Kham dialect, chortling like a schoolboy and making his boys clutch their sides with laughter when I couldn't make out a word. I was as respectful toward him as they were, but at ease in his house like no other. He helped me understand some philosophy texts and we even traveled together to the International School at Kodai Kanal, where he taught an introduction to Buddhism.

Geshe Kayang, however, wasn't destined for greatness. The threadbare bushes that marked the edge of his little courtyard encompassed the entire extent of his authority. On my way to and from this surrogate home I was more than once beset by well-wishers who warned me of his poor scholarship and low standing. Aware that my democratic sensibilities were out of place, I didn't respond. As I grew more familiar with daily life at Sera, I saw more examples of normal human pettiness to which I'd once presumed the Tibetans immune.

"We're going back," said Thomtok's servant.

"Who? Where?"

"All of us. To Tibet. Kundun[96] will lead us." His tone belied his defiant words; he was hoping beyond hope, expressing loyalty, not conviction. The Dalai Lama still assured his people regularly that compassion and understanding for their oppressors would prevail, while in the meantime he reached out to the leaders of the free world. The Western powers tut-tutted in private and arranged aid for refugees, but didn't lift a political finger or even acknowledge Tibet's desperate plight. They were bending over backwards to remain on speaking terms with the Chinese.

The Tibetan-born generation could hardly bring itself to accept the hopelessness of Tibetan independence, but the youngsters, especially the secular ones, were frustrated by the passivity of the old guard and wanted to take up arms. Nevertheless, the great mass of Tibetans, both in exile and in Tibet, stood solidly behind their spiritual leader. While they hailed him as a living Buddha, he described himself as a simple monk.

The Tibetan communities in India had by now passed beyond refugee status. Despite the poor sanitation, the monastery and its surrounding lay settlements were already better off than their rural Indian neighbors. They lived in brick houses, not straw huts, and the population was on the rise. They never stopped building and were determined that if Buddhism was to be eradicated from Tibet, as the Chinese vowed, they'd replant it elsewhere. In a corner of the monastery grounds a small compound and house was reserved for The Dalai Lama and other high-ranking lamas. Spick, span and usually empty, it boasted its own outhouse and flush toilet, though there was no sewage system to connect it to.

Less than ten years before, the spot where I stood in Thomtok's courtyard had been jungle, now cleared and pushed back several kilometers to make room for the refugee communities. Their annual crop of maize helped provide for the three hundred monks.[97] New houses and temples were under constant construction.

The monastery was also helped by the worldwide diaspora as well as the growing numbers of Western converts to Buddhism. One morning during communal prayers I recognized the garbled names of some Swiss acquaintances and realized that Geshe Rabten had passed some donors the way of his alma mater.

Understanding this, I advertised the fact that I was one of those Westerner with no wealth to speak of, and the number of dinner invitations

GESHE KAYANG: perpetually pensive

fell quickly. This left me with mixed feelings. On the one hand, I was glad
to be free of uncomfortable formalities; on the other, it shone an unflattering light on my hosts.

I'd never been particularly comfortable in Thomtok's house and was
relieved when, several weeks after my arrival, the schoolhouse was finally
completed. Along with it came the schoolteacher's room. Since I was to
teach English, and the authorities were beholden to me for what they
perceived as the sacrifice of leaving Tharpa Chöeling, I moved right in.
It was tiny—a plus, for unlike most living space it could never be shared.
It even had a bolt and padlock on the door. I had visions of privacy even
though it opened onto the large veranda where the youngest boys worked
daily on their handwriting and memorization.

They sat in dusty robes with chalkboards on their laps. Diligent in
the presence of their elders but unintimidated by me, they occasionally
sought distraction by running their fingers curiously up and down the
golden-brown hairs of my arm and asking why I was hairy as an ape and
had such a big nose.

I was delighted at first by the familiarity of so many sweet, smiling
faces, but soon began to crave my privacy again. I couldn't lock the door
from the inside, nor close the shutters without being stifled. Barred but
not glazed, the windows offered no resistance to incoming sound. I told
the boys to clear off, but they laughed at my absurdity.

The attendance of my most enthusiastic students, teenagers who
already spoke a little English, was sporadic at best, and slowly dwindled.
I went to their houses to find out why. Visibly uncomfortable in the presence of their housemasters, they claimed their debate studies occupied
all their time. Their tone of voice belied the words, and I suspected their
teachers' mistrust of cultural contamination.

This wasn't idle speculation. Walls in the monastery were posted
with Indian calendars featuring futuristic cityscapes and aircraft-filled
skies. Tinny transistor radios sat raucously on windowsills screeching
out Indian pop songs from early morning till late at night, and clunky
watches adorned the wrists of all but the poorest monks—the more
knobs, the better. Although the important hours were announced by the
blowing of conch shells and the clanging of gongs, and adornment of

THE BOYS: worked daily on their handwriting

any sort is a transgression of the monks' rules, the abbot never intervened. I watched, but kept my Caucasian nose out of it.

All were gregarious, and I heard stories almost daily about the good old days of Tibet. When they were done, the monks would encourage me to speak of home as if my need to unburden myself was as urgent as theirs. They were being friendly, but such maudlin exchanges tried my patience. Geshe Rabten spoke of the old country, but never obsessively.

For a bit of peace one day, instead of taking my afternoon walk in the shady pathways of Sera Jey and Sera Mey, I ventured down an old rutted track to the edge of the jungle. The clearing ended and the dense undergrowth began abruptly, as if I'd passed into another world. Trees struggled upwards against invading mosses and vines. Creatures rustled in the shadows. I wasn't sure what I was stepping on. The air was thick and humid, the light an opaque daytime dusk filled with motes and bugs. As reckless as I sometimes was, I had to admit how easily I might get lost. If I was looking for a quiet place to meditate, this wouldn't do.

Heading back, I saw a group of monks pointing at me fretfully from the edge of the compound. As soon as I came within range, a couple of boys were sent out to grab my arms and pull me back to safety.

"What's up?" I asked.

"You mustn't go there," admonished an older monk. "There are elephants."

"I was just walking," I said.

"Walking where?"

"Just walking. Nowhere."

This produced looks of consternation.

"That's not good. Walking alone for no reason? Anyway, it's dangerous in there. There are elephants."

"Elephants?" I'd heard that people were periodically maimed or killed by angry elephants.

With some difficulty, and frayed nerves, I extricated myself from their clutches, deciding that I'd have to secure myself some dependable peace and quiet. Otherwise, sooner or later, I'd erupt.

At the very edge of the monastery grounds, in the yard of the great temple shared by both colleges, was a ramshackle hut.

"It's uninhabited," I said.

"That," the caretaker explained patiently, "is because it's uninhabitable."

I prevaricated. "Could I look inside?"

He grabbed a Dickensian ring of keys, waddled past the temple's two cows and crossed the temple yard.

One side of the room was filled with traditional wooden printing blocks, about thirty inches long and an inch thick. Each was carved with the reverse image of a page, its surface hardened to a metallic sheen by ingrained ink. He picked one up and held it respectfully against his inclined forehead. Among Tibetans the printed word represents the buddha mind and, in theory at least, is esteemed over and above even the most valuable statue.

A coarse mesh covered the window. It would keep out most birds, but locusts and small creatures could crawl through. There was a roof but no ceiling, and daylight poured under the tiles, illuminating cobwebs and insect carcasses. Deep in the woodblocks I heard a rodentian scurrying.

"It's perfect," I said.

He looked at me as if I were cracked, shrugged and pointed questioningly at the room's precious contents.

I put my hands together and bowed the respectfully towards the woodblocks. This apparently satisfied him, for he walked away without a backward glance.

If I'd moved from Thomtok's house into this hovel or, even worse, from the generous hospitality of the college schoolhouse to Gen Kayang's shabby house, I suspect there would have been an uproar. Now, however, no one suggested that my move from the brand-new teacher's room to my remote hut had directly insulted anyone, it was so bizarre as to confound judgment; I was peculiar, even for an inji.

It wasn't an easy place to live. The fields, which doubled as the communal toilet, lay just beyond my window; there was no way to block the constantly renewed reek of several hundred daily bowel movements. Mosquitoes passed easily though the broad mesh and rats scurried playfully around the room at night, even chasing each other over my prone

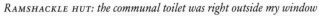

RAMSHACKLE HUT: *the communal toilet was right outside my window*

body when I lay still for long enough. Still, I was on my own at last, and didn't receive many visitors in that remote corner. At least there were no boys yelling their recitations, monks chattering outside my door, or unannounced visitors. I had a kerosene stove, a flat bunk and my own water pot, which I learned to refresh daily; otherwise, I'd find larvae squiggling though it. I usually took shelter under a mosquito net draped over my bed but, prize of prizes, I had my own door, and it could be bolted from the inside.

29

HEALING

I WAS IN BYLAKUPPE and had just ordered a coffee and a masala dosa[98] when a tall Caucasian man about my age walked in. He pulled up a chair and ordered the same.

"David," he smiled, putting out his hand.

"Hello," I answered. "Steve. Australian?"

"New Zealander," he grimaced.

"Whoops! Sorry,"

"It happens all the time," he said with good-natured disgust.

"So," I continued after a polite pause. "What are you doing in the wilds of Karnataka?"

"Live here," he said.

"Really?"

"Near Sera."

"Really? I live at Sera."

"I know."

"You do? How?"

"Are you joking? An Inji monk at Sera? Heard about you weeks ago."

David was married to Vivian, the Anglo-Indian girl I'd met at the library years before. They'd been part of the Dharamsala crowd until their son, Jampa, had reached school age, when they'd asked Geshe Ngawang Dhargyey whether they should put him in a monastery. Who knows what they expected, but Geshe assented, and here they were. Jampa was now nine and fluent in Tibetan. David, however, wasn't happy.

"He can't add," he said. "Or subtract. He can't spell. He's not getting a proper education."

"But he's learning debate?"

"Not all monks turn out to be great debaters," he said. "And Jampa's lazy. All he wants to do is play."

"He's just a boy," I said.

"He still needs an education."

David lived with Vivian on the main road to Sera, and we walked back together. My fluency in Tibetan had certainly benefited from immersion among Tibetans, but as I left him just outside the monastery I realized how relaxing it was to chat in English for the first time in weeks.

There were no paved or asphalted surfaces in the compound, and like everyone going about in light sandals I occasionally scraped and cut my feet. I'd injured my toe within days of my arrival; it became infected and remained that way during my year and a half at Sera. Gen Kayang and his boys watched with fascination as I applied antibacterial ointment and replaced the dressing daily. Their usual policy was to wait until a mosquito bite or scratch had become septic, then embark on an expedition to the local Indian doctor, or even to the hospital in Mysore. As I swabbed my skin with Dettol I lectured them on hygiene and the importance of cleanliness, especially since the surrounding fields, the communal toilet, were rank with human excrement.

Naturally, Gen responded with long tales of the cold hardships of Tibet and the natural healing properties of Tibetan blood, which was rapidly achieving mythical proportions.

"If Tibetans are so tough," I retorted, "How come they die?"

"Aro! You got me there," he chuckled.

What was more likely was that the mountainous climate gave bacteria less opportunity to proliferate. In fact, a native Tibetan's immune system was probably *more* susceptible to tropical infections than a local Indian's. When I tried to explain this I received looks of incomprehension.

Almost all the boys bore the unmistakable marks of ringworm on their scalp, body and nails. Intestinal worms were common, and the mosquito population varied in intensity throughout the year without ever completely receding. Tibetans often allow the bloodsuckers to take their fill and fly off, in the name of compassion for mother sentient beings.

Living creatures are known as "mother sentient beings" because, in countless rebirths since beginningless time, we've all purportedly shared every conceivable relationship with one another, including that of mother and child. Contemplating the love of one's mother is supposed to arouse feelings of indebtedness and lead to compassion—the lynchpin of Mahayana Buddhism. As with most religions, the value of sacrifice is exemplified in the lives of its saints, particularly Avalokiteshvara,[99] Tibet's patron buddha whose well-celebrated mantra is *om mani padme hum*.

I thought it possible that this laid-back attitude towards mosquitoes might temper the physiological response—produce less irritation and more rapid healing—but it was just a matter of time before some puncture or another became infected and painful. Further dangers included malaria, black-water fever and amoebic dysentery. The journey in and out of the communal toilet every day contaminated everyone's footwear or bare feet with fæcal matter. There were no wells or water purification. All sorts of bacteria, viruses and parasites were transmitted through mud in the wet season and air-borne dust during the remainder of the year.

In these conditions, the boys' bodies grew under constant stress. Milk was a luxury, consumed only as an ingredient of tea, and the lack of fresh food and vegetables left them with virtually no regular vitamins or nutritional variety. The supposedly robust Tibetan immune system was simply starved of raw materials. The tetracycline[100] sold in the monastery shops was known as *inji men* (Western medicine), and popped indiscriminately by anyone who felt poorly but didn't want to pay the doctor a visit.

There were two Tibetan doctors in the area. Their diagnoses were surprisingly accurate and the traditional herbal/mineral remedies effectively treated the widespread stomach and liver ailments, but outcomes for other afflictions were mixed at best.

One night, receiving a gentle knock on my door, I opened it to a rotund, sad-eyed geshe who asked for *men*.[101]

"What for, Gen?" I asked.

"Oh, it's nothing," he responded. "It's just . . . my leg hurts."

I opened the door wider. "Come in then. Let's have a look."

"No, no," he begged. "Just give me medicine and I'll be on my way."

"Well," I negotiated, "I have to know what sort you need."

After a courteous argument he came in. It was funny to feel authority over a geshe. He sat on my cot, propped his leg up and pulled back his robe. The cause of his pain was obvious; his calf was swollen to the size of his thigh, the skin stretched as taut as a drum. "How did that happen," I asked as I washed my hands.

"A mosquito bite," he said. "I know you shouldn't scratch, but I couldn't help it. It tickled so," he giggled and winced.

I turned him on his side and sure enough, there was the entry point, barely distinguishable from the dark red inflammation that lay beneath the length of his lower leg. I looked around the room for something absorbent. I had no spare clothes or rags. There were no newspapers. I realized I'd have to sacrifice my carefully hoarded supply of cotton wadding from Boots.[102]

"This'll hurt just a bit, Gen," I said.

"That's okay. I don't mind."

I sterilized a pin above a candle flame and carefully loosened the scab. It was extraordinarily hard, deep and stubborn, like a plug.

"Oww," he moaned quietly.

The yellow, viscous pus oozed out and quickly saturated half of the cotton wool. I grabbed my spare cotton undergarment and stuffed it under the wound.

"How's that?" I asked.

"You know," he said, "I think it feels better already."

I put my hands around his ankle and pressed gently, working up his leg like a toothpaste tube. The pus flowed out evenly.

"Oh, ooh!" he exclaimed with a mixture of pleasure and pain.

Twenty minutes later, the flow was finally tinged with blood, by which time the ruined garment had absorbed a good half-liter of pus.

He was almost crying with relief. "Oh thank you, thank you so much. The pain's completely gone. Boy, you're a great doctor. You're an expert!"

"Not at all," I said. "More like, you're a really bad patient. How long have you been walking around like this?"

"Oh, a month, maybe two ...," he avoided my eye.

"Maybe three?"

He laughed sheepishly. I covered the wound with antibacterial cream, bandaged it and gave him oral tetracycline with some boiled water. He grimaced. "That water's no good."

"It tastes lousy," I said, "but it's safe."

He looked at me doubtfully.

Without the reminder of constant pain I knew he'd abandon the course of pills as soon as he felt better, so I announced I'd be over twice a day with more. Three weeks later, his leg was right as rain and I'd made a friend for life, who nevertheless continued to ignore all my advice on hygiene and preventive medicine.

From then on, day and night, a steady trickle of monks and local Indians sought me out, mostly with infected wounds. I was soon obliged to take the crowded bus to Mysore to replenish supplies.

By this time I'd become a frequent visitor at David and Vivian's house, and Vivian took a personal interest in setting up a regular dispensary. She sold some jewelry to raise money, and no one was more surprised than I when she went to the Sera Jey abbot and got everything she demanded— a permanent room, unrestricted access for all monks and boys and approval for a layperson to assist me. The fact that her son lived in the unsanitary monastery gave her the maternal gumption to dig in her heels. Wisely, she let her victory sink in before announcing the following week that the assistant would be Sonam, a pretty Tibetan girl. She could enter the compound only during the day, could only treat young boys and couldn't wander around, but she was admitted.

Vivian's success was particularly astounding to me because at this point my relations with the abbot had reached a low. I'd been caring for a stick-thin six-year-old with an infected foot. Timid, tiny and miserable, the child was pining for his mother. I first saw him limping barefoot through the dusty monastic lanes, wearing no sandals and looking thoroughly miserable. He'd never have found the nerve to visit my hut so, as he dragged his bare feet through the dusty monastic lanes, I called to him. He turned towards me with a look of terror.

"It's okay," I said. "I want to help you with your foot."

He glanced at it.

"Fix it up."

His eyes were dull.

"You're new here, right? When did you arrive?"

He shrugged.

"Your mother, right? Your mother brought you here?"

His eyes filled with tears. He wiped his nose on the back of his arm.

"Where's your house?"

He looked startled and lied in a clear voice, "Don't know."

I coaxed him to come with me, and after a few steps asked me to carry him. He shrugged once more but as I picked him up he clung tightly to my neck. By the time we'd arrived at my hut he was less tense. I sat him on the edge of the cot, rinsed the caked dust off his upper foot and took a closer look. A pus-filled crater extended from one side to the other.

"What happened?" I asked.

He mumbled, "Dunno."

"An insect bite?" I ventured.

He shrugged listlessly.

I changed his dressing regularly and ten days later a dry scab had formed over the shrinking wound. A week later, however, the wound was again open and weeping. I suggested a visit to his room to look into living conditions. Panic filled the boy's eyes, but I now had his trust. It turned out that his housemaster had selected his wounded foot as a site for special punishment, meted out with a wooden baton.

I went directly to the abbot,[103] thinking how lucky the poor lad was to have an advocate in me.

The interview was short and not sweet. "It's none of my business," he shrugged. "What can I do?"

"You approve of this?" I blurted out.

"Approve?" He was bewildered and offended. His servant cursorily escorted me from the room.

Gen Kayang listened to my story, tapped his fingers on the table and looked worriedly out the window. "The boy stays in his uncle's house," he said. "There's just the two of them. Nothing you can do about it. It's okay, the boy's just pining for his mother. He'll get used to being here."

"He'll lose his foot," I said angrily.

I went directly to the boy's house, hoping I wasn't making things worse.

A grimy door curtain concealed a tiny room, black with soot and grime. On the floor lay the boy's bedroll, and on the lone cot sat a tall, stone-faced man, his yellow skin stretched into a suspicious grimace.

I introduced myself. "I'm trying to fix your nephew's foot."

"Thank you." He smiled ingratiatingly.

I quietly assured him that I knew why it wasn't healing and that although the monastic authorities wouldn't intervene, I'd be watching. His gaze shifted back and forth from the absent boy's bedroll to me as he scratched his neck. We glared at each other for a few moments and I announced that I'd be back.

For the next six days I visited the nervous boy each evening and examined his foot in full view of his uncle. On the seventh day the boy was gone.

"His mother took him home," the uncle announced with disgust.

My actions had deprived a young boy of a blessed monastic life, and this episode blackened my already doubtful reputation in the monastery, but I was delighted.

The maize was waist-high when I was shaken from a deep sleep one night by the clattering of pots and pans, shouts, whistles and ululations. Heavy footfalls and the threatening thump of staves drew near. The distinct sound of rocks and stones scattered among the immature crop. Had the Tibetans finally inflamed the local population to rise against them? I jumped out of bed, pressed myself into the corner of the room and listened. As the crowd tramped past my window, I heard voices, Tibetan. I was sure I recognized Kalsang Wangdu, one of my older students. With a sigh of relief I was heading outside to confront the pranksters when, with a sudden shout, they veered away at a run. As they faded into the distance

I climbed back under my netting and traced their movements around the field for another hour or so before falling into merciful asleep.

Next morning, bleary eyed, I wondered at my dream. Or had I been awake?

I asked Kalsang Wangdu in my senior English class that afternoon, expecting a sheepish response and conspiratorial grins, but all I got was an exhausted look of assent.

"Yes sir," he nodded. "We were near your hut last night."

"You came to wake me up?" I offered, smiling indulgently. "As a joke?"

"Oh no, sir. No, no." They reverted in alarm to Tibetan as they balked at the suggestion. "Oh, sir, we would never do that. We were on pig beat."

It took them a moment to register my blank look. "The pig beat. He doesn't know." They erupted into exhausted laughter and tripped over each other's words, trying to explain.

"The pigs."

"From the jungle."

"Come to steal the maize."

"Yes, into the fields. At night."

"To eat our maize."

"Yes, and so we chase them."

"Scare them."

"Make them go away."

"Otherwise, all the maize, gone."

"Yes, finish."

We all had a good laugh, but in the next weeks I saw it was no joke. Half the monks spent one day after another in a stupor of sleep deprivation. Gen Kayang confirmed that things were much harder here than they'd been in Tibet, where the monastery's land holdings, combined with the support of the lay population, enabled the monks to concentrate entirely on study, debate and ritual. Now even the monks were refugees, and had to protect their food supply from marauding swine.

30

The Curtain Falls

I'D BEEN AT SERA for barely nine months and was sitting on my stoop reading Steve's latest letter. My correspondence with him and Brian had helped keep me in touch with my own roots, for by now it was clear that in this hotbed of medieval tradition, I was an anomaly.

Brian had written the week before about the Dalai Lama's recent visit. He'd officiated over public teachings, private ceremonies and a mass ordination of monks, a veritable circus of events. Brian had served as the Tibetan leader's personal chauffeur and had spent dozens of hours one-on-one with him. He was still bathing excitedly in the afterglow. By contrast, Steve's letter was a long, dry missive—a lengthy working out of ideas with little in the way of personal feelings. However, his thoughts grew out of daily events in the world to which I'd soon return, and his intellectual dilemmas reflected my existential ones.

Things at Tharpa Chöeling were now considered to be returning to normal, but Steve believed that beneath the surface they were in fact disintegrating—not that the forthcoming situation would affect him directly. He'd just accepted a full-time position in Hamburg, Geshe Rabten was heading to India for a prolonged visit and—big news—Alan had left.

Not just left, but disappeared.

Alan, Geshe Rabten's presumed closest disciple, translator to the Dalai Lama, elder monk, a shining example to all, ostensible leader of the community, most fluent in Tibetan and the darling of the Geneva sponsors, had slipped out one December morning to pick up groceries, and never came back.

Having wished for a long time to enter retreat, Alan had finally decided his time had come. Geshe however, as I learned from Alan decades later,[104] had insisted on secrecy, and the departure was a mystery to everyone. There hadn't been the slightest warning, even to Arnie, and the effect was only reinforced by Alan's natural reserve. The detachment that had lent him an air of dedicated single-pointedness now rebounded; a shockwave of gossip ran through the community. Some said that Alan had plunged a dagger into Geshe's back, that Geshe didn't eat for days and that he never pronounced Alan's name again. Steve and Brian, on the other hand, reported that Geshe took it in his stride. It seems the lay community was outraged on Geshe's behalf. They didn't grasp the fact that, unlike Christian abbots, Geshe didn't hold his monks in a vow of obedience.

Sitting thousands of miles away in the heartland of Gelug scholasticism, it now seemed the grandiose mission we'd conceived for Tharpa Chöeling all those years ago had been farfetched. Here at Sera I'd seen what Geshe envisaged for us, and it couldn't have been less compatible with our shared aspirations. I'd put up with Sera thinking I'd return to Tharpa Chöeling refreshed and reinvigorated, but I'd been kidding myself, recalling the center as we'd conceived it, not as it had actually evolved.

My path lay through doubt, not certainty. I could easily reconcile that with the original teachings of Buddha, but I still hoped for personal guidance. Lama Yeshe's opinion had been that I should study with Geshe Rabten, and although I trusted Geshe to explain the Sera-Jey textbooks with great clarity, I didn't feel the same about his personal judgment.

Wandering in small circles under the hot sun, a stream of thoughts charging through my mind, I reread the letter.

"One of the most disappointing side effects of learning Tibetan," Steve wrote, "is that one becomes conscious of the limits of [our teachers'] field of conceptual reference."[105]

He was right. It was easy to maintain incongruous hopes and illusions when our teachers were remote and incomprehensible to us. We'd figured this out years before; but never had the simple truth been so charged. Who would even understand my doubts, let alone address them? How is guru devotion not an exercise in willful self-deception? What's the point of Buddhist psychology[106] if it doesn't address fear, guilt and disappointment? Isn't studying to overcome the inner dialogue like eating to lose weight? Should Awakening really be spelled with a capital A? What's the role of creativity on the path to Awakening? As inexpressible as these questions were at Sera, they were crucial at Tharpa Chöeling.

I now recalled something Lama Yeshe had once told Massimo about Sera. Hands together at his heart he'd said, "I have much, much respect for these monks, but ... I really feel they're wasting their time." Perhaps he meant that scholarship too easily became a substitute for practice.

Letter in hand, I stared at the clump of Sera's houses and temples. Red-robed old geshes waddled to and fro on daily business. Teenagers in their prime walked with a spring in their step, dazzled by visions of debating glory. Younger boys took breaks from memorizing unintelligible strings of syllables to play in the dusty laneways, animating discarded bicycle wheels, sticks and stones with their imaginations. While they accepted their lot without question, I was afflicted with the freedom to think and do whatever in the world I wanted.

On the back of the envelope was a Hamburg address. Steve had made his move, and by now enjoyed on-demand, uncomplicated access to a good geshe, no strings attached. He was writing his book. He had time to read and reflect. He's also made friends with a German bhikkhu[107] with whom he swapped doubts. What conversations they must be having ....

I sat there restlessly sliding the folded letter in and out of its envelope, watching the sun set over the Dalai Lama's residence.

The Dalai Lama's junior tutor was visiting a large Tibetan settlement at Mungod, an overnight trip away, and Thomtok suggested I accompany him there. I'd heard about Ling Rinpoche from Brian, and hoped to meet him. Who knows? I might make a personal connection. Also, Mungod was the site of both of Sera's sister monasteries, Drepung and Ganden.[108]

SERA MONASTERY: The sun sets over the Dalai Lama's residence

Traveling with a contingent of Sera monks was awkward; they cramped my style by huddling together in an extraordinary display of insecurity and calling out my name whenever I wandered from the pack. Eventually, I slipped away and completed the trip on my own, wondering how they could have so quickly lost the nerve that had taken them over the dangerous passes of the Himalayas and into India.

The trip was a disaster. I was sick as a dog in Mungod. I attended only two days of teachings and on the third was woken by a stomach ache so violent that I couldn't get up. I took some of the Tibetan medicine that I kept on hand for intestinal problems but, for once, the bitter black pills didn't clear it up. A fever came on and my attempt to get to the rooms of the nearby doctor left me prone on the deserted ground while everyone was engrossed at the public teachings. A few steps at a time, I made it safely back to my borrowed room and felt my energy trickle away in short breaths. I couldn't eat. Even water nauseated me. I fell into a blackness, not caring whether I saw the light of day ever again.

But I did. Waking up to spine-chilling cramps, I staggered to the outhouse and watched dark liquid pour from my guts. I was drenched in sweat and weak as a rag. Compared with this, hepatitis had been easy.

Every half hour my fever rose and I lost my wits. It plummeted and I reencountered my pain-wracked body. My innards seemed to be scraped with broken glass. I craved the fever and it obliged. I longed for death, but dreamed of Mum receiving word and relented.

Each time I opened my eyes I saw the worried gaze of a girl in a Tibetan dress, but a Caucasian. She sponged me down and spooned water into my mouth. She summoned traditional and conventional doctors who were both baffled. The fever ran its course for three days and the modern doctor gave up. The traditional one pored over medical texts and furrowed his brow. Finally he jumped up with a page in hand. "I think I've found it," he said, "Hold on!" He spoke in whispers with the girl.

"Where'd he go?" I gasped.

"Darjeeling," said the girl.

Darjeeling was a three-day journey, each way.

"Hold on," she demanded of me.

When he returned at the end of the week I was still breathing—much to his obvious relief. He smiled bravely, forced an unimaginably bitter black paste into my mouth and held my jaw shut. Then he sat and spoon-fed me hot water for hours.

Next morning, the fever broke.

As I took my first nourishment in days, he tried to describe the medicine. It challenged his English and my Tibetan, and when he pointed to his throat we figured it had something to do with the thyroid gland of an elephant or rhinoceros; at any rate, a very large mammal.

Months later in England, Doctor Tom listened carefully to my story and surmised I'd had black water fever, though he couldn't explain the remedy. "You're a lucky fellow," he said over the rim of his glasses.

I knew that. What I didn't know, and have never since rediscovered, are the names of my benefactors—the girl, who I believe was Canadian, and the Tibetan doctor she brought to my bedside. They saved my life.

The Dalai Lama's junior tutor had by now finished his teaching and left, but Geshe Ngawang Nyima, whom Mum and Dad had met, had just become abbot of Drepung's Gomang college, and I stayed a while to study Tenets. This is a systematic arrangement of different interpretations of emptiness[109] into a philosophical hierarchy, in which each version is slightly less flawed than the previous. In dialectical style one eventually arrives at the pinnacle, the "correct" and intellectually elegant view of the Prasangika-Madhyamika school. This was one of my most fruitful studies whilst in Tibetan orthodoxy, and maintained my interest long after I left. It illustrates with great originality that the project of Buddhism transcends any particular belief system or philosophy.

I returned to Sera unwillingly but in fairly good spirits, for my health was returning and my term was almost up. There, I found a letter from Sigrid, announcing that she was on a whirlwind tour in India and would soon be paying me a visit. It seems that Alan's behavior had stirred up a vigorous discussion about what the monks should and shouldn't be doing, and she had learned that my removal to Sera was not Geshe's idea. Some supporters of Tharpa Chöeling and its monks, including Sigrid, were indignant. She arrived in a state of great displeasure.

She swept her eyes up and down my gaunt appearance and fixed a gaze on the cheap plastic sandals on my feet and the grubby bandage covering my toe.

"You should keep clean your feet. How filthy they are," she sniffed.

I pointed out the feet of passing monks. Such were the conditions and customs of Sera.

"Then set an example," she said imperiously.

I almost pointed out that the natives had a mind of their own, but instead let her get to the point.

"I learned that you left Tharpa Chöeling against Geshe Rabten's wishes."

I nodded, waited.

She grew defensive. "It is impossible for me to continue sponsoring you." She rushed through a long list of financial reasons.

I didn't argue. She was entitled, and anyway it would be undignified. When she finished I thanked her for her assistance over the years.

She looked at me as if from a distance.

I felt sad, but smiled. Her disappointment was real, but I was undaunted. No matter how others saw me, I knew I was trying, in my way, to be real. I got to my feet, still not my normal self. The interview had exhausted me.

She told me I'd have three more months, then got into her hired car and disappeared in a cloud of dust. I felt vaguely abandoned, but content to pay the price for following my instincts.

I muddled on until it was time to leave. Westerner Buddhists were now making their way to Sera, and their good behavior would only make my nonconformity more conspicuous. A recently arrived American monk asked in half-jest, "What ever did you do to become such a persona non grata around here?"

"Oh, you know," I said.

"Actually, no I don't," he said.

"Just try thinking for yourself. You'll understand."

"So it's true what I heard." He looked scandalized.

I didn't ask what he'd heard.

"What about the geshe training?"

"I'd rather be a Buddhist," I said.

"You seem to have your own idea of what a Buddhist is."

"Of course. Don't you?"

He looked at me blankly.

"Buddhist," I echoed, "Buddhism—just terms. Aren't they supposed to be empty, mere designations?" This was the pinnacle of Prasangika-Madhyamika thought.

He shuffled his feet warily.

I stared at his robes, feeling out of place in mine. "You think you're standing on holy ground," I challenged. "Don't you?"

"Well!" he said with finality. He crossed his arms and took a step back, out of the quagmire of independent thought.

31

FULL CIRCLE

I WAS LOOKING FORWARD to my remaining three months of freedom. Before returning to Tharpa Chöeling, I'd go into a Sri Lankan[110] retreat to shake out my mood and recover my balance. Then I'd revisit Dharamsala.

Captivated by the old-fashioned rhythms of rural India, I trundled southwards with the lightest of baggage—a towel over my shoulder, a change of light cotton robes and a toothbrush in a bundle. Life was as simple as it gets. From Tuticorin I crossed the Gulf of Mannar on a rusty old ferry and then bussed it down the long road to Colombo in "Reserved for Clergy' seats. This was a predominantly Buddhist country and I received a warm welcome, even from uniformed officials. It was a nice change from feeling like a crackpot, as I did in India. People bowed as I passed, though with curious stares at my maroon robes. Here, the monks wore saffron.

I went directly to Kandy, Ceylon's beautiful capital at fifteen hundred feet above sea level. There I spent a few days exploring temples and a culture as distinct from Tibetan Buddhism as Catholicism is from Calvinism.

Then I headed down to my main destination, the Kanduboda Meditation Centre, just outside Colombo.

This wasn't a bustling center of learning but an austere outpost of Theravada[111] Buddhism set in a leafy tropical compound. There was no library, no iconography and no ritual. The raison d'être of this monastery was the practice of meditation, pure and simple, to turn each moment of sitting, lying, walking, eating, excreting and washing into a seamless exercise of mindful awareness.

We were awoken each morning at 3:45 with a bowl of tea, after which I usually sat in meditation posture and fought off sleep. Breakfast came at sunrise, a bowl of gruel with a lump of raw brown sugar. If I'd succumbed to my drowsiness, I was reawakened with a disapproving "tut." More meditation followed breakfast.

The midday meal was a singular daily diversion. A dozen and a half monks lined up in rank, and a donor family served a vegetarian meal consisting of a half-dozen attractive, sizzling vegetarian curries, several

KANDUBODA & RESIDENT INSTRUCTOR: an austere outpost of Theravada Buddhism set in a leafy tropical compound

rice dishes, pickles and chutneys. Sweets and fruits followed, along with tea, coffee and biscuits.

The rest of the day was uneventful and, whether I sat, or practiced the ponderous walking meditations, the quiet of the monastic compound and the meager daily stimulation were mixed blessings. They were calming, but also a reproachful backdrop to the clamor of my inner chatter.

I didn't enjoy the blissful absorptions described so alluringly in the Tibetan textbooks, but I did begin to experience the sanity of being in touch with my senses. No matter how distracted I might be, my attention eventually returned to the in-breath and out-breath.

Each morning the cycle of boredom and distraction started over and I often found myself fixated on remote memories, trivial incidents or the pain in my knees. The elder monk who visited me each afternoon to follow my progress pounced on this last item and counseled me to watch the sensation closely. I was surprised to find that although the feeling of pressure and tightness was constant, the intensity of the pain itself depended on my mood, and at times even disappeared; more precisely, it became something for which the word "pain" was simply inappropriate. When I reported this, the faintest smile escaped his usually grim expression and he urged me to keep at it.

I learned a lot about my mind at Kanduboda, and came away with the curious realization that samsara's a racket befitting any con man. The thing is, we're fooling ourselves. The midday meal and the discomfort of going without dinner were the high and low points of each day, fulcrums on which my cravings turned without the slightest friction. I knew better than to follow the cycles of anticipation and disappointment, but new illusions of satisfaction lay in ambush around every corner, and I was the sucker, reborn every minute. Cyclic existence is the constant search for something unambiguously satisfying, while meditation is imprecise and unpredictable. That's why it often feels so discouragingly unmeditative.

After two months of this I left the compound in a state of heightened slow motion, sensible to every movement of my body and to the roar of every in-breath and out-breath. I approached the bus stop, acutely alive to the universe of my own body and mind. The sounds of the jungle, the wind in the high palms and the crunching of the dust beneath my feet overwhelmed my senses. In this moment of excruciating clarity, I stood outside the monastery gates awaiting the Colombo bus.

From the bowels of the earth I felt a vibration that grew into a diesel roar and the screeching halt of the great vehicle in a cloud of dust. I placed one foot on the lower step, transferred my weight, slowly lifted the second and grasped the handrail. With a good-humored sigh, the driver let me climb aboard before pulling away as fast as the ancient motor would allow. I lurched from side to side, trying to follow the movement of my center of gravity, until a sudden swerve threw me conveniently into an empty seat. In the moment before I dropped my head in contemplation I noticed that everybody on the bus was talking, twitching, scratching and getting on and off at extraordinary speed. The passing countryside was a blur.

Bustling Colombo was more than I could handle. I headed north-wards for Anuradhapura, an ancient capital filled with colossal, spectral stupas. There, I wandered for a couple of days, regaining my balance.

While crossing the channel back to India, my newfound focus gradu-ally unraveled. According to the scriptures, Awakening is supposed to be immutable, but what I'd achieved in Kanduboda was provisional at best—a product of the environment, dashed to pieces by the ordinary pace of life. I was disappointed but, deep down, unsurprised.

There's nothing quite like an interminable Indian rail trip in which to contemplate the loose threads of your life. I spent the next three days swaying from side to side, thinking about tantric mysticism and critical reflection, universal love and personal salvation, endless study and endless meditation. For a while it was Northern Buddhism versus Southern, and then, I wondered, why? Any contradiction was mine to resolve. I owed no allegiance to the Sri Lankans, and if I felt a debt to the Tibetans it seemed more appropriate to reciprocate it by cultivating personal integrity than by trying to satisfy the hopes that others happened to invest in me.

In this state of mind, I arrived in Dharamsala. Over the years I'd heard Brian recount the stories of his time with Serkong Rinpoche, Trijang Rinpoche, Ling Rinpoche, the Dalai Lama and other great lamas. I wanted my time with them too, if it wasn't too late.

*ANURADHAPURA: filled with
colossal, spectral stupas*

I was afraid it was. Measuring the change in me since I'd first turned up here six years earlier, just after hitting rock bottom, things were indubitably better. But there was no hint of self-mastery. My newfound stability was little more than a result of fitting in and feeling secure, and even that was fraying. Once again I was losing trust in the status quo. A part of me would have given anything to remain starry-eyed; it was a weaker part.

Awakening, that's to say real freedom, is the end of views. Faith, belief and devotion are means to an end. When they became ends in themselves, you're lost. But it seemed too soon to let go. I was fully ordained now, spoke Tibetan well and was ready to start teaching. Why did I still feel like a novice?

Shaking off my doubts, I turned my attention to the excitement of being in Little Tibet with its big lamas. Here were the mythic giants of Tibetan Buddhism, each with dozens of former lives to his credit. The invading Chinese had broken their idyll, and now they lived in modest circumstances, accessible even to lowly foreigners.

I knocked on the door of a small stucco house. The Dalai Lama's personal secretary opened it and assigned me an appointment the day after next.

All I knew about this man was what I'd read. First of all, his book *The Key to Madhyamika* made the most difficult of Buddhist teachings clear and succinct, in just a few pages. Then there was his autobiography[112] about a young Tibetan tulku who was uncharacteristically curious about the outside world, who enjoyed tinkering with old watches, and was interested in science. Other things set him apart from the mainstream; he'd even expressed half-joking thanks to the Chinese for freeing him from the gilded cage of the Potala Palace.

I went next to the house of his junior tutor, Trijang Rinpoche, a venerable, wrinkled lama of exceptional poise and dignity. I was taken off-guard when his servant swept me straight in, and there I stood before him. Sitting on the floor with just a thin mat to cushion his ancient bones, he wore a beatific smile and held my eyes inquisitively.

Overawed and unprepared, I covered my confusion with three prostrations and sat down uncomfortably, wondering what I should say. Had he heard about the persona non grata at Sera?

"Where did you come from?" he asked.

"Sera," I answered. "Well, Tharpa Chöeling originally. I'm one of Geshe Rabten's monks."

"Rabten, yes," he nodded in recognition.

He filled the uncomfortable silence with small talk and nodded genially when I got up, looking vaguely relieved.

Once outside, I was mortified by my gormless performance and immediately began to draft a list of topics for my visit to the Dalai Lama. There were scriptural questions, matters of personal practice and some direct questions about how much study was too much and how little meditation was not enough. Perhaps I was hoping he'd flush away the after effects of my mind-numbing blackwater fever. At least, I hoped, I'd regain some faith.

His Holiness welcomed me in a simple room. I peeled back my robe to make the routine prostrations but he grabbed my arm instead and pointed laughingly to a chair facing the plastic sofa on which he perched himself. "No need for that," he said, shaking his head as if I'd just tried to stand on my head and juggle. He watched me keenly and waited, just like his tutor Trijang Rinpoche had done.

But this time I was prepared. I pulled out my list and began at the top.

He took his time on each topic. Apparently my questions inspired him to speak. It was a good meeting, but not for the reasons I'd expected. His answers really were illuminating, but what I'd instinctively come to him for, and what I was getting, had nothing to do with explanations. Still, my questions kept up a flow and put my insecurities at arm's length. Finally, he stood up, took my hand and thanked me.

I thought about this man who passed hardly a day without meeting a few strangers, sometimes dozens, and never showed any sign of impatience. In one sense he was typically Tibetan, generously lubricating the conversation with youthful laughter. And yet he was refined in ways that took me by surprise, even after my year and a half in Sera. Perhaps I was projecting my desire for him to be special. Perhaps he really was more inscrutable than other Tibetans. Or, perhaps, I was just under the influence of his significant personal charm.

A few days later I watched him preside over a public ceremony. Hundreds of visitors lined up to present a scarf and be tapped on the head or grasped by the hand. Every one left with his or her own personal gift, secured for life in a downcast, private reflection.

I strolled often through the bazaar of McLeod Ganj, remembering the ingenuous young man I'd been six years earlier. Feeling guilty for delaying my return to Tharpa Chöeling, I looked into the smiling faces of the Tibetan merchants for ulterior motives.

The sight of a trio of bronze statues[113] stopped me in my tracks so visibly that the shopkeeper feigned disinterest. "In fact," he said preparing the ground for a high price, "they're not really for sale."

I was about to ask him what he meant by "not really," when a huge American voice boomed in my ears.

"Hi there ... beautiful statues!"

Burly and grinning, a glass eye discomfortingly awry, the man looked like a lost tourist. The elegant woman at his side made him look even more out of place.

I nodded toward him silently, thinking that once he saw me conversing fluently in Tibetan, he'd show a little respect. Instead, he leaned over my shoulder and, in perfect Tibetan, convinced the merchant to hand over the goods for a bargain-basement price.

The old man sighed as he held the statues toward me.

"Are you sure?" I asked.

The merchant shrugged sheepishly, but the American scoffed, "He's got another dozen sets like that under the counter."

And so I met the Thurmans. Little did I know it at the time, but they were already the stuff of legend. As we left the shop together he extended a burly hand and thundered, "Hi, I'm Bob, and this is Nena."

"Well, Bob," I said. "Thanks." He was such a big loud American that it didn't seem right to like him, but there was something warm and very real about him. Nena was utterly charming.

I learned he'd been the first Westerner ordained in Dharamsala, quite some years ago, and although he'd long ago given back his robes he remained close to the Dalai Lama and was now a professor at Amherst University in Massachusetts. At his request, His Holiness had agreed to conduct a private ceremony in his personal chapel, and Bob asked if I'd like to come along. I needed no persuading.

They asked about me, and when I explained I'd just spent a year in Sera, they wanted to know what it had been like. I was tempted to vent, and wondered how far I could go. "It surprised me."

"Go on," he sat back.

I described one or two of my most galling experiences and saw that he wasn't fazed. He commented that one couldn't expect miracles of ordinary people, Tibetan or otherwise.

"That makes sense," I said.

"And yet . . . ," began Bob.

"You're still upset," said Nena. "You need time to digest your experiences."

"I like you guys," I said, surprised at myself.

Bob laughed. "Really? In that case, perhaps you feel like babysitting."

It was my turn to laugh.

"No, really," he insisted.

I looked at Nena. She shrugged.

"You've got a baby here in Dharamsala?"

"Two boys—"

"Actually three," Bob interjected.

"Stop confusing the issue Bob," Nena reproved. She turned to me. "We left Mipam behind. Too young."

"Mipam?" I asked. They gave their child a Tibetan name?

"We brought Ganden and Dechen. Eleven and nine. Come. Meet them."

Down the street and up some steps, we opened the door to an unholy mess and boisterous shouting. Bob roared, to no effect. Nena strode between us and pushed each boy sternly into a wicker chair. They twitched, but remained seated.

"You'd trust me with them?" I asked.

"You can handle them," Bob chuckled.

"Why would you trust me?"

Nena turned to me. "Are you untrustworthy?"

"No," I shook my head in protest.

"Well then?" she asked, satisfied.

"Well, okay."

"You mean okay, you'll look after them?" Nena asked expectantly.

I nodded.

They broke into relieved smiles.

"Just for a day," said Bob.

"A day?"

Bob nodded. "Is that too long? Are you busy?"

I shrugged. "Not at all."

"Well then it's settled," said Nena.

The boys looked me up and down.

The boys were energetic and quick-witted, and I envied their uncommon childhood. Thinking of my own, I realized I'd become moribund once again. Half-Italian in England, half-English in Italy, half-Tibetan Buddhist, half-Theravadin, a foreigner in Asia and quite out of place at home. It dawned on me that my conflict was just a habitual story running through my head. There was nothing to resolve. Tibetan Buddhism hadn't made me any less the fretful English-Catholic boy who'd set out to hitchhike across Asia; in fact, the question of to what extent it had been a positive influence was just more unnecessary baggage.

After years of feeling unable to accept my emotions, I understood that my path lay at my feet. Where else? My feelings were what they were and no argument or logic would change them. If Bob could give up his robes, marry, have children, pursue a career and be so damned cheerful, then maybe I too could follow my own nose. In the few days I'd known Bob, he'd become an honest-to-goodness role model for me.

Still gravely thin and unlikely to withstand another tropical disease, I looked forward to the healing airs of Switzerland. It actually felt like going home, though I didn't expect that feeling to last. I looked forward to putting my Tibetan to good use. I was ready to teach, and anticipating the accelerated learning it would entail.

A day or two before leaving McLeod Ganj I recognized from a distance the familiar loping stride and pensive gravity of Alan. He greeted me as an old friend and quizzed me about Sri Lanka's suitability for his planned retreat. I asked him in turn about Tharpa Chöeling, but he was circumspect.

Knowing that his responsibilities at Tharpa Chöeling had weighed on him, I felt his relief. Still, I kept my own pool of negativity to myself. I wouldn't feel comfortable sharing my doubts about trust, devotion and faith with him. Mixed up as they were with anger and loneliness, it was dawning on me that moral safety was just another fiction. If this really was my path, where was it leading?

32

THE SENIOR MONK

THE STREETS OF GENEVA were so quiet it seemed like a Sunday afternoon. In fact, it was a weekday morning; I'd simply grown accustomed to the dense population and great bustle of India.

With low rumbles and electric clicking, a barely swaying CFF train conveyed me along the familiar North-West shore of Lac Leman; then the Vevey funicular carried me up Mont-Pèlerin. I was back in the cool air.

Geshe's welcome turned businesslike as he took stock of my new skills, and I of his diminished resources. He remarked on my thinness and suggested I take a few days to recover. Alan, Steve and Brian were gone. A dozen new monks had arrived. He asked about some of his colleagues and students from Sera, but didn't talk about my old friends. I mentioned that I'd need a new sponsor, and within days my needs were met by a Bernese lady who turned up one day in search of a monk.

I translated classes and personal interviews, but wasn't privy to the organizational matters of Tharpa Chöeling. Helmut continued to work discreetly on various projects with Geshe, and any details that escaped were immediately obscured behind his dissimulating laugh. Now I realize that all the secrecy might not have been his idea at all, but Geshe's.

Meanwhile, Arnie's work as the administrator and manager of the center had led him to quit his studies. Also, he'd contracted tuberculosis and the toll of the intense medications on his meager frame was terrible. He smiled wanly at his misfortune.

"If I can't study, at least I can help create a conducive environment for others," he said.

"What does Geshe think?" I asked.

Arnie shrugged. "Someone's got to do it."

"Did he ask you to give up studying?"

"It was my decision."

"To give up everything?"

"Next life," he stared with a blank look of exhaustion.

Perhaps others found this commendable. It made me sad.

With a pained expression, Arnie confessed to knowing nothing about Alan's departure. He held Alan in high esteem and, more than any of us, had counted him as a friend. "I know," he continued, "that Alan's wanted to go into retreat for a long time."

"And Brian?" I asked.

"Brian's gone to Hamburg. Took over from Steve."

"Steve's off to Korea, then?"

"Yes."

"So it's just you and me?"

"What d'you mean?"

"From Schwendi. Just you and me left."

"Yes, I suppose so."

"Who's here then?"

Arnie reeled off the names of a few younger monks who'd been there when I left, plus a long list of unfamiliar people. One significant addition to the community was a small group of nuns.

"Why d'you think everyone's gone, one by one," I asked. "D'you ever wonder if you'll be next?"

Arnie explained away each case as a separate, personal issue, as if they were all disconnected, and resisted my attempts to identify a common malaise. Steve's letter still resonated clearly for me, and I was convinced that here in Tharpa Chöeling the East-West crucible had bubbled over in ways we should have foreseen. I'd go next probably, and I presumed that Arnie too would sooner or later discover a part of himself that couldn't find expression here. I didn't convince him of that, but he did grudgingly accept that there might be a widening gap between Geshe's goals and the mandate we'd once conceived for our center.

Our center indeed—things were different from the Schwendi days when we had so much drive. It was pretty lackadaisical around here now. Monks had televisions in their rooms and went to the cinema in lay clothes; some didn't even put on a show of studying. Geshe seemed fine with it; at least, he made no objection. He was away often, and the community was fragmented—you might say neglected. The present incumbent was the friendly but unimpressive Geshe Kayang, my old friend from Sera, and no sooner had he arrived than a scandal had cost him his credibility; he was accused of having touched one of the nuns improperly.

Geshe continued to welcome prospective monks without question, but when Delphine, a young Swiss woman who'd been close to the center for years, requested ordination, Geshe found himself in a predicament. Like any Tibetan abbot, he would naturally have sent nuns elsewhere,[114] but there were other precedents in the West. Dharma centers like Lama Yeshe's had grown out of grassroots organizations that were managed and shared equitably by men and women. Quarters were segregated into ordained and lay, male and female, and if there was only one roof, then all slept under it.

Whether Geshe ever considered this sort of arrangement or not was a moot point, for a far more strident voice rose up to settle the matter. Anila Ansermet rejected a place for the nuns out of hand, not just under the monastic roof but even within the organizational compass of Tharpa Chöeling. They were told unceremoniously to rent their own quarters and meet their own expenses. In short, they would not be given the same leisure to study, or not, that their male counterparts enjoyed. Most of the nuns made their way by cleaning houses.

It wasn't unusual for women of Anila's age and class to be antagonistic to women's rights—Swiss women only got the vote in 1971. Far more disconcerting was the attitude of the monks, although it wasn't just a matter of male chauvinism. Arnie and all the others I spoke to confessed to feeling bad for Delphine's group, but helpless. Geshe made it clear that this was none of my business and that it would be a major breach of monastic etiquette to argue. What upset me was that, rather than just accepting this as a de facto matter in which we had no say, the general consensus went one step further and decided that Geshe was exercising a wisdom beyond our ken. It was considered good "guru devotion" to believe that his reasons must be just and proper, if not transcendant.

Intellectually, I was amazed by these self-imposed blinkers. Emotionally, I was appalled. Here were people claiming to be Buddhists, but so dazzled by exotic thinking and ritual as to be unable to exercise their own critical judgment. Western Buddhism would sooner or later have to develop its own feet, and it was beginning to look like the sooner the better. Once again I recognized that, just as a child pulls away from its parents, my time was coming.

Shortly after my return, on one public Sunday afternoon, I fell into conversation with Tara, a periodic, enthusiastic visitor from Paris. I didn't know her well. Passionately devoted to Geshe, she'd brought him a snappy little Spitz that Geshe took a surprising shine to.

"Welcome back Steve, how are you," she asked earnestly. "How did you find it down in Sera?"

Tara was of a type who wears her heart plainly on her sleeve, which was perhaps why I had no difficulty allowing my feelings to tumble out in one curt line. "Don't ask me how I am; I don't want to talk about it; I'm still much too angry." I delivered this, she told me years later, with "clenched teeth and burning eyes." I immediately regretted my outburst, "I'll explain later ... still too tired," and changed the subject. I'd regarded her ardor as the badge of the sort of dogmatic follower I wasn't inclined to suffer, but there was more to her than that. She was merely at a loss for words, and neither closed nor indignant. In fact, I noticed as she narrowed her eyes, she was intrigued by my outburst. Nevertheless, she let the subject lie, and we talked of less explosive things.

The next I saw of her was when she joined my scriptural Tibetan class one weekday afternoon. She'd moved to the area for an extended stay, to

THE AUTHOR PUTTING ON A FRONT:
"Don't ask me how I am. I don't want to
talk about it. I'm still much too angry."

be more involved. Women were welcome to study, if not to lodge in the
monastery. Delphine was there too, together with a handful of monks.
We welcomed Tara and got down to work on a Buddha-nature text.

I'd never learned so intensely. I had to prepare more thoroughly as a
teacher than as a student, but now had open access to Geshe. My hesitations about him never extended to his command of the textbooks or his
ability to articulate them,[115] and he was always a pleasure to work with.

Other duties included interpreting Geshe's classes to the younger
monks and translating public teachings. Everything I'd learned by
watching Steve and Brian now reminded me of how isolated I felt. If
Tharpa Chöeling had been a home to me it was because of my associa-
tion with those two friends. And although our friendship certainly left
me feeling cared for, its significance went further. From day one it had
touched on the very nerve of my thoughts and feelings as a Buddhist and
as a monk. Each of their personalities had tugged me in opposite directions, one devotional, one skeptical, in a dialectic that always eventually
resolved itself. Left to my own devices however, the inner counterparts of
these alternate attitudes had a way of tearing me apart. Decades would

pass before I understood, and accepted, how stubbornly the head denies the primacy of the heart.

I meditated. I walked. I read and I worked the Buddha-nature text into a book. I corresponded with Steve and Brian, but even several letters a week weren't enough. My dilemma wasn't simplified; if anything, it fell into a more strangled focus than ever. The possibility of hanging on to both my self-respect and my robes seemed less and less feasible. I tried to understand, but could only *feel*—something inside me was tearing.

I needed someone to talk to. I'd resigned myself to never expect such a relationship with Geshe, even though that had been my main reason for learning Tibetan. I got along well enough with most of the monks, but seemed to scare them off whenever I tried to explore the outer limits of faith, belief and the Tibetan way. By now, the topic had gained a volatile foothold in my emotions.

One person who didn't try to steer clear of me was Tara. She told me I was a good teacher and laughed at "the mad glow of my stare;" I was still stick-thin and sallow skinned from my fever. I took her genial mockery as a complement, and was drawn to her. She lingered after classes with questions and intense conversation, never small talk. When she'd first met Geshe, her passion had been yoga, and she spoke wide-rangingly of Hinduism, Western philosophy and the Jewish and Christian Bibles. She'd studied for years and had vigorous opinions on most things, all of which she expressed with a certainty that was hard to crack. She wove the threads of Buddhism into those of other religions—too casually for me, but intriguing nonetheless. Her faith in Geshe and the Tibetans was childlike, but she didn't flinch when challenged, nor when I shared disturbing stories from Sera. I came to trust her. At what seemed a considerable risk to her own faith, she reflected my glowering inner landscape in a sympathetic eye. This sustained a process that had begun with Bob and Nena's unquestioning acceptance of me at face value, and which would go on for decades as I came to accept myself.

Tara's devotion to Geshe was ardent, and others took exception to her unreserved ways. She looked to Geshe for advice on everything, not just Buddhism, and stoutly presumed that her intense love for him was reciprocated. On the occasions when I translated their meetings, I found

Geshe's manner cool. As she leaned forward, he leaned back. She either didn't notice, or chose not to.

Like everyone, Tara dreamed of speaking to Geshe without the mediation of a translator, and put her limited Tibetan vocabulary to the greatest possible use, sometimes with hilarious results. She was unabashed and apparently oblivious to the fact that she was widely considered a dilettante.

Tara had no time for insincerity and bemoaned the dry academics that gathered around Tibetan lamas. She had particularly low opinions of Alan and Steve, but reserved her greatest scorn for Helmut and those who played the realpolitik of East-West dharma. She believed that money should never trump heartfelt devotion, and watched with disgust as those with wealth found Geshe's ear more easily. The fact that Tara was vivacious and beautiful didn't help, for many of Geshe's biggest supporters were elderly matrons, old-fashioned and judgmental.

Tara and I grew far too close for the comfort of Tharpa Chöeling watchers. We met in Vevey and went for walks. I had coffee with her. One day we took a picnic lunch to Les Pleiades, built a large bonfire and chatted like old friends until nightfall. I said, "I don't want to be part of that set-up any more. I couldn't forgive myself if I became like them." She didn't comment, except to repeat my words back to me. I hadn't uttered such thoughts to a living soul before, not even to myself.

Others might have cared for me, but she took the time to drain my feelings in a sort of bloodletting that left me giddy. I gave her private Tibetan lessons and she coached me in French. We spent hours alone in her rooms, fully aware that our liaison was no secret. She seemed to think that because we never broke the letter of the monastic law, that our time together was entirely innocent. In fact, I was indeed breaking all sorts of supporting rules by being alone in a room with a woman and making direct eye contact. And although it's never stated in these terms, it was quite against the spirit of celibacy to form a one-on-one emotional bond, and that we most certainly did.

Strangely, she seemed to expect that our familiarity would stay under wraps. I harbored no such illusions, and was ready to pay the price of disapprobation; without her I'd have exploded in far more alarming ways.

Tara eventually received a letter from "a well-wisher," advising her that her antics were common knowledge and that she was corrupting my innocent young flesh. Livid with indignation, she compiled a short list of suspects and kept her hawk eye peeled, in hopes of exposing them. We presumed it was written by one or some of Geshe's benefactors— the Church Ladies— self-appointed caretakers of communal morals and owners of the bricks, mortar and monks of Tharpa Chöeling.

Things now imploded in more ways than one. My appreciation for Tara devolved into an anxious dependency, and she eventually had to push me away. She was blunt and I was hurt, but there was nothing to be done—I'd started using her as a crutch. This was when, she proudly announced, she told Geshe that I was the best monk he had, bar none, and that he was wasting my talents. This conversation must have saddened him; the thought of it surely made me cringe.

I slunk into Geshe's room to clear up the matter. He asked if I'd committed a "defeat," meaning the destruction of the monastic vow—in other words, intercourse. He accepted my word that I hadn't, and also that I wouldn't see Tara alone again. But I withheld the most important truth of all, that I no longer saw a future to my monkhood. The trouble was, I saw no future outside of it either; I was stymied, and needed to clear my head before I could anticipate my next steps.

I had no intention of abandoning Buddhism. In fact, it was clearly my practice that had brought me to this brink. In my heart, I knew that although circumstances might change, my path would be unbroken. Still, as clear as this explanation was, my feelings were muddied and compounded by guilt. The next months would be tricky.

At that moment I was granted a temporary reprieve. The Dalai Lama was giving the Kalachakra initiation in Wisconsin, and the young Frenchman Alain Levy, whom I'd met at Coniston Priory just after my ordination, offered to take me along. I accepted at once.

It was an exciting diversion that prolonged the torture. Everywhere I went as a monk, I received free accommodation, preferred seating and other perks. There was no refusing, no way I could not wear my robes until I formally renounced them, even though I traveled in lay clothes.

Arriving at Cornell University in jeans and a shirt, I changed into my robes for the first stop on the Dalai Lama's tour. There I bumped into Bob Thurman, who bulldozed away my angst and made me thoroughly welcome. Afterwards, he packed me in a van with his family and drove me to his handmade, mandala-shaped house in upstate New York. During that brief respite I was shadowed by the momentous question that hung over me like an anvil frozen in time over Wily Coyote's head.

Then in Madison there was the Kalachakra initiation. It was a huge gathering at the time, though a pale shadow of what was to come when the Dalai Lama became a Nobel laureate two decades later. With a stage at one end of an open field, the atmosphere was like a sixties rock festival, with Chinese brocade. The crowd felt blessed, and it was all very catholic.

After two years apart, Brian and I laughed happily in each other's company again. He meant to return to Hamburg afterwards but, like me, was counting down his days as a monk. Still, his plans for a graceful exit were more strategic and less guilt-ridden than mine. He was negotiating a place for himself at the Deer Park center right there in Madison,[116] where he could attend university at the same time. With one foot in each camp he'd make the transition at his own chosen speed.

We talked about the old Schwendi group and what had become of it. Steve had left and was now living in a Zen monastery in Korea. Alan was snuggling up even closer to the Tibetans, especially the Dalai Lama. Unsurprisingly, Helmut was still with Geshe Rabten, and would remain for life.[117] Arnie was still at Tharpa Chöeling too, though he'd been talking for years of studying medicine.

They all had some sort of plan, however vague. I looked into my future and saw a black hole. Bob had offered to get me into a graduate program at Amherst College in Massachusetts, and for a few minutes it sounded grand. I was no scholar, however, and certainly didn't have the temperament to work among academics. My wish to teach was, if anything, stronger than ever, but what I envisioned was far more personal than theoretical. Nor was I in any mood to join another Dharma community. Everything I could think of that might ease the transition seemed like a cop-out, and I wasn't about to compromise myself. Besides, I was confident I'd find my own way though, Lord knows, I couldn't explain why.

Back in Tharpa Chöeling, Anila Ansermet had dropped a bombshell. In the few weeks I'd been gone she'd renovated a corner of the first floor and moved in directly beneath Geshe's quarters. The nuns were outraged; having been effectively barred they now watched helplessly as the old doyenne flagrantly disregarded her own inconvenient rule.

"I am an old woman," she said. "No monks will be corrupted by me."

She had a point. Except for Arnie and me, the monks were a younger and far more docile lot than we'd been.

Tara fumed with disgust as she lost her respect for Geshe, but I was quietly, skeptically, unshocked. The awkward silences greeting both her outrage and mine drove us further from the community and kept us connected, at least for the time being. She was planning a prolonged stay in India with Song Rinpoche, one of the great old lamas of the Gelug tradition with whom I'd become acquainted in South India. She, once again, adored him and believed he adored her too.

Hitherto, I'd assumed that Sera Monastery's orthodoxy was the result of fifteen hundred years of gradual petrification. I now watched as the vibrant community that had once been Schwendi-22 settled into moribund complacency after just a few years. In its informal early years it had infused us all with energy. Now, it too seemed lifeless.

Still unprepared to make my move, I took Tharpa Chöeling one day at a time. When Lama Yeshe went to Zollikon to teach, I visited Frau Kalff and secured a few minutes alone with him.

He sat exhausted on the throne in the large, empty meeting room as I knocked at the open door. He beckoned me.

I sat down and tried to collect my thoughts.

His fatigue seemed to vanish. He leaned forward with a conspiratorial schoolboy grin and said, "Hello darling."

I crumpled in laughter.

"What can I do for you?"

"I think you've already done it," I said.

"All right dear. Thank you. Thank you." He didn't seem puzzled by my cryptic statement.

"I . . . I just wanted to understand what had happened to me in Sera."

His eyes went up theatrically. "You were in Sera?"

"For a year and a half."

He shook his head in astonishment. "Did you have a good time?"

I shook my head. "Neither did they," I said.

"The monks of Sera? My brothers?" He had a twinkle in his eyes.

"Yes. They were happy to see me go."

"I see. I see. Must be very difficult for you. Very old place, Sera. Like Tibet. So now you speak Tibetan?"

I answered, "Yes," and we exchanged a few polite phrases.

"Good, very good," he nodded approvingly. "You're back with Geshe Rabten now?" He put his hands together and bowed as he spoke his teacher's name.

It was odd to see Lama Yeshe behaving with such hierarchical correctness. For a moment I wondered whether he wasn't being sarcastic, but that would have been equally out of character. He was utterly Tibetan, an ineluctable advocate of guru devotion.

I said, "Yes, I'm translating and teaching at Tharpa Chöeling."

"And debating?"

I shook my head uncomfortably. "Not really."

"Perhaps debating inside, with yourself?" he tapped my chest.

I choked on my own saliva.

When my coughing subsided Lama leaned forward and took my head in his hands. He touched my forehead with his own and muttered some syllables. For the first time in my involuntarily Catholic life, I experienced communion. There was no light show, no pumping heart beat. I simply felt whole, able to deal with anything, sure of my path, willing to make any sacrifice. He trusted me and that was enough.

He put a ceremonial scarf around my neck and dismissed me with a pat on the cheek.

Back on Mont-Pèlerin I spent sleepless nights writing poetry, pouring out my anger, frustration, heartbreak and confusion in raw verse. It wasn't just therapeutic, it also revived my latent creativity—something, I realized, that could flourish only with trial and error. Far from abandoning Buddhism I now had to explore it on my own terms. I had more than enough theory under my belt.

I decided I'd become a writer. Tara was encouraging. My first book would be about the rise and fall of a Buddhist monk, a Westerner who became a Tibetan Buddhist—well, not a Tibetan, but a Buddhist Would I use a capital B? First person or third? The angles were endless. How would I decide? Who would narrate it? Should it be fictional?

First though, I had to make my move. I was nervous. The thought of finding a way to support myself and securing a place to stay seemed about as likely as sprouting wings, but I checked the classifieds and visited apartments for rent, telling myself that if these things were possible for the vast majority of people, they would be for me too. I just had to believe it.

As a first step, I needed to meet people outside the monastery, and I began by visiting the house of Tharpa Chöeling's lay students. Their situation too had undergone changes over the years. Only a handful of the group that now shared a large house was regularly connected with Geshe and the monks. It was an anarchic, open household, a good place to start reconnecting with the world outside. I also joined Professor Jacques May's Sanskrit class at Lausanne University. This confirmed, as if it was necessary, that an academic career held no allure for me. Still, I met more people, sat with them in cafés and began to improve my French. Gradually, my wings unfurled.

Tom Tillemans, my very first Tibetan teacher, had been teaching the language to a Lausanne doctor, and now asked me to take over from him. This was my first paying job in ten years. It was a big step to accept money for what I'd always received, and so far passed on, for free. In doing it, I realized that nothing came without a price, and that in the world I was returning to, money, although a burdensome form of exchange, was more democratic than the currency of monastic duty. It brought in just a little pocket money, but it was a good start.

At Geshe's request, and to my delight, I continued the tradition started by Alan, then Steve and Brian, of traveling to Geneva once a week to teach. I drove down in the monastery station wagon and delivered the same systematic teachings I'd interpreted so often for Geshe. There I was, in the robes, representing the Tibetan tradition under the ægis of Geshe Rabten. The group had been following a well-known text, and in spite of the long interruption since their last class it wasn't difficult to pick up where Brian had left off. I was on a low teaching throne and everyone sat back to listen. I kept it orthodox and noncontentious. Actually, I thought my delivery was rather wooden. Afterwards however, a woman raised her voice in praise: "Such wisdom! And in one so young!" This was greeted by a rustle of nodding assent.

I shuddered inwardly. I'd longed for the day when I'd finally begin to teach, not just language and philosophy but the bread and butter of the path to Awakening. Now I'd earned the right—and was on my way—but felt like a fraud. All I'd delivered were words. If they could see inside me they'd find no wisdom; just confusion. Who'd have thought that praise for my teaching would become the last straw?

My experience as a monk, my seniority and my position as a teacher led younger monks at Tharpa Chöeling to look up to me, and I was acutely aware of my potentially seditious influence. While I wanted to be forthright about what I'd seen and what I felt, I didn't think it fair to undermine their innocence. Let them learn for themselves, I thought. One afternoon in the refectory I was chatting cautiously with some of them about how my sense of devotion had changed over the years, when suddenly their heads bowed and shoulders hunched. I looked over my shoulder to see Geshe making a rare visit to the communal area.

"So, what are you lot up to?" he asked intently.

"Just talking . . . relaxing," I said.

"You know," he began as if delivering a prepared speech, "Could be you all talk together too much."

"Yes, Gen," I said. "We should get back to our studies."

"You see," he ignored me, "sometimes young monks get together and talk too much. They stir things up," he made motions of mixing a cauldron with a big stick. "It just introduces doubt and uncertainty. If you want to test Lord Buddha's teachings, you should debate."

This was an unusual interjection for Geshe. He rarely walked in on our conversations or volunteered an opinion unasked. Unsure how to respond, I nodded mutely until he asked me to translate. I did so.

He went on. "You don't know how lucky you are. You don't have to go to work or deal with family problems like those people in Geneva. You don't need to work for money. Money and sex cause so many problems; you wouldn't believe the stories I hear. You can just sit back and put your feet up, and they'll provide food, shelter . . . everything. Your time's your own. All you have to do is study a bit and say a few prayers. You've got a life of leisure. You have it so much easier than those lay people. Why don't you enjoy it?"

I could hardly believe my ears. Didn't he understand how disreputable this made monkhood sound?

"You don't even have to study if you don't want to," he continued. "You can do nothing. Just being a monk, you accumulate more merit than any layperson."

I hid my amazement by translating, and muttered deferentially, "Very well, Gen."[118]

Geshe gave us one last look and a strangely intense smile before walking away.

The thought of lying back and doing nothing, of taking advantage of the sponsors' generosity wasn't just low on my list of priorities, it was a strong disincentive. If I'd needed any further impetus to leave the dependent life of a monk, this was it. Over the years I'd developed a new, hard-won focus on self-respect and integrity, and this was an appeal to self-indulgence.

Of all the things I'd seen in my experience with the Tibetans, this was the saddest. I didn't know what to do, and wished it had never happened. It cast me into a profound gloom.

Outside the center I now put it out loud and clear that I was ready to leave. Word would sooner or later get back to my fellows, but by then, hopefully, I'd be gone. As soon as she heard of my decision, Diane Lavenex, a fellow Sanskrit student, promptly offered me the spare room in her apartment. Another friend found me some part-time hours teaching English as a second language. Pathways appeared.

I knocked on Geshe's door. He responded with a curt, "Yes," and I went in.

His prayer book was in front of him. I had to force my lungs to breathe and my words to take shape.

"Gen?"

"Thubten Sangye," he eyed me cautiously.

"You know, Gen ... ," I began.

In a single gesture he flicked the cloth cover over the pages of his prayers and leaned back.

I remembered the first time I'd sat across from him like this and he taught me my first debate. A wave of gratitude washed unexpectedly over me. No matter how things had worked out, he'd given generously of his time and attention. I remembered him joking around as Brian and I lost our hair. Those eyes that were burning into me right now had been filled with laughter.

I bumbled on. I don't remember my words, such a muddle was I in.

Eventually I stopped, and his response is etched in my memory. He turned sharply away and gazed out the window to the distant mountains. Without looking he said, "I don't want your vows. I won't take them. Go give them to Kayang."

"Geshe. I'm sorry." I wanted to explain myself, to tell him it wasn't his fault, but every thought I had sounded ridiculous. I backed out, numb.

"Thubten Sangye," he called me.

I turned around.

He looked uncomfortable. "Can I ask you one thing?"

"Of course." Were we to end on a positive note after all?

"When you have ... ," he made an awkward gesture, "you know, with a woman ... "

"Sex?" Where was this going?

"Don't do it in the daytime."

"Huh?" I thought my Tibetan had failed me.

"No sex during daylight," he said. "It's better that way."

Yes, I'd got the words right, but I didn't for the life of me understand. Sex was the furthest thing from my mind. For a split second I considered explaining that to him, then dismissed the idea.

Geshe Kayang was in his room, also saying prayers.

"Thubten Sangye," he welcomed me straight-faced, as if he was expecting me. He hadn't called me Aro for some time, preoccupied as he was with his own troubles. When I said that Geshe wanted him to take my vows, he sat up and looked businesslike.

"Are you sure?" he asked.

"Yes."

"Then it's already done," he answered. "But if it makes it clearer for you, just tell me three times."

"Should I go down on one knee?"

He shrugged. "If you like."

I did so and repeated the simple statement three times. "I no longer wish to be bound by the monk's rule."

That's it," he said matter-of-factly.

"Thanks, Gen," I said.

"Go slowly, Thubten Sangye," he looked me squarely in the eye.

I backed out, hardly breathing.

I returned to my room, removed my robes and lay them on the bed. Everything else, I packed into a battered suitcase. Autumn was settling in as I stepped out into the damp twilight. How would I cope? I knew that the customs and culture I'd absorbed would fade from disuse. I also knew that these eight years had marked me for life. My apprenticeship was unorthodox by any standards, for I'd bucked the Tibetan system no less than the Western one, but I'd acquired much to sustain me. The task ahead was to pick the gold out of the dross. Time alone would tell whether I could live a worthwhile life.

The door closed behind me as I crossed the lawn down to the road. I glanced back. The building was like a fist, clasping my dreams. Tears cut through the mist that settled on my cheeks, and I walked away.

Wander forth, O monks. Let no two go the same way.[119]

—THE BUDDHA

EPILOGUE

He who lives more lives than one
More deaths than one must die.

—OSCAR WILDE
The Ballad of Reading Gaol

NEVER BEFORE HAD MY PATH been so clear: I'd closed all doors behind me; I was alone. I didn't hesitate, though had I foreseen what the next two decades held in store, I'd have thought twice about it. But what am I saying? I'd already thought a thousand times about it. It didn't change the reality—I was as green as a sapling.

I'd abandoned not only the robes and monastic environment, but also my teachers, friends and vocation. The Buddha's claim to Awakening still charged my imagination, but I saw Buddh*ism* as another matter. I'd learned much, and already knew that parts of it were useful, but the mass of it was all dressed up in the cloak of Tibetan mysticism, and only a winnowing of unpredictable proportions could guide me to an authentic practice. This decision was raw, unpremeditated and unfounded—a leap of pure faith. I'd never heard of any such process of distillation.

My only recognizable skill was command of an obscure Himalayan language, and my only resource in Canada, where I'd moved, was the former Tharpa Chöeling monk Georges Ostiguy, who found me a job in his own workplace. I entered the Montreal labor force on a lowly rung, managing the seedy office of a pen-shooting[120] company.

Mercifully, I soon found work teaching English, and bought a desktop computer to use as a teaching aid. Instead, I learned the novel tool of word processing. This was timely, for I was ready to put the story of my time with the Tibetans on paper—or so I thought.

My years of celibacy had somehow cured me of awkwardness with girls. I now had confidence, and no trouble gaining their attention, though I'd still no idea how to manage a mature relationship. I married rashly, separated within weeks, and fell into a nervous depression.

My long absence from consumerism set me apart. I learned not to speak of my past; it tended to create barriers and attract ridicule. Meanwhile, the drive to write this unborn book kept me going, though I struggled fruitlessly to get it past the embryonic stage; I was still too close to the story and my writing lacked momentum. I thought occasionally that I might have been fooling myself all those years, but in the end, only the Buddhist perspective enabled me to make sense of my present circumstances. Whether it felt like it or not, I decided, I must still be on track.

One attempt after another to write this story ended up in the waste paper basket. For years I had nothing to show for having been a monk, let alone to justify the calamity of giving it up. I cast my mind back to the early days in Switzerland, imagining some lucky young monk shuffling around my old room. Years passed, and Father Cunliffe's prophesy about my way of doing things the hard way proved to be the understatement of a lifetime. I grew accustomed to living with no taste for life.

I continued to acquire new skills. I was at ease now with technology, and writing software manuals for a living. My experience with Tibetan had been good practice for translating the arcane language of engineers and programmers into plain English. I discovered that concise prose takes time, and that there's a fine line between confusing readers and patronizing them. I learned the nuts and bolts of writing.

With the proliferation of computerized tools there were new opportunities to practice typesetting and digital illustration. I acquired most of my new skills for the sheer fun of it, and put profitability second. I was especially fascinated by typography and its place in the history of communication.

Within ten years I was working as an editor, illustrator and designer, compiling complex scientific books from the comfort of my home office, putting far more time and effort into upgrading my skills than was financially justifiable. I kept going as the Internet grew into a chaotic warehouse of knowledge and, when the time came, studied web design.

I realized that I just liked learning, especially through autodidactic trial and error. Making endless mistakes and retracing the same ground repeatedly creates a far broader contextual web and greater flexibility of understanding than plodding through a syllabus compiled by established "experts," even though one's range of knowledge is uneven.

I had an advantage when it came to understanding the graphic messages that barrage us day and night. Having lived beyond the fringes of consumer society for so long, I could easily objectify the enticements of consumerism and modernity, although I was surprised to see what a sophisticated consuming machine I remained anyway. My years apart had barely dented the instinct to seek happiness in shiny new stuff. I had to *keep* resisting; the effort was endless. I was just as skeptical of the impulse to look back nostalgically on my Tibetan years. Both lives were unsatisfactory, but they were all I had. I placed my faith in writing, knowing it would be somehow cathartic. This book danced at the edge of my imagination, stubbornly refusing to emerge, and yet I knew it was there; without any recognizable foundation, my confidence grew. I digested my experiences and learned something every day.

As a would-be writer I nurtured the usual pretensions about the purity of creative writing, as opposed to the whorish, mundane money-grubbing of subsistence jobbing, but at least I was writing. In my spare time, as I groped for the literary thread to carry me though, I realized I had yet to find a voice; I'd been trying too hard to write *well*. I had to take a back seat and let the story speak for itself.

Creative writing courses at university helped, and brought me badly needed human contact. I made new friends and met women, but still felt like a stranger to the world I inhabited, torn by a lingering foreignness I was reluctant to give up even though it pained me.

This psychic distance meant I took less for granted, and saw angles on life to which others were oblivious. North American society was strange indeed. On the surface it offers unprecedented freedoms, but its day-to-day operations encourage those raised on television and pop culture to huddle in consensus and flock to the malls for succor. Even academe is subverted to job training, and although I met some enlightened teachers, they seemed powerless against the tide of conveyer-belt education. I saw prospective young graduates who, rather than preparing to explore the world, were setting up timetables for building wealth and predictability. They expressed amazement at the risks I'd taken, but I was infinitely more amazed by their myths of security and permanence.

Day by dispiriting day my nonconformity lost momentum. I had no soul to share it with. A lifelong attempt to live by my convictions seemed to be failing me. I began to think that the search for ultimate truth was a mind game. Perhaps Dad was right and nothing ever would change. The life being lived around me was, quite simply, what was available.

I lost my nerve.

It was time to grow up, face reality and become a full-fledged citizen, and I chose my second wife accordingly. She was both a product and a promoter of the glamor industry, well-turned out and attuned to the outer signs of the times. Determined to make her dream my dream, she protested her love vehemently, dressed me in finery and lent me ambition. She knew exactly what sort of man she was looking for, saw just what she wanted to see in me and never suspected what remained. Taking her cue, I placed my trust in her and tried with all my might to believe that her dream would satisfy me. For a while we even prospered, but in the end our cosmetic rewards turned to ashes.

Since the second year of this doomed marriage I'd sought out psychological guidance, but most of the certified counselors I met with seemed more lost than I. They confirmed my cynicism, unwittingly rebuilt my walls and artlessly diminished my self-worth. When I finally found a real healer I was primed for the long process of peeling away my defences. He was Allan Putterman, and although he had a PhD to his name, he was no dry academic. He was a man I came to trust.

Almost eight years had passed—a period as long as my sojourn with the Tibetans. In that time, all I had to show for my sacrifice at the altar of mammon was the stubborn relief of being, once again, on my own. Every alley seemed blind, life itself a disappointment. I woke up each morning startled and oppressed by the coming day. I didn't care to work and focused increasingly on writing. My income diminished perilously.

Allan was no idle solution peddler. He listened to me describe myself as a frustrated seeker of truth. He asked for more and still more until, I felt self-deceptively, all my hopes and fears must have been laid bare. What others squirreled into their life savings or homes I spent on psychoanalysis, even relying on credit card advances. There was no point in living long and wealthy if life had no taste. Our sessions seemed at times to be little more than chitchat, but he got to know me, my quirks, my defenses and my clever avenues of denial.

Eventually he spoke. "You know, most people who sit in that chair," he pointed to where I sat, "pour their hearts out. Some of them literally break down in tears. That's why they come. But you just sit there and tell me that everything's all right."

For a few moments every valve in my heart seemed to be opening and closing at the same time. My recovery was underway.

As I came to my senses, I saw that I'd used beliefs as convenient tools of denial, and my monkish ego to inoculate myself from normal human failings. The more I'd tried to point my anger away from myself, the more it turned full circle. It wasn't easy to look down the barrel of my own gun but there, on Allan's couch, I acknowledged my duplicity, and the sense of devastation subsided. In time I came to see myself as a relatively average, partially adjusted individual with the rather typical neuroses of an incompletely outgrown childhood.

As depressing as it sounds, this banal truth put everything in perspective and gave my writing the simple shove it needed. I'd been struggling with the story off and on, both with and without my creative writing peer group, for more than ten years. Although I'd managed to animate the exotic passages, real continuity was elusive. It only gradually dawned on me that I was being undermined by my own agenda; I still saw myself self-righteously as having been stymied by the monastic establishment, and was trying to bend the facts to my defence. The lesson was clear—worthwhile stories either speak for themselves or die a turgid death.

At this time I was living in a small apartment overlooking Mount Royal, and the initial elation of leaving my miserable marriage had devolved into a sense of general isolation. What friends I had, possessed little understanding of where I was from or whence I was going, and I refused to volunteer anything to those who didn't care enough to ask. I frequently came close to full-blown despair, but I'd found my voice, if not my rhythm, and the writing was a tonic and friend.

This was when I unexpectedly met Caroline, a woman who was to become pivotal both in my life and in the evolution of this book. We shared our experiences of bitter divorce, and the growing conviction that "true love" was a fiction. There was also her own book, a novel about the multiple sclerosis she'd been diagnosed with seven years before and the effect of that diagnosis on her family. We helped each other with suggestions and encouragement, and in the process became friends with a bond that neither of us had known before.

The book had progressed to about a hundred pages when she suggested some minor adjustments, and I startled her by announcing that I was going to start over. Afraid that her criticisms had thrown a spanner in the works, she tried to dissuade me, but her fears were ungrounded. This time I had a steady hand from page one, and out flowed the fluent memoirs of an unapologetic amateur, the oh-so-catholic confessions of a would-be Buddhist. It was long-winded, at times pitiful, but its stories entwined each other like the strands of a single thread. I was on track.

I rose at four every morning to bathe my memory in those reflective hours. Meditatively, I stared into the nooks and crannies of my life and saw just how much I'd brushed under the carpet. It wasn't easy, but it was a therapeutic eye-opener, the counterpoint to my meetings with Allan.

Mum, lamenting Dad's unwillingness to share his story, had often said, "Never mind. When you grow up you'll have an exciting life and write all about it." Now, the seed she'd planted decades before was coming to fruition. *Exciting* wasn't the word I'd have chosen, but then, what was finally happening was more than just a writing project.[121]

When she learned that I was finally at it, she begged to see, and after some hesitation I handed over an early draft. Never have I seen her so single-pointed. She read it the way a starving person eats—laughing and crying, furrowing her brow and not stopping until she'd consumed everything. Then she looked up and said, "Well, it would have been nice if you'd had a bit more support when you were young, wouldn't it? Don't you think it would have made a difference?"

I was floored. This breathtaking understatement and Mum's unexpected frankness opened up a whole new resource for me. Not only did it get me past my own suppressed version of events, it also dissolved a lifelong resentment and marked the beginning of real intimacy between us. Suddenly, I was no longer a bad-tempered sociopath but a product of circumstances, angry for a reason, torn between the age-old call of independence and the demands of one's elders.

The first draft was a log of everything I could recall, and came to almost a quarter of a million words. Caroline knew my audience better than I, and helped massively with cutting and editing. As we turned the long-winded confession into a tight narrative, my self-image was reassembled and I acquired the subtle skill of doubting myself without losing self-esteem.

In the five years it took to complete this unwieldy draft, I and my circumstances changed entirely. My friendship with Caroline grew into the sort of trust I never expected to experience. I moved in with her and became a step-father to her two daughters; two boys had grown and left home already. In time, a firm bond blossomed in spite of ourselves, and we became man and wife. By sharing our resources, we both came to accept our imperfections, and so I learned the purpose of family life—no den of seclusion but a hive of busyness and confusion, misbehavior and laughter. Allan called it domestic bliss, and I loved it. It showed me once and for all that real change doesn't take place in the ideal circumstances we imagine. Gone were the days I craved a remote mountain retreat.

The family in which I'd grown up had had its share of internal troubles, but whether we wore our hearts on our sleeves or kept them bottled up, the issues were never addressed in the cool light of day. Hence the dearth of emotional intelligence in our childhood. Now, I'd found a

different way altogether, one that felt, at last, like *home*. Trust enabled
me to stand back from denial and see it as an integral component of
the unexamined life, an ingenious pretender of self-control and a self-
obscuring suppressor of personal freedom.

Finally, I was able to shoulder everyday stresses without disdain. I
discovered that a healthy, reflective life had been growing in me all these
years, although it wasn't the transcendental bliss I'd expected. I continued
to discard former beliefs if they didn't meet the standards of plain honesty
and practicality. It wasn't difficult. All that really went out the window
were my expectations of Buddhism, not the Buddha's message. His words,
twenty-six centuries old, were clarified by every experience. I understood
a new willingness to look at unhappiness, recognized the attitude of
turning inwards for meaning and saw that others weren't so different
from me after all. The meditative mind turned out to be preposterously
obvious; it had been under my nose all the time. The ordinary became
extraordinary. I was living exactly the way I'd worked so hard for so long
to avoid, and it was anything but meaningless. Life was full—almost.

Caroline was a born fighter. When told she had an incurable disease, she
refused to accept that nothing could be done, and turned to complemen-
tary medicine and the new-age movement for alternatives. She was open-
minded, but no fool. Over the years she'd developed an eye for popular
culture and its perception. She understood that consumerism works by
showing people what they want to see, and that my story would have to
both use this ploy and subvert it at the same time. She was an advocate
of the reader, and gave me invaluable insight into how the story would
sound in the ears of strangers. She helped me understand how it might
encourage them to distrust appearances and look deeper.

I wasn't seeking a qualified audience in the Buddhist press, or trying
to convert anyone. I was just writing for those who wrestle with their
doubts. My family and teachers had blamed my troubled childhood on
my urge to question what they took for granted. Even when I distrusted
myself, I knew they were wrong. The bigger problem, as Mum belatedly
realized, was that I staked my claim as an outsider and isolated myself
even further. What enabled me to eventually write was the recognition

that those gnawing doubts in the dead of night were not signs of madness. From the ability to play the game of life without being taken in grows a reserve of insight and empathy.

Caroline convinced me there were plenty of readers out there who didn't want to be patronized or preached to; nevertheless, it wasn't something I could take for granted. The growing Western interest in Buddhism was distracting. More than just fashionable, it was becoming mainstream, even institutional. Dozens of books were emerging from monks, scholars and practitioners every year, some as lightweight as a powderpuff, others packed with terminology and doctrine. Between those extremes lies a challenge to express the experience of the Buddha's message in plain English. That's where I hoped The Novice would find its place. Years of technical writing had taught me how to address a broad audience, as opposed to the linear process of writing for specialists in specialist jargon. I had no desire to write yet another book on Buddhist theory.

Life with Caroline was a new experience for me; I was happy. The constant chatter of family life with a wife and two children was distracting and confounding, but it melted away years of rigidity and raised laughter from depths I'd forgotten I had. I began to wonder why I'd gone to such lengths for so long to avoid domestic life. On the other hand, my office was my retreat, the pursuit of uninterrupted flow still a driving force.

When Caroline read my first draft chapters about Steve and Brian she asked one of her trademark questions, simple and easy to answer but loaded with innuendo. Why, she wondered, wasn't I in touch with them?

Any lingering resistance vanished. I googled their names, e-mailed them and received enthusiastic welcomes. Brian was now working with children and their families as a school social worker in Wisconsin. Steve had made a name for himself as a writer and iconoclastic reinterpreter of Buddhism. His bestseller, Buddhism without Beliefs, had upset establishmentarians by questioning the point of introducing notions of karma and reincarnation to Westerners. The exchange of a few e-mails with Alan revealed, unsurprisingly, that he had little patience with Steve's work. Alan was a full-fledged academic, a scientific advisor to the Dalai Lama, president of the Santa Barbara Institute for Consciousness Studies and on a mission. His talks featured the same bristling energy that drove him thirty years ago. His books are intense and urgent. I also turned up Arnie, living a lonely life in California, his wife on the East Coast. Eckart lived a low-key existence in Germany as a translator, and it was with him in the end that I had the most frequent contact, though Brian is ever my brother, bound by our joint ordination all those years ago.

Just how out of touch I'd been was brought home when I learned of a schism in the ranks. It was precipitated by the reversal of fortunes of an invisible dharma protector known as Dolgyal, and hit the public stage when the Dalai Lama announced[122] that, "it has become fairly clear that Dolgyal is a spirit of the dark forces." Mayhem erupted, followed by the savage murder of a prominent monk and his two assistants. Old friend-ships and guru-disciple ties were severed. Being a Tibetan affair, the political machinations underlying this schism were almost completely obscured by doctrinal cover stories. Few Westerners were positioned to understand what prompted the peace-loving Dalai Lama to unleash such divisive forces, and yet a surprising number felt it necessary to take sides.

Helmut, still a monk and in every other way a pillar of the establish-ment, publicly distanced himself from his beloved Dalai Lama. Being asked to abandon this practice so dear to Geshe Rabten, and the price of tantric disloyalty being so high, it must have torn him apart. Steve shrugged off the Dolgyal affair as just another episode in the machina-tions of Tibetan religio-politics, many precedents for which litter the gruesome annals of Tibetan history.[123]

Shortly afterwards, the Tibetan leader was awarded the Nobel Peace Prize and became a celebrity of huge stature. Accounts of the Dolgyal affair in *Newsweek* and elsewhere came and went without tarnishing him, while his most vociferous opponents only drew scorn on themselves. It was sad, but I recognized the almost indecipherable Tibetan game of public face and behind-the-scenes subterfuge, and wasn't surprised.

If I'd had any doubts over the years about my decision to leave insti-tutional religion alone, this finally laid them to rest. Still, I was delighted to open the door once again to news from my old friends and the world we'd once inhabited. Buddhism was flourishing, and the substratum of loners and outcasts looking for a place to belong had remained more or less constant, but there was also growing mainstream interest in what was broadly regarded as this *nonreligion*. The pace of life in the industrial West had been accelerating for decades, alongside a growing willingness to live without beliefs. Now, the information revolution was literally decimating the average attention span, and more and more secular, thinking people were seeking ways to resist the self-regulating acquisition of goods and knowledge. Here was my target audience.

Knowing they'd never be able to divert social currents head-on, they focused instead on adjusting their response to them. They had little interest in philosophy, exotic cults or big questions, but they knew stress firsthand. These were educated people, interested in sanity, family and the material as much as as non-material sides of life. They were about to become of very immediate interest to me.

I put down the phone after a long chat with Steve one day and mentioned to Caroline that he spent much of his time giving meditation courses. She quizzed me a little about this, then popped one of her heart-stopping questions. "Couldn't *you* do that?"

"What?" I asked. "Teach meditation?"

She raised her eyebrows, waiting for an answer.

"Well yes, of course. I suppose I could."

She looked rather pleased with herself, and I realized it was, after all, high time I picked up where I'd left off.

We signed up thirty people and met once a week in a church hall. I was surprised by the turnout. Caroline wasn't. On the other hand, she was impressed by how naturally I sat down and began teaching. My initial talks were pretty raw, for I'd underestimated just how subversive the Buddha's message is, not to mention the sorts of resistance it provokes. Some people are offended by the notion that life on Earth is treacherous, fueled by the willful illusions of its human inhabitants. Caroline sat in on hundreds of workshops over the following years. She listened carefully to what I was saying and advised me in no uncertain terms as to what, by contrast, my students were hearing. Her ear, far more attuned to the mainstream than mine, helped me adjust my delivery. In the process I learned that, as I'd hoped when I left Tharpa Chöeling, the clutter of ideas, beliefs and confusion was being resolved. While, to my vague dismay, my scholarly and ritual knowledge had faded with disuse, the meditations and reflections sank in daily, ever more effectively. The chaff was being winnowed from the wheat.

I get a little better at it each year. Nevertheless, I'm sure of very little. I think the core teachings are deeply relevant to our hurried, fragmented world, but reincarnation strikes me as unlikely and I don't see the point of Awakening if it's beyond plain human experience. I'm deeply inspired by the Buddha but don't call myself a Buddhist, mainly because I don't identify with any establishment, and don't want to.

What do I believe? That we have an instinct for right and wrong, and push it aside when it's inconvenient. That the more deeply we're motivated by emotion, the more insistently we pass it off as reason. That denial is a force to be reckoned with, and our principal obstacle. That ethical codes are as likely to produce hypocrisy as goodness. That belief is precarious, especially when it demands certainty. That no religious, scientific or academic faithful can be trusted that can't laugh at itself. That the only way to respect truth is to take it with a pinch of salt. That life leads nowhere until we consciously take the direction it provides.

My job is to reverse, undermine and overturn preconceptions—first and foremost the notion that meditation is an escape, a mere blocking of stress or emptying of the mind. Concentration alone isn't enough. Moments of quiet focus feel great, but without a foundation they're circumstantial and impossible to maintain. The Tibetan distinction between concentrative and contemplative meditation is paramount, and I use the term *mindful reflection* to encompass both. This spotlights another preconception, that *mindfulness* means merely "bare attention." Again, the crucial skill of being simply, nonjudgmentally aware is not sufficient in itself. Without using our mental capacities to the full, without taking a full-bodied, reflective approach to the inner life, we'll never get to the root of the human condition. What's the value of all our technical and scientific "progress" if we have no more handle on brutality and war, poverty and starvation than our ancestors of five millennia ago?

Underlying all our attitudes and objectives are our accumulated, self-administered illusions about life and happiness, an interdependent web of automated patterns and subconscious denials that today empower us to obliterate the biosphere. As civilized humans have always done, we act as if everything's just fine.

Those who sign up for my mindful reflection workshops are ordinary people stressed out by busyness and anxiety. They don't really want to hear that taming the restless inner dialogue is only the beginning, that finding the quiet mind is a question of retooling their conscious and subconscious mental pathways. The mere belief that the restless mind can be slowed down is already a huge leap of faith. This hands-on approach to personal improvement, without any pseudo-religious delusions of grandeur, isn't easy, but most people are more easily motivated to do that than to sit for prolonged periods in cacophonous silence. Of course, we benefit best by doing both, but my concern is to provide strategies that leave my students less inclined to quit just because they can't be still. The epidemic of restlessness can't just be discounted. I explain that the point is to change the world, starting with oneself. They don't bat an eyelid.

I have the greatest affection for these people.

Buddhism has come to the West without imposing itself. In that alone, it's unlike any religion. It shares with science a suspicion of absolutes, a view of the universe as interdependent cause and effect, and faith in the empirical method.[124] Nevertheless, its Asian forms are unambiguously religious and beguiling. Many an otherwise skeptical Westerner has turned to Buddhism as a panacea. Those with scientific training aren't immune, and some researchers are clearly on a mission to validate, rather than merely examine, its methods. Much has been made of the observable changes in the brains of meditators even though the same is true of musicians, tennis players and, presumably, computer hackers. We should approach scientific "proof" of meditation with caution. It's ultimately beside the point, although it may help open some closed minds.

Making Buddhism a part of life means understanding the cyclic and short-term nature of temporal happiness. The complacent will never be interested in what the Buddha had to say about suffering. Only those who suffer stress or trauma *and acknowledge it* come to meditation in earnest. While science is the pursuit of objective knowledge within a coherent logical system, what the Buddha taught is not a belief system or a philosophy; it's a practice, and a highly subjective, tricky and paradoxical one at that. Liberating the mind requires enormous creativity.

Scientists aren't the only ones with an agenda. In England, the New Kadampa Tradition (NKT) has emerged as a player in the Dolgyal affair, a vocal opposition to the Dalai Lama and a cult to be reckoned with. Its founder, the Sera Jey monk Kelsang Gyatso, was installed as a spiritual advisor for Lama Yeshe's Manjushri Institute back in the early eighties, and promptly commandeered it. That Tibetan imagery and lore can be turned to such forms isn't at all surprising, but its growth is astonishingly so. The NKT is firmly established in more than two dozen countries, with assets running into the hundreds of millions. Back in 1982, I translated a seven-day course for Geshe Kelsang Gyatso in the Lama Tzongkhapa Institute in Italy. I found him a pedantic teacher and an irascible man, one of very few Tibetan teachers to whom I took a visceral dislike.

I've corresponded with several NKT members who initially took up arms against my provocative little web page on the topic. In the end, they admitted that they were in search of a sympathetic ear, and ultimately a way out. This is a guilt-driven rather than a military-style cult, making its web both insidious and sticky. Rather than challenging its members, it's best to ask about their allegiance and let them formulate their rationalizations out loud. Given time, the skilful design of the Buddha's teachings seems able to penetrate even such convoluted trips.

As for the threads of the past, I heard—though nobody would corroborate the story—that when Geshe Rabten died in 1986, his body was propped up in his car as if asleep, driven across the border to Austria and ceremonially cremated. The Swiss authorities would not have been sympathetic, but Geshe would surely have had a good laugh. His tulku[125] Tenzin Rabgye lives in Switzerland under the tutelage of Gonsar Rinpoche, and what was Tharpa Chöeling is now Rabten Chöeling. Lama Yeshe's reincarnation was recognized in a Spanish boy who was carted off to Sera as a boy, and as a young man unceremoniously quit the geshe training to study cinematography in Madrid. Lama Yeshe's worldwide organization[126] has grown under Thubten Zopa Rinpoche, though he's still hard to understand. The Dalai Lama is an international superstar whose forte is heartwarming messages about love and compassion. The Chinese authorities continue to demonize him, disenfranchize his followers and glower in denial. The transplanted Sera Monastery has multiplied its population tenfold since I left. Tibet is no longer a country on any map.

This is the story of my life so far, thirty years in the writing. At times I think I've discovered more by telling it than by living it, mostly because through the process I worked out so many demons and became rather simply happy. I love my wife and family. I love my teaching and writing, and finally I learned to love my mother in ways I thought had forever escaped me. Although it's been devilishly difficult to let go of my expectations of others, that process too is underway. What liberation I've found can certainly be explained in Buddhist terms, but it's the product of the soul-searching that started well before, and continued well after, my monkhood. My purpose is not to be Buddhist but to be true, and the greatest praise I can muster is to call someone or something "real." I tell my students that if they don't cultivate integrity they'll end up grumpy old men and women, and that there's no third option. There are exactly as many ways to find mental freedom as there are ways to shut it down.

In one way or another every life is a whole, but certain events stand out. I'm most proud of my decision to leave behind my robes so definitively, though if I'd known what was to come I would have at least *tried* to avoid it. Thankfully, out of the turmoil a foundation emerged. Writing and teaching have reunited my past and present, and my students are my greatest inspiration. I keep my beliefs to a minimum and make no secret of what few I have, though they're quite unremarkable and have nothing to do with an afterlife, or transcendental reality. I live in the same stressful, painful world as my students and if I have a mission, it's to help them question the very things they believe in most earnestly. After all, if I've learned one thing it's that the pursuit of truth has more to do with letting go of certainty than finding it.

NOTES ON THE TEXT

[KEY: Skt = Sanskrit; Tib = Tibetan]

1 The wife vowed to "love, honor and obey," her husband, " . . . 'till death us do part."

2 Gloucester relishes the grisly death of its heretic Bishop Hooper. The straw and wood faggots that eventually consumed him were so damp they had to be relit three times. An eyewitness wrote, "But when he was black in the mouth and his tongue swollen that he could not speak, yet his lips went until they were shrunk to the gums, and he knocked his breast with his hands until one of his arms fell off, and then knocked still with the other, what time the fat, water and blood, dropped at his finger ends, until by renewing of the fire his strength was gone and his hand did cleave fast in knocking on the iron upon his breast. So, immediately bowing forwards he yielded up his spirit." [See visit-gloucestershire.co.uk]

3 Gaetano Donizetti, *Don Pasquale* (1843).

4 The Dismissal: *Go, the mass is ended.*

5 The Response: *Thanks be to God.*

6 Short for *navigators*: road-construction laborers.

7 Chocolate-coated balls of crunchy malt.

8 From Catholic Truth Society, *A Catechism of Christian Doctrine*; three hundred and seventy articles of faith framed in question and answer format.

9 A civil engineer's assistant.

10 Timothy Leary, Press conference in New York City (September 19, 1966): "Like every great religion of the past we seek to find the divinity within and to express this revelation in a life of glorification and the worship of God. These ancient goals we define in the metaphor of the present—turn on, tune in, drop out."

11 Before the days of integrated keyboards and display monitors, data was input and retrieved from processing systems with punched cards.

12 The part of the London Borough of Enfield where the campus was located. Enfield Polytechnic is now known as Middlesex University, and has moved.

13 Bob Dylan, *Ballad of a Thin Man* (1965): "You know something is happening here but you don't know what it is—do you, Mister Jones?"

14 Carlos Castaneda, *Journey to Ixtlan* (Simon & Schuster, 1972, ISBN: 0-671-73246-3). Don Juan was immortalized in this and other books by the same author.

15 Richard Wilhelm (translator), *The I Ching or Book of Changes: A Chinese Oracle* (Princeton University Press, 1967, ISBN: 069109750).

16 The great mathematician, 1906–1978.

17 Pronounced *Dolgethly*.

18 At Aberffraw, on the Isle of Anglesey.

19 The goal of the Buddhist teachings; an end to views: freedom from conditioned existence and suffering.

20 The ritual casting of fifty sticks is a more meditative preliminary than the less elaborate use of three coins.

21 The astronomical tables used to calculate astrological charts.

22 Warner Brothers, *Lust for Life* (1956).

23 When he finally returned he became the Ayatollah Khomeini, establishing theocratic rule, crushing all opposition and launching a cultural counter-revolution that forced Mehdi's class into silence or exile.

24 See note 14.

25 TIB: *bde bar bsegs pa*; SKT: *sugata*: one who has fared well, an epithet for *buddha*.

26 From HINDI: *bilayati*: "foreign," also "England."

27 From the region now encompassed by north-western Pakistan, with extensions into the lower valleys of the Kabul and Swat rivers.

28 Street-vendors' barrows.

29 Thirty years later, that figure doubled.

30 Hindi and Tibetan respectively. For the latter, see note 95.

31 TIB: *dge bshes*; SKT: *kalyanamitra*: spiritual friend, also a scholastic degree in the Tibetan Gelug tradition and the title accorded a graduate.

32 TIB: *kun rdzob bden pa*; SKT: *samvrti satya*): the everyday reality of appearances. Ultimate truth (TIB: *don dam bden pa*; SKT: *paramārtha satya*) is non-dualistic and therefore cannot be rendered in words or ideas; nor is it divisible as an object of consciousness from consciousness itself.

33 Geshe Rabten, *The Preliminary Practices* (Library of Tibetan Works & Archives, 1974, ISBN: 81-85102-62-7).

34 By the eleventh century CE Buddhism had spread into most of the Asian countries where it flourishes today, and began a decline in its native India that was accelerated in the following century by Muslim raids, especially upon the great monastic universities at Valabhi and Nālandā. Both were destroyed.

35 Eloquently expressed by Chögyam Trungpa in his seminal book *Cutting Through Spiritual Materialism* (Shambhala Publications, 1974, ISBN: 0-87773-050-4).

36 TIB: *skyes dman*:the everyday word for *woman*; literally, one born *lower* or *lesser*.

37 A 24-hour pledge to avoid killing, stealing, sex, lies, intoxicants, accepting homage, eating more than once, using ornaments and indulging in music or dance.

38 As Geshe later clarified, he was not a tutor but an occasional sparring partner to the Tibetan leader as he prepared for his geshe examination.

39 TIB: *byang chub sems dpa*; SKT: *bodhisattva*: one with the mind for Awakening (bodhicitta—see note 50.)

40 The Dalai Lama. Even before receiving the Nobel Peace Prize and becoming an international superstar, a cult of personality surrounded the Dalai Lama. He is charismatic, friendly, curious and engaging, with far broader interests than most Tibetans of his generation.

41 TIB: *rtsam pa*: barley grain, but also the prepared meal in its ground, dry-roasted form.

42 TIB: *rding ba*: like the robes themselves, the mat is made with cloth strips to resemble the stitched rags used in the Buddha's time.

43 See note 36

44 Since the early 1960s, S.N. Goenka has taught rigorous ten-day Vipassana Meditation courses in the tradition of Sayagyi U Ba Khin to thousands of people.

45 Traditionally, a monk's worldly possessions would not exceed the three robes, a begging bowl, a cloth

belt, a needle and thread, a razor and a water filter.

46 Taking refuge in *buddha* (Awakening), *dhárma* (practice) and *sangha* (community of like-minded) distinguishes individuals as Buddhists.

47 Most were employed by AG Heinrich Kuhn metal goods, manufacturers of kitchenware. The first European country to receive Tibetan refugees (in 1961) was Switzerland, where brothers Henri and Jacques Kuhn provided employment, shelter and cultural support to the fledgling community while the plight of Tibetans was ignored by Western governments.

48 TIB: *rlung*; SKT: *prāṇa*: a source of vitality in several oriental physiologies.

49 This was just before the Sony Walkman introduced personal music.

50 TIB: *byang chub gyi sems*; SKT: *bodhicitta*: the intention to reach Awakening not simply for one's own sake, but for all sentient beings.

51 The path to Awakening, said to ordinarily take three countless great æons, is also said to be attainable in as little as three years through the extraordinary class of tantric practice (TIB: *bla na med pa'i rgyud*, SKT: *anuttarayoga*).

52 See note 51.

53 TIB: *dorje*; SKT: *vajra*: can take either noun or adjectival forms and has a plethora of meanings, including "thunderbolt" and "indestructible." There is no real English equivilant. A giant double (crossed) dorje is embedded in the foundations of divine mansions, the abodes of tantric deities. As an implement, it is usually cast in bronze together with with a bell, and the two make a ritual pair. The finger drum is double-headed

with attached clappers that strike the skins (preferably human) with a flick of the wrist.

54 The Teeth of the South (midday).

55 TIB: *a ni lags*: respectful form of address for a nun.

56 Place of Liberation Studies/Centre for Higher Tibetan Studies.

57 Paul Tillich, *Systematic Theology*, in one volume (University of Chicago Press, 1963, ISBN: 022680336-8).

58 Each monk spread his own seat-cloth. See note 42.

59 TIB: *blo rigs*: types of mind. See note 68.

60 TIB: *rtags rigs*: types of reasoning.

61 Tib: *shes rab gyi pha rol tu phyin pa*; Skt: *prajñā pāramitā*: The Perfection of Wisdom; an aspect of the path of a bodhisattva; also the shorthand title of a philosophical treatise on the realization of ultimate truth (see note 32).

62 Both mean "you."

63 TIB: *dbyin ji*: "English," but also more generally, "westerner."

64 SKT: *Bodhicaryāvatāra* by Śāntideva; *A Guide to the Bodhisattva's Way of Life*, trans. Stephen Batchelor, p 47. (The Library of Tibetan Works and Archives, 1979, ISBN: 8185102597).

65 Ibid., VIII, 60–61.

66 TIB: *khams pa*: one from the native East Tibetan province of Geshe Rabten, known for its horses, its provincial culture and its rustic accent.

67 TIB.: *rab du rten pa*: well-grounded.

68 TIB.: *blo rigs The Mind and its Functions*, trans. Stephen Batchelor. (Edition Rabten, 1992, ISBN: 3-905497-46-8).

69 See note 64. Stephen Batchelor was at that time translating the text into English.

70 SKT: *Nālandā*: a Buddhist center of learning in Bihar, North India that flourished from the fifth to ninth centuries CE. See note 34.

71 SKT: *Bodhicaryāvatāra* by Śāntideva; *A Guide to the Bodhisattva's Way of Life*, The Library of Tibetan Works and Archives, 1979, trans., Stephen Batchelor, VII 58-59; ISBN 8185102597.

72 The left foot rests on the right thigh, and the right foot on the left thigh.

73 Tib: *bshes gnyen bsten pa*; Skt: *guru-shishya*: guru devotion, or spiritual teacher-student relationship is one of the most misunderstood aspects of Tibetan Buddhism. The Sanskrit term guru literally means "heavy" (with presence) but in practice refers to a "spiritual friend." Any teacher-student relationship begins with respect, but may go much farther, depending on exactly what's being learned. At its most consuming, it means interpreting all one's teacher's activity as fully enlightened behavior. According to the tantric scriptures this is by no means incompatible with watchfulness and critical reflection, but Westerners do not typically struggle with that particular subtlety. Consequently, many simply abandon judgment out of eagerness or ignorance. They also fail to distinguish between teachers from whom they learn theory, preceptors who guide their practice and tantric gurus to whose influence they open themselves unconditionally—all different relationships with different stakes and outcomes. Skilled students of the Buddha never abandon their critical faculties, and both mahayana and tantric scriptures establish their credentials on the practice of critical

reflection (Pali: yoniso manasikāra). See Alexander Berzin's Relating to a Spiritual Teacher: Building A Healthy Relationship (Snow Lion, 2000, ISBN: 1-55939-139-1).

74 One of the "big-three" monasteries in the Gelug (TIB: *dge lugs*) tradition that originated within walking distance of Lhasa. The three are Sera (TIB: *se ra*), Ganden (TIB: *dga' ldan*) and Drepung (TIB: *bras spungs*), and had a combined population of more than twenty thousand monks.

75 Helmut published an extraordinary statement in 1999 about the Dorje Shugden schism, entitled *Dalai Lama Dorje Shugden*, in which he describes how he tried to "keep my distance" (page 4) from the Dalai Lama. The document is available as this book goes to press at http://www.schettini.com/gassner.pdf.

76 TIB: *thabs*; SKT: *upaya*: means, usually implying "skillful" or "expedient" means; loosely "tactful teaching," a way that places less importance on philosophical exactitude than on nudging people in the right direction, especially if the "correct" answer will fall on deaf ears.

77 See note 46.

78 From the Kalama Sutta, trans. Nanamoli Thera: "Do not be satisfied with hearsay or with tradition or with legendary lore or with what has come down in scriptures or with conjecture or with logical inference or with weighing evidence or with liking for a view after pondering over it or with someone else's ability or with the thought, "This monk is our teacher." When you know in yourselves: "These things are wholesome, blameless, commended by the wise, and being

adopted and put into effect they lead to welfare and happiness," then you should practice and abide in them."

79 From there he published initial drafts of his first book, *Alone with Others, An Existential Approach to Buddhism*, Grove Press, 1982, ISBN: 0-8021-5127-2.

80 Now *Mumbai*.

81 The recognized reincarnation of a famous teacher or meditator.

82 TIB: *dge rgan*, teacher: familiarly, *gen*, also used to refer to a housemaster.

83 Those named by Geshe Rabten took Jampa, not Thubten, as a "family" name.

84 See note 63: corruption of "English," but also a generic, familiar and sometimes derogatory term for any westerner.

85 Tib: *spun skya*: an imprecisely fraternal relationship between two males of more or less equal rank.

86 SKT: *mañjuśrī kumāra bhūta*; Tib: *jam dpel dbyangs*: The buddha of wisdom.

87 What wasn't typical though, was that he went further and committed to heart Tsong Khapa's entire, three-inch-thick *Stages of the Path to Awakening* (TIB: *lam rim chen mo*), a prodigious feat.

88 Also, a monk who successfully defends an unacceptable tenet, such as the thesis that plants are sentient beings, is accorded great respect—as long as he doesn't take it too far. For an intriguing and disheartening example read the story of Gendun Chopel in *The Madman's Middle Way* by Donald S. Gomez Jr., page 9 (University of Chicago Press, 2006 ISBN 0-226-49316-4).

89 An authentic, detailed description of the ritual is available at http://www.thdl.org/essays/dreyfus/physicality.html.

90 The Tibetan calendar has twelve 30-day months. An extra month is added every 3rd year and certain days are then cut out of the calendar. The new-year's day falls in the northern spring and is the most important day in the calendar.

91 TIB: *mtshan nyid*: literally *definition*. Every significant term in every branch of study is defined in each monastery's textbooks, and debate is largely about these terms and their relationships. I was therefore disconcerted to learn, for example, that a *valid cognition* is defined as "any cognition that apprehends a valid object," and a *valid object* as "anything apprehended by a valid cognition." I questioned this circularity, but it didn't seem to worry anyone else (except for Stephen Batchelor, who sighed wearily). I approached several geshes on the topic, all of whom dismissed it as insignificant, since we could all depend on Lama Tzong Khapa (*tsong kha pa blo bzan-grags pa*, 1357-1419), the progenitor of the Gelug school. Years later, I learned about Gendun Chopel (see note 88), an outspoken early twentieth-century Sera monk who took issue with this and other questionable debating practices. He was imprisoned and ostracized.

92 See note 76.

93 In this view our world is one of four continents surrounding, in mandala-like symmetry, the central, hourglass-shape Mount Meru—a description irreconcilable with scientific accounts. Gotama adapted this from the prevailing views of his day.

94 A broad-spectrum antibiotic.

95 TIB: *bkra shis bde legs*; a traditional New Year wish, often used by

Westerners as an everyday greeting.

96　TIB: *sku mdun*: presence, used by most Tibetans to refer to the Dalai Lama.

97　By 2006, the population of Sera Jey alone, the larger of the two schools of Sera, had grown to well over three thousand.

98　A savory pancake of fine-ground rice and mashed, fermented black lentils; usually served with potato curry and coconut chutney.

99　TIB: *chenrezig*, SKT: *avalokiteśvara*.

100　See note 94.

101　TIB: *sman*: medicine.

102　A British pharmacy chain.

103　TIB: *mkhan po*: "abbott" is a misleading translation, though the kenpo is the titular head of the monastery.

104　Alan wrote that Geshe "was not pleased at my decision and told me not to tell anyone else at TC or in Geneva (where I had been teaching regularly) that I was going away for anything more than the holidays. So I packed up my books in boxes, and took with me just what I thought I'd need when I went to India. I felt very bad about this, for it felt like I was sneaking away, as if I'd done something wrong. But I deferred to Geshe Rabten's request. He had been my closest teacher for years, and I was (and still am) deeply indebted to him for his kindness and generosity in guiding me in my studies and practice of the Dharma." Email message to author from B. Alan Wallace, February 19, 2004.

105　Letter to author, postmarked Hamburg, January 28, 1980.

106　Tib: *blo rigs*, (types of mind).

107　A monk of the Southern Buddhist (Theravadin) tradition, a more austere and generally less ritualistic tradition. See note 109.

108　See note 74.

109　SKT: *śūnyatā* TIB: *stong pa nyid*.

110　What was Ceylon at that time is now Sri Lanka.

111　The "Doctrine of the Elders," Theravadin is the school of Buddhism that draws its scriptural inspiration from the Tipitaka, or Pali canon, which scholars generally agree contains the earliest surviving record of the Buddha's teachings.

112　*My Land and My People* by The Dalai Lama. (McGraw-Hill, 1962, ISBN: 0-446-67421-4).

113　Tsong Khapa (TIB: *tsong kha pa*) and his two disciples.

114　Tibetan nuns were routinely advised to pray for rebirth as a man, though some were renowned as great meditators; I heard no mention of any women-scholars.

115　In his autobiography as a geshe in training, Georges B. J. Dreyfus describes an altercation with Geshe Rabten over a point of philosophy that led Dreyfus to seek a more flexible teacher. See, "The Sound of Two Hands Clapping" (University of California Press, 2003. ISBN: 0-520-23260-7).

116　Where Geshe Lundrup Sopa was resident teacher.

117　As this book goes to press, Helmut is indeed still a monk closely connected with Geshe Rabten's heir Gonsar Rinpoche, who is raising Geshe Rabten's tulku. However, a rift has developed between former colleagues and even between teachers and students. See notes 75 and 122.

118　Tib: *colloquial expression, spelling untraceable, pronounced 'low luss;*

usually accompanied by a sharp intake
of breath; deferential, often servile.

119 Sutta-Nipata 1.12.213, trans., H.
     Saddhatissa p.23.

120 A long-distance telephone scam
     selling cheap pens for a high price
     to businesses in distant cities, usually
     by manipulating clients – known as
     mooches – with worthless free gifts.

121 Dad died in 1984, before I'd written a
     single paragraph, and Mum in 2007
     after a struggle with Alzheimer's
     Disease. She'd nursed her own father
     through dementia for over a decade
     and knew what was coming, so when
     she had a stroke she was spared her
     worst fears. Although it was painful to
     stand by helplessly, she comforted me
     by laughing at her affliction, and we
     became unprecidentedly close in her
     final years.

122 Full name, Dorje Shugden (TIB: *rdo
     rje shugs ldan*) The Dalai Lama said
     on March 21, 1996, "Recently I have
     conducted a number of prayers for the
     well being of our nation and religion.
     It has become fairly clear that Dolgyal
     is a spirit of the dark forces. Therefore,
     during the Hayagriva invocation last
     year, I specifically mentioned Dolgyal
     by name and an incantation was made
     to ward him off." He continued: "I
     wonder if any among you here today
     continue to propitiate Dolgyal and
     still feel comfortable receiving this
     Hayagriva empowerment. This is
     the reason why I suggested yesterday
     that it would not be appropriate
     for those who propitiate Dolgyal to
     attend this empowerment. When the
     protector concerned is disloyal to its
     commitments, the person concerned
     becomes disloyal in turn. As I said
     yesterday, this gives rise to a breach of

commitments which carries with it a
definite threat to the life of a Lama.

If any among you here are
determined to continue propitiating
Dolgyal, it would be better for you to
stay away from this empowerment, get
up and leave this place. It is improper
for you to continue to sit here. It will
not benefit you. On the contrary it
will have the effect of reducing the life
span of Gyalwa Rinpoche (The Dalai
Lama), which is not good. However, if
there are any among you who hope
that Gyalwa Rinpoche will soon
die, then you can stay." [Reported on
the web site of The Government of
Tibet in Exile: http://www.tibet.com/
dholgyal/dholgyal2.html.]

123 See *Tricycle* The Buddhist Review,
     Spring 1998. Stephen Batchelor *Letting
     Daylight into Magic: The Life and Times
     of Dorje Shugden.*

124 These parallels were formulated by
     the Dalai Lama in a talk given at the
     annual meeting of the Society for
     Neuroscience on November 12, 2005
     in Washington DC. See mindandlife.
     org.

125 Officially declared reincarnations.

126 The Foundation for the Preservation
     of the Mahayana Teachings (FPMT).
     See fpmt.org.

127 Jan Tschichold, *The Form of the
     Book*, (Hartley & Marks, 1991, ISBN
     0-88179-0346).

NOTES ON THE PICTURES
[by page number]

by John Hill; GNU Free Documentation License, Version 1.2 [http://en.wikipedia.org/wiki/File:Swayambhunath,_1973.JPG]

164 Lama Thubten Yeshe; by Carol Royce Wilder; © Vajrapani Institute 1983; by kind permission of Lama Yeshe Wisdom Archive

166 Lama Thubten Yeshe at Kopan Meditation course, March 1974; by unknown; © Lama Yeshe Wisdom Archive; by kind permission

173 "Thubten Sangye;" by author using Tibetan Machine Uni Font 1.901; General Public License

182 Interior of The Don Pasquale restaurant with proprietor publicity image; from the estate of Gwenda Schettini; © Stephen Schettini

211 Geshe Rabten and Western students at Rikon Switzerland 1975; by anonymous; General Public License [Left to right: Author, Marie-Thérèse (lastname unknown), Pierro Cerri, Arnold Possick, (unidentified), Claudio Cipullo, Massimo Corona, Georges Drefus, Aldo (lastname unknown), Elio Guarisco. Geshe Tamdrin Rabten, Bruno LeGuevel, Tom Tillemans, Alan Wallace, Brian Grabia, Stephen Batchelor, Charles Genoud, Shelly Tillemans]

216 Lamas Yeshe and Zopa with attendees of meditation course at Coniston Priory (Manjushri Institute) September 1976; © Lama Yeshe Wisdom Archive; by kind permission

222 Thanka painting of Yamantaka (Vajra Bairava); © Mima Gallery Vancouver; by kind permission

230 Geshe Jampa Lhodro, Gonsar Tulku and others in Tharpa Chöeling Temple 1978; by Fred von Allmen; © Fred von Allmen; by kind permission

233 Page fom handmade Tibetan phrase book 1977; by the monks of Tharpa Chöeling; General Public License

238 Tibetan Book, by Jan Thijs 2007; © Stephen Schettini

243 Shantideva, by Robert Beer; © Robert Beer; by kind permission

247 The Dalai Lama with Geshe Rabten at Tharpa Chöeling Switzerland 1980; by Fred von Allmen; © Fred von Allmen; by kind permission

251 Geshe Zangpo with Geshe Rabten 1980; by Fred von Allmen; © Fred von Allmen; by kind permission

264 Sera Monastic University India 1980 by author; © Stephen Schettini

267 Geshe Ngawang Dhargyey debating at the Tsuglakhang, 1975; by Sean Jones © Sean Jones; by kind permission

269 The road from Sera Monastic University to Bylakuppe India 1980; by author; © Stephen Schettini

271 Geshe Kayang at Sera Monastic University India 1980; by author; © Stephen Schettini

273 Boy monk at Sera Monastic University working on handwriting 1980; by author; © Stephen Schettini

275 Author's hut in the outermost reaches of Sera Monastery 1981; by author; © Stephen Schettini

288 Sunset over Sera Monastic University; by author; © Stephen Schettini

293 Kandubodha Retreat Centre, Sri Lanka with resident instructor; by author; © Stephen Schettini

296 Anuradhapura stupa 1981; by author; © Stephen Schettini

306 Author at Sera Manastic University 1981; by Geshe Kayang

Back cover photograph: Sera Monastic University India 1980 by author; © Stephen Schettini.

ACKNOWLEDGEMENTS

First and foremost, with grudging but sound reason, I thank my childhood teachers for unwittingly instilling in me the questions that triggered my quest for the real.

My bountiful thanks go to the Tibetan community in exile and their leader Tenzin Gyatso, the Dalai Lama, for sharing so freely their Buddhist canon; in particular, Geshe Ngawang Dhargyey, Lama Thubten Yeshe, Lama Zopa Rinpoche, Geshe Tamdrin Rabten, Geshe Jhampa Lhodro, Venerable Lati Rinpoche, Geshe Ngawang Nyima, Kyabje Kalu Rinpoche, Kyabje Trijang Rinpoche, Kyabje Ling Rinpoche, Kyabje Song Rinpoche. I am also indebted to the monks and patrons of the Kanduboda Meditation Centre in Sri Lanka. My debt to them all cannot be measured.

My warm and sentimental thanks go to friends and fellow monks from Schwendi in the 1970s and early 1980s, just for being there; notably, Stephen Batchelor, Piero Cerri, Claudio Cipullo, Massimo & Carol Corona, Georges Drefus, Charles Genoud, Brian Grabia, Elio Guarisco, Dora Kalff, Martin Kalff, Bruno LeGuevel, Arnold Possick, Gonsar Rinpoche, Lotti Sanders, Dorli Schriever, Tom & Shelly Tillemans, Fred von Allmen, Alan Wallace and Eckart Zabel.

I thank my benefactors Sigrid Kremzow and Elizabeth Arzoner, as well as Anne Ansermet and Tharpa Choeling's Geneva Group, who by sheltering and feeding me during those formative years granted me the extraordinary leisure to study and meditate; for additional material help I'm indebted to David Skitt, Hans Beck, Igrid Racz and anonymous others.

Thanks to Diane Lavenex, who eased the difficult transition from a life of financial dependence to one of independence. For the same reasons and in even greater measure also to Georges Ostiguy, who secured my subsequent foothold in Canada.

Thanks to Kerrith MacKenzie, who handed me a castaway but invaluable pocket camera as I headed off to South India. I am especially indebted to Fred von Allmen for photos from the Tharpa Choeling years and for an unfailing response to all my requests. Thanks also to Doctor Nick

Ribush and the Lama Yeshe Wisdom Archive for retrieving photographs and recordings from the early 1970s, and permitting their use.

For pictures illustrating my overland trip, when I carried no camera, I turned to strangers who were there: Philip Game, Imran Rashid, William A. Ring, owners of proprietary images who generously permitted their reproduction; also to Stephen Shephard, John Armagh, Paula Santos, James Mollison, Markus Koljonen and John Hill, who made their photographs freely available on the internet through the GNU General Public License, the GNU Free Documentation License, the Creative Commons Attribution ShareAlike 2.5, Attribution ShareAlike 2.0 and the Attribution ShareAlike 1.0 licenses. Special thanks to Robert Beer and Vancouver's Mima Gallery for images of their paintings. [Credits and appropriate links are listed in the Pictures section on page 340.]

Kudos to Gavin Kilty for initiating the Old Dharamsala Wallahs social networking site. The stories, photos and links to old friends jogged memories and introduced me to Sean Jones, to whom I extend my gratitude for the use of his photographs.

Thanks to B. Alan Wallace for sharing private thoughts and lowering ancient veils; to Stephen Batchelor, for long, intense monospace letters from the days before electronic mail, as well as for checking my ever atrocious Tibetan spelling in the notes; to Brian Grabia, Eckart Zabel and Ingrid Racz for long phone conversations and email exchanges.

Most personally, to Stuart James, for letting my hair down; to Tom Butler, for so genially gutting my childhood beliefs, to Annemette, for the slap in the face; to Tara, for believing in me when no one else did; to Allan Putterman, for true counsel; to Steve, Brian and Ekki, for friendship; to my sister Yolanda, for steady and enthusiastic encouragement; to Hassan Elshafei, for punctilious criticism, copious suggestions and warm, intense hours of tai chi, green tea and dim sum. Thanks.

Most emphatically, to the dozens of old-school publishers and agents who, by roundly rejecting The Novice, passed it on and into the nurturing hands of the Greenleaf Book Group. In particular, I extend special thanks to Greenleaf's Tanya Hall, who made my work so warmly welcome and who so effortlessly conceived the perfect cover image for my memoir.

For their thoughtful and generous endorsements, thanks to Bob Thurman: for all his intellect, a man of heart; and to Glenn Wallis, who shares my mission to shine new lights on old truths.

Finally, to my wife and partner Caroline, who watched over this book, nurtured its growth, helped me cut it in half and knock it into shape and constantly, when self-doubt reared its shrunken head, assured me without the slightest shadow of doubt that readers would care.

COLOPHON

This book is set in Linotype Sabon® Next. In creating this typeface, Jean François Porchez revived a revival. The original Sabon typeface designed by Jan Tschichold was itself a revival of Claude Garamond's 16th century types for the 1960s. By referring to the original metal versions of Sabon for Linotype casting, Monotype machines and hand-setting, as well as Garamond's 16th century pages, Porchez has created a digital typeface of great utility and beauty.

CG
＊ JT ＊
JFP

As designer of this book as well as its author I'm indebted to Jan Tschichold both for this typeface, as well as for the broader inspiration of his essays collected in *The Form of the Book*,[127] subtitled, *Essays on the Morality of Good Design*. Tschichold's hilariously rigid principles have gravely influenced my ability to communicate visually and literally. The selection of Sabon is a design decision, but also homage to this artisan whose greatest ambition was that his work be transparent.

For more information, stories and articles about and by the author visit

www.schettini.com